The Privilege of Love

The Privilege of Love
Camaldolese Benedictine Spirituality

Edited by

Peter-Damian Belisle, O.S.B. Cam.

Introduction by

Michael Downey

THE LITURGICAL PRESS
Collegeville, Minnesota

www.litpress.org

Cover design by David Manahan, O.S.B. Cover illustration courtesy of Thomas Matus, O.S.B. Cam., Painting of Saint Romuald, Abbot, by unknown artist, 1705, Camaldoli Monastery, Italy.

1	2	3	4	5	6	7	8

Library of Congress Cataloging-in-Publication Data

The privilege of love : Camaldolese Benedictine spirituality / edited by Peter-Damian Belisle ; introduction by Michael Downey.
    p. cm.
  Includes bibliographical references and index.
  ISBN 0-8146-2773-0 (alk. paper)
    1. Camaldolese—Spiritual life. I. Belisle, Peter-Damian, 1947–
BX3085 .P75 2002
255'.14—dc21
                                                2001038062

*Dedicated to the memory of
our confrere Aelred Squire (†1997)
who cherished our charism
and would have delighted in
contributing to this volume.*

Contents

Acknowledgments

I wish to thank The Liturgical Press for the opportunity
to publish this book on the Camaldolese Benedictine tradition.
These essays tell the remarkable story of our little Congregation
within the larger Benedictine heritage.
The bibliography at the end offers readers and scholars alike
for the first time anywhere and in any language
a comprehensive list of Romualdian/Camaldolese source material.

The contributors are to be commended
for their willingness to devote time,
consideration to endure deadlines, and
patience to suffer the swipe of editorial scissors.

Gratitude also goes to Michael Downey for his generous help,
enthusiastic encouragement, and warm friendship.

Lastly, a word of thanks to Prior General Emanuele Bargellini
for his animated support and personal vision.

Peter-Damian Belisle

Introduction

Michael Downey

"It is a small place. But it opens up to a universal space." While I was visiting Camaldoli in the hills of Tuscany, this is how Bernardino Cozzarini, superior of the Camaldolese community there, described the Holy Hermitage several miles up the road. His few words spoken in faltering, broken English, may indeed convey the richness and the depth of the Camaldolese Benedictine spirit: These men and women are hermits living by a monastic rule, committed to both solitude *and* community life, giving witness to the magnitude of God's love loose in the world.

Are they hermits? Or are they monks? There is a difference. And the Camaldolese are both. Their life combines a strong measure of solitude and silence that is cultivated, nurtured, and sustained through the discipline of living alone in a hermitage. But they embrace the *Rule of St. Benedict*, praying and working day by day alongside others in a community of brothers or sisters. Theirs is a rich heritage, unique in the Church. This particular form of life makes provision for the deep human need for solitude as well as for life shared alongside others in pursuit of a noble purpose. But because their life is ordered to a threefold good, the discipline of solitude and the rigors of community living are in no sense isolationist or self-serving. Rather, both of these goods are intended to widen the heart in service of the third good: The Camaldolese bears witness to the super-abundance of God's love as the self, others, and every living creature are brought into fuller communion in the one Love.

The flourishing of different kinds of spiritualities has been one of the greatest riches of the post-conciliar Church. In earlier periods, "spirituality" and the "spiritual life" were sometimes thought to be the prerogative of vowed religious, monks, nuns, and clergy. It is now more commonly recognized that the Spirit is awash in a variety of life forms, and that all the baptized are called to the fullness of Christian life, indeed to a life of holiness. And Christian holiness is found in the perfection of charity—the flourishing of love by which we share in the communion of the three in one Love. Indeed the life of love is a privilege, for it is in and through love that we participate in the divine life itself, the very life of God whose name above all other names is Love (1 John 4:8).

One of the great achievements of the century just past was its return to the sources of Christian faith and life. It is because of this *ressourcement* that we now have a deeper appreciation of the monastic impulse that runs long, deep, and strong in the Christian tradition, and well beyond it. What's more, in its Christian expressions monasticism is, at its origins, a lay movement. In no small measure, it is this realization that has led to a renewed interest in monastic spirituality on the part of people in all walks of life. Further, of late, there has been a resurgence of interest in those Christian spiritual traditions that place less emphasis on the communal dimensions of the monastic impulse and more on the importance of aloneness, silence, and solitude in all spiritual growth and development.

Perhaps the most significant Catholic spiritual writer of the twentieth century is Gethsemani's most celebrated son, Thomas Merton. His own spiritual heritage as a Trappist Cistercian is decidedly cenobitic, communal. But Merton himself dug deeply into the sources of that heritage to retrieve the currents of the eremitic, solitary life, within it. It may well be that the reason for Merton's enormous influence lies in his ability to articulate the struggle to combine these two irreducible elements of the mature spiritual quest. The "cenobitic" and the "eremitic," evocative of the monk and the hermit to be found at the core of the deepest self of each one of us, are blended in a distinctive fashion in the particular form of life that is the Camaldolese way.

The enduring image of Merton in our own time is not that of the monk in choir singing the divine office together with his brothers in community, but of the solitary figure of "the hermitage years," whose aloneness as well as his struggles with human relationships opened him up and out to the wider world awaiting a word of unrestricted mercy. It is intriguing to note that as Merton's commitment to the life of solitude deepened, he became more and more open to the religions of the East. In his desire to combine the cenobitic and eremitic strands of the monastic impulse, as well as in his ecumenical and interreligious sensibility, Merton's life is deeply resonant with the spirit of the Camaldolese. In both we recognize that solitude and the privilege of loving relation widen the human heart so it may be brought into a deepening, eternal communion in one Love.

Merton is impossible to pigeonhole. And so are the Camaldolese. As this collection of essays demonstrates, there are many paths on the Camal-

dolese way. This is a charism quite varied in expression. The diversity of expression is itself a manifestation of the magnitude of God's creating, animating, bonding love. This bonding is the Spirit's own gift, weaving
together the many voices found in these pages—voices of women and men,
of monk, hermit, and layperson, from Camaldoli in the hills of Tuscany and
from Camaldoli's most fruitful seed sown in the United States—New
Camaldoli Hermitage in Big Sur, California. The voices speak of historical
roots and ecumenical routes, of the gold which is found in solitude and the
grit of community life which is the test of its purity, of the psychological
strength required in any serious pursuit of God, as well as the weakness and
vulnerability of the human heart which is the home for wisdom's Word.

It is a singular delight for me to introduce this collection of essays. Although I do not know the Camaldolese all that well, I have had occasion to
share in their life of solitude and community, both at New Camaldoli in
Big Sur, California, as well as at Camaldoli in the Tuscan hills. Theirs is a
distinguished heritage. But it is little known in the United States. Because
of the initiative, coordination and editorial skill of Peter-Damian Belisle,
O.S.B. CAM., and due to the ongoing commitment of The Liturgical Press to
a fuller appreciation of monastic traditions, the riches of Camaldolese
Benedictine spirituality are here made available to a wide readership in the
English-speaking world for the first time.

Why the abiding appeal of the monk? Of the hermit? Because each
seeks in a distinctive way to live in the presence of God. Above all else. It is
this for which every heart longs. This is the deepmost of the deepest
human desires—to listen long and lovingly to the beating of the heart of
God. But our own deepest desires are unrecognized, unnamed, unclaimed
if we are strangers in that country whose name is "solitude." Yet the very
God for whom we long is the God who is toward us, for us, with us, in us
and in all. Our destiny is to be brought into communion, to live in right
relationship with others and, in so doing, to be made holy by the presence
and power of the Spirit. Thus, by living in the grace of this holy communion, whose very seedbed is the solitude in which we know ourselves to be
in loving relation, we bear testimony to the enduring privilege of being in
love with Love itself, which is first and finally Love's own gift to us.

Part One

A Vision in Context

Overview of Camaldolese History and Spirituality

Peter-Damian Belisle

1. Eleventh-Century Background

When Saint Romuald of Ravenna began drawing disciples to himself, gathering isolated hermits and eremitical groups into community, making monastic foundations, refounding already extant houses under reformed principles and speaking out against ecclesiastical decadence slightly over one millennium ago, little did he realize that his movement would develop into a religious order. He had no intention of founding an order. He intuited needs to be met in the second half of the tenth century into which he was born and committed himself to meeting those needs until his death (1027) in a small hermitage near the monastery of Valdicastro.

The tenth and eleventh centuries formed a period of serious Church-state relational problems. A gradual strengthening of the crown was occurring and problems concerning succession to the imperial crown were being ironed out—such as the crisis occasioned by the untimely death of Romuald's friend and follower, Emperor Otto III. With all this imperial turmoil, an emperor spent the lion's share of his time stabilizing various territories against secessions, rebellions and unwanted strategic alliances. The nobility, including many bishops, were clutching a feudalistic world in which they could continue to be local "lords" with the keys to life and death, let alone taxation, justice, etc. And so, it was a time of constant strife—a seemingly endless stream of local civil wars. To fill the constant need for money to feed all the war machines, monasteries and abbeys became prime targets of the rulers—both civil and ecclesiastical! A considerable lack of justice existed because so much depended, quite simply and at times brutally, on money. Those who could pay could receive so-called "justice." Within the Church structure, moneyed people were buying their way into bishoprics, parishes and abbacies. Here again, those who could pay simony's price often received the positions and power, thus infuriating the reform-minded Church leaders who felt themselves constantly fighting an uphill battle. Family-based alliances, usually cemented in contracted marriages for financial gain and military advantage, often ruthlessly overwhelmed the populace with their demands for more fodder to feed the war machine of this confusing and conflictive period. Whether one was pro- or anti-emperor in any given historical situation often depended on such alliances.

The Church was unfortunately, in many ways, a product of its times! The various vying "family" factions waged war in order to control papal elections. Scandals, often of a sexual nature, abounded. Schism was rife. But the picture was not totally black. These centuries were also a time of incredibly rich monastic reform in a Church badly in need of far-reaching reforms. The foremost of these monastic reforms was that of Cluny (important to St. Romuald who received his monastic formation in two Cluniac houses: St. Apollinare in Classe at Ravenna and St. Michael of Cuxa in southern France). This Cluniac Reform would eventually encompass some 1,100–1,200 houses. Characterized by centralization and uniformity, the reform covered England, France, Italy, Spain, and Germany. The evident strength of the movement stemmed from the presence of five strong abbots during a two-hundred-year period. But Cluny was not the only impressive monastic reform at that time. There were also the Lorraine reforms, centered at Gorze Abbey in the south and Brogne Abbey in the north. The Abbey of Fleury attracted many houses to its reform. Anglo-Saxon monasticism took its cue from Fleury and initiated many important reforms at the Council of Winchester. Our Lady of Einsiedeln Abbey in Switzerland proved yet another center of reform. And of course, we can add the Romualdian reform movement, the Congregation of the Holy Cross at Fonte Avellana and St. John Gualberti's Vallombrosan reform.

During these centuries in which the Romualdian founders lived, one pressing question for reform-minded clergy became: "How can we stabilize the papacy without making the Church a department of the empire?" What ultimately became known as the "Hildebrandine" or Gregorian Reform was the answer. Pope Leo IX (r. 1049–54) was a reformer concerned with spreading the influence of the papacy beyond Rome to other parts of the empire. Basically by means of extending the ongoing Cluniac monastic reform to the Church as a whole, Hildebrand helped Leo to begin that process. Through a series of decrees and local Church synods, they worked against the abuses of simony, clerical marriage, and concubinage, thereby beginning to establish papal supremacy which history would try to assert over all of Christendom, including the Eastern Church. The papacy had begun its ascent as a temporal power in the Empire.

At the Lateran Synod of 1059, the Church finally determined a precise method for canonical papal elections rather than trust imperial whim or the local factional disputes of the Roman populace. St. Peter Damian was a highly influential Church reformer and papal legate during this period. Popes Alexander II (r. 1061–73) and Gregory VII (r. 1073–85) used papal legates to work Church reforms on a local basis, also reiterating decrees against simony, clerical marriage, clerical incontinence and lay investiture. All three great Italian monastic reformers during this period (St. Romuald ca.952–1027; St. Peter Damian 1007–72; St. John Gualberti 995–1073) were outspoken opponents of simony. Two monk–cardinals became the main articulators of theology against this heresy: Humbert of Silva Candida who wrote three books against simoniacs and Peter Damian of Fonte Avellana whose theology Leo IX ultimately accepted for his reform work.

Realizing that many of the clergy were buying their ecclesiastical positions or had them forced on them by well-meaning families, it is hardly surprising to hear that such clerics found ascetical disciplines like celibacy and sexual continence most unappealing. Many of these ecclesiastical benefices became, for all practical purposes, dynastic in the sense that fathers passed them down to their sons. Nicolaitism was sporadically rampant: married clergy; priests living with concubines; priests living together in homosexual relationships; and various other forms of incontinent behavior.

This is the situation into which the early Romualdian founders were born. This is the Empire with which Romuald and Peter Damian became intimately involved: Romuald with Emperors Otto III and Henry II; Peter Damian with the ecclesiastical forces aligned with imperial interests and politics. Even more poignantly, this is the Church badly in need of reform, within which Romuald worked his reform movement—primarily within the monastic world, but also in the area of anti-simoniac Church reform. This is also the Church within which Peter Damian worked tirelessly for reform: monastically, by furthering Romualdian principles of reform; ecclesiastically, by actively opposing simony, clerical incontinence and ignorance.

2. Romuald of Ravenna

The greater part of our knowledge of Romuald lay in two documents: Peter Damian's *The Life of Blessed Romuald*[1] and Bruno-Boniface of

---

1. The critical editions of this work are: (a) St. Petrus Damianus, *Opera Omnia*, PL 144-5 (1853), (b) St. Petrus Damianus, *Vita Beati Romualdi*, ed., Giovanni Tabacco (Roma, Istituto Italiano, 1957). An English version is available which I will use: Peter Damian, *The Life*

Querfurt's *The Life of the Five Brothers*.[2] Both authors bring to their works their own polemical slants and ideologies. Peter Damian is interested in answering a question related to his own reform activities: "What is true eremitism?"

> Using Romuald as his vehicle, which does not mean that Romuald would not have agreed with him, Peter Damian shows how true eremitism is a combination of Saint Benedict of Nursia and Saint Antony of the Desert, that is, the hermit is not selfish but truly lives a love of neighbor and is able to live to the fullest a monastic ascesis as well as a personal relationship with Christ within the hermitage cell. True eremitism is the *group dynamic* hermitage: hermits living together.[3]

As Tabacco indicates, "Romuald represents the creative and visibly dynamic moment of an experience which Peter Damian wishes to prolong."[4] Bruno of Querfurt calls Romuald the "father of rational hermits who live according to the Rule."[5] Romuald received his initial monastic formation at the Benedictine abbey of St. Apollinare in Classe where his personal fervor only occasioned the resentment of his fellow monks in this newly Cluniacized monastery. With the permission of his abbot, Romuald then lived an Eastern model of abba-disciple relationship at the feet of a somewhat rustic hermit named Marino in the Ravenna countryside. The years spent near the Benedictine abbey at Cuxa where Romuald and companions lived the eremitical life together in the nearby forest were crucial to Romuald's development as a spiritual mentor. He studied the monastic sources and taught his companions the wisdom stemming from his own intense life of prayer and solitude. He was later appointed abbot of Classe, but Romuald's reacquaintance with life at St. Apollinare lasted only a little over a year when he resigned in disgust in December 999.

---

of Blessed Romuald in *The Mystery of Romuald and the Five Brothers* (Big Sur, Hermitage Books, 1994). Hereafter VR.

2. The critical editions of this work are: (a) Bruno-Boniface di Querfurt, *Passio Sanctorum Benedicti et Johannis ac Sociorum Eorundem*, ed., Wojciech Ketrzynski, *Monumenta Poloniae Historica* 6: 388-428 (Cracow, 1893), (b) S. Bruno di Querfurt, *Vita dei Cinque Fratelli e Lettera a Re Enrico*, trans. B. Ignesti (Camaldoli, Edizioni Camaldoli, 1951). An English version is available which I will use: Bruno of Querfurt, *The Life of the Five Brothers* in *The Mystery of Romuald and the Five Brothers* (Big Sur, Hermitage Books, 1994). Hereafter V5F.

3. Peter-Damian Belisle, "Primitive Romualdian/Camaldolese Spirituality," *Cistercian Studies Quarterly* 31:4 (1996) 414.

4. Giovanni Tabacco, "Romualdo di Ravenna e gli inizi dell'eremitismo camaldolese," *L'Eremitismo in Occidente Nei Secoli XI e XII* (Milan, SEVEP, 1965) 83.

5. *V5F* 88.

Romuald followed up this short-lived abbatial service with an amazing period of foundation in Istria (Dalmatia) where he lived as founder and recluse for some three years. Otto III promoted his "mission to the East" idea with its "novel approach to the eremitical life through the *triple good*: cœnobium, hermitage, and evangelization/martyrdom."[6] Though somewhat reluctantly, Romuald allowed a few of his disciples to take up this mission to Poland where they later suffered martyrdom.

> During this period, Romuald is brought clearly to the fore by the primary sources as a Wisdom figure whose gift of tears flows from a profound comprehension of God's mystery. This description is not mere sentimentalism but a reference situating Romuald within the context of the monastic and mystical traditions vis-à-vis the gift of tears (for example, Origen, Evagrius Ponticus, John Cassian, and Symeon the New Theologian [949–1022], Romuald's contemporary in the East).[7]

Another period of foundation ensued, then a lengthy stay with the monks of Saint Mary of Sitria,[8] followed by yet another of Romuald's journeys of monastic foundation. Camaldoli was, if not the last, certainly one of the last foundations of Romuald's, dating to 1023.[9] We are told that Romuald was sensitive and humble, living in a radically prophetic manner radiating holiness to others who seemed drawn to the hermit wherever he traveled. He was a charismatic, free person who trusted in Divine Providence for all decisions. True son of Benedict, Romuald centered his life on the Word, as can be seen in his love for the psalms in the so-called "*Brief Rule of Saint Romuald*,"[10] his life with Marino and their scriptural devotion,[11] Romuald's own personal praxis,[12] and his famous teaching regarding

6. Belisle, *Primitive*, 415.

7. Ibid.

8. Romuald stayed four times at ValdiCastro and four times at Sitria during his later years. Cf. *VR* 35, 39, 45, 49, 52, 64, 68, 69.

9. The document deeding the church of San Salvatore to the early monks of Camaldoli after having lived there some years is dated August 10, 1027. Cf. Giuseppe Vedovato, *Camaldoli e la sua Congregazione dalle Origini al 1184; Storia e Documentazione*, Italia Benedettina 13 (Cesena, Centro Storico Benedettino Italiano, 1994) 126.

10. *V5F* 158. "The path you must follow is in the Psalms—never leave it. If you have just come to the monastery, and in spite of your good will you cannot accomplish what you want, then take every good opportunity you can to sing the Psalms in your heart and to understand them with your mind. And if your mind wanders as you read, do not give up; hurry back and apply your mind to the words once more."

11. *VR* 178–79. "Marino sang the entire Psalter every day. Rising early, Romuald with him, he would wander aimlessly, stopping now and then to sit under a tree and sing twenty Psalms, then moving to another tree to sing thirty more."

12. *VR* 182–88.

praying the psalms.[13] "Romuald was eminently a man of solitude who cared about the salvation of others, particularly other solitaries living without the support of communal fellowship, the discretion of a superior, or the guidance of the *Rule*."[14]

Romuald also enjoyed mystical gifts. Besides the previously mentioned gift of tears, he experienced ecstasies, prophetic utterances and the reportedly total comprehension of Sacred Scripture. Tabacco views Romuald's gift of tears as "expressing both ineffable grief and great certainty"[15] and holding a prominent place in Romualdian spirituality's need to speak with God in solitude:

> Before the solemn decorum of Cluniac monks praying long hours in choir united to realize the idea of perfect community, stands the heightened voluntary penance and secret prayer of Romuald and his hermits, the restlessness to travel from one solitude to another, the conversation between souls with an exceptional ability to love and an unquenchable thirst for tears.[16]

Romuald is said to have experienced this gift of tears while praying the psalms, celebrating Eucharist and during contemplation. Peter Damian also speaks highly of the connection between prayer and tears. In his "On the Perfection of Monks" (Opus XIII), he connects contemplation with the gift of tears: "O tears of spiritual joy, sweeter than honey and better than any other nectar! You renew minds raised to God with the sweet delight of a delicate taste while watering dry and shriveled hearts with the flow of supernatural grace. . . . The taste of divine contemplation completely fills us inwardly, gives us life and sweetness."[17] "Tabacco insists that prayer with tears finds a place not only within the patristic and medieval traditions, but also specifically within the context of Romualdian spirituality, where it is conspicuously connected to the need to speak to God."[18]

3. Romualdian Spirituality

By the Romualdian reform movement, I am considering those monastic houses which were either founded, refounded or reformed by Romuald and his followers, including the houses which Fonte Avellana

13. *VR* 188. "Better to sing one Psalm with feeling . . . than to recite a hundred with a wandering mind."

14. Belisle, *Primitive*, 416.

15. Giovanni Tabacco, "*Privilegium amoris: aspetti della spiritualità romualdina*," *Spiritualità e Cultura Nel Medioevo* (Naples, Liguori, 1993) 178.

16. Ibid.

17. Petrus Damianus, *De Perfectionis Monachorum*, PL 145: 309.

18. Cf. Tabacco, *Privilegium*, 178.

founded or reformed during the time before the canonical erection of either the Camaldolese Congregation[19] or Avellanita Congregation.[20] This movement joined the spirit of the early desert monastic tradition to the Benedictine way of life. "Based on greater solitude, silence and fasting, the Romualdian system of life imitated the ancient Egyptian anchoritism in the penitential ascetical sphere; for the rest, it faithfully referred to the observance of the Benedictine *Rule*. It was an organized eremitism."[21] "This reform movement within the Benedictine world was not antagonistic to Benedictinism, but it wanted to extend the influence of the *Rule of Saint Benedict* to those drawn to solitude."[22] "Montecassino . . . recognized Romuald's institute as legitimate and authentic. . . . In fact, in 997 Abbot John II retired to a nearby hermitage 'with five of his monks' where John Gradenigo, Romuald's disciple, had been since 988. The Romualdian eremitical movement did not come to be considered antagonistic to Benedictine monasticism, but even a magnificent fruit of it."[23]

Certain essentials for the Romualdian reform can be discerned: the *Rule of Saint Benedict*, the union of hermits and cenobites under a hermit superior, silence, fasting, prayer, solitude. "But there is also another interesting phenomenon characteristic of both Romuald's own foundations and Peter Damian's later Romualdian foundations out of Fonte Avellana: almost all Romualdian foundations were relatively small."[24] Romuald himself established an incredible number[25] of hermitages, monasteries, cells and churches under various auspices and patronages. "Even during those last years when he was surely suffering the pains and frailties connected

19. The Camaldolese Congregation was established under Pope Paschal II (r. 1099–1118), whose bulls *Ad hoc nos* (1105) and *Gratias Deo* (1113) confirmed the congregation as an autonomous union of monasteries and hermitages under Camaldoli.

20. The Avellanita Congregation (Congregation of the Holy Cross, Congregation of the Dove; Little Doves) was established by Pope Gregory VII (r. 1073–85) with a bull dated April 10, 1076. This congregation was suppressed by Pope Pius V (r. 1566–72) and joined to the Camaldolese Congregation.

21. Mansueto Della Santa, *Ricerche Sull'Idea Monastica di San Pier Damiano* (Camaldoli, Edizioni Camaldoli, 1961) 168.

22. Belisle, *Primitive*, 417.

23. Della Santa, *Ricerche*, 169.

24. Belisle, *Primitive*, 418.

25. Major foundations or reformed houses include: Longadera hermitage near Cuxa; Veghereto di Bagno di Ravenna monastery; St. Apollinare in Classe monastery; Pereo hermitage and monastery; St. Michele di Lemmo monastery; a hermitage somewhere near Rome, most likely in the suburbs or between Tivoli and Rome; Valdicastro hermitage and monastery; St. Elena dell'Esino monastery; Santa Maria della Sitria hermitage and monastery; Montepregio hermitage; St. Vincenzo al Furlo monastery; Pietrelata hermitage united with St.Vincenzo; a monastery near Orvieto; Camaldoli hermitage; still others of which we do not know specifics.

with old age, there he was: still traveling from one side of Italy to the other, founding and building all the way."[26] Camaldoli itself, from which the great congregation would takes its name, was established during these last few years of Romuald's life.

John of Lodi[27]—Peter Damian's successor as prior of Fonte Avellana and his biographer—relates that Peter Damian acted in much the same way. When housing conditions became cramped at Fonte Avellana, the prior would set off on a founding journey, dropping off one or two monks at each location, which he designated a new foundation. All[28] part of the Romualdian world, these Avellanita foundations were built on a small scale. Only some of the larger monastic houses that later joined the movement (e.g., Pomposa) were exceptions to this rule, during those years before Fonte Avellana and Camaldoli had been erected on a juridical congregational basis. "It seems to me that the fact that all these houses were rather small says something about the movement's spirituality, especially since so many foundations were being made rather than concentrating on building up certain houses into large, prosperous monasteries. There was no rule mandating smallness, but surely the fact that most Romualdian houses were small says something about the lived reality of Romualdian spirituality."[29] The quality of spirituality had to be sound and the fraternal bonds, strong, for the movement to last.

Solitude certainly characterized Romualdian spirituality and was intrinsically central to the heart and spirit of Romuald himself. He was deeply drawn to greater solitude throughout his life and felt compelled to devote it to providing the possibility for other solitaries to live a monastic life which would be formational, accountable, and juridically approved. Romuald was allowing hermits to live alone together, but under the *Rule* and obedience to a superior. Before Romuald, those hermits not living alone in the wilds were attached to an established monastery, under obedience to the superior of the cenobitical house. But Romuald accented the importance of solitude

26. Belisle, *Primitive*, 418.

27. Ioannes Lodensis, *Vita B. Petri Damiani*, PL 144: 113-80.

28. Major foundations and reformed houses include: St. Vincent al Furlo monastery; Holy Trinity of Monte San Vicino hermitage near Frontale; St. Nicholas of Corno hermitage near Ocri; Montepregio hermitage; St. Barnabas Gamugno hermitage; St. John Baptist Abbey at Acereta; St. Bartholomew of Camporeggiano monastery; St. Gregory in Conca monastery. Still other Romualdian houses helped by Peter Damian include: Holy Mary of Sitria; Holy Savior Monastery near Perugia; St. Emiliano monastery in Congiuntoli; an unknown monastery named St. Benedict. Cf. Giuseppe Cacciamani, "Le fondazioni eremitiche e cenobitiche di S. Pier Damiano; Inizi della congregazione di S. Croce di Fonte Avellana," *Ravennatensia* V (Cesena, 1976) 5–33.

29. Belisle, *Primitive*, 418.

in his spirituality by placing cenobites and hermits living together under a hermit superior. Hermitages came into their own ecclesiastical standing, with the *Rule*, a superior, novices and professed monks. Pierucci[30] considers this evolution a consequence of Romuald's experiences with Marino in the wilderness, as well as those years spent near Cuxa when he was superior over a small group of solitaries. Tabacco adds, "Again, it is among Cuxa, Ravenna and Venice that the formation of the Romualdian eremitical experience occurs: a small group of solitaries bonded *pro privilegio amoris*."[31] I believe this is a core statement about Romualdian spirituality: a small group of solitaries bonded for the privilege of love (i.e., loving God and sharing that love within the *koinonia* of monastic community.

But why is solitude so important?

> Followers of Romuald are drawn toward solitude for two main reasons: to speak with God, and to challenge evil openly. The desire to speak with God, to hold spiritual conversations with God on a regular basis, to center clearly on the Word of God, and to converse with that Word with tears stemming from both compunction and joy: this is the Word-centered reality of Romualdian solitude, which ran the gamut from short periods of solitude to permanent reclusion.[32]

The second motivation for solitude evokes the spiritual combat of the desert tradition. Here is the "white martyrdom" of Egypt where the solitude of eremitical life is peopled with demons.[33] To enter the hermitage is to challenge evil openly in the voluntary martyrdom of Romualdian spirituality. "Just like the gift of tears, battling demons is a time-tested theme of monastic literature and tradition; so this theme repeatedly comes to the fore in the *VR*."[34] Traditional hagiographical imagery and experiences aside, the encounter with evil is surely germane to the solitary's quest and thus, an intrinsic part of Romualdian spirituality's accent on solitude.

Given that accent, it seems a bit paradoxical to find Romuald traveling so much! Judging by the *VR*, there is a clearly discernible restlessness in Romuald to journey forth in apostolic mission. For a reclusive hermit, he is "on the road" a good deal of the time! Tabacco refers to the "restless life of Romuald [that] seems to witness a continuous contrast between the needs for action and contemplation."[35] He is either living in seclusion or helping a mo-

30. Cf. Celestino Pierucci, "La riforma romualdino-camaldolese nelle Marche," *Aspetti e Problemi del Monachesimo Nelle Marche* I (1982) 39–59.
31. Tabacco, *Romualdo*, 106.
32. Belisle, *Primitive*, 419.
33. Cf. Petrus Damianus, *De Fuga Dignitatum Ecclesiasticarum*, PL 145: c. 455-464.
34. Belisle, *Primitive*, 420. Cf. *VR* 7, 16–18, 32–33, 49, 58, 60-63, 70.
35. Tabacco, *Privilegium*, 194.

nastic foundation to find its footing on contemplative ground. "He wanders from one solitude to another solitude, living or fashioning for others an organized approach to the solitary monastic witness."[36] There were plenty of little churches and chapels[37] peopled and served by Romualdian solitaries, just as there were plenty of hospices and hospitals[38] sponsored by later Camaldolese hermits and cenobites during the thirteenth and fourteenth centuries. Various documents, including sets of Camaldolese constitutions, stress the need for hermits to perform apostolic ministry, particularly in the areas of guest ministry and care of the sick. Both Romualdian and Camaldolese spiritualities accentuate this apostolic concern. But here is a paradox: Romuald's eremitical life is more open to the world than other extant forms of hermit existence. "There were many other forms, thus the need for Romuald to fashion and give integrity to the eremitical monasticism in the Church of his day. But Romualdian monasticism is also most definite about its rejection of the world and its ways—open to the world, but not engulfed by it; grounded in that world, but not buried by it."[39]

The interplay between solitude and apostolic work—action and contemplation—in Romualdian monastic spirituality may be understood more clearly vis-à-vis the unique context of the mission to the East[40] proposed by Otto III. The emperor encouraged Romuald to send monks to what is now Poland where they could build a monastery in some secluded spot situated in Christian territory but near enough pagans for the purpose of evangelization. They could then live the "triple good": a cœnobium for monks beginning their monastic formation; solitude for more experienced monks desiring the fruits of the hermit life; the possibility to evangelize pagans and perhaps, suffer martyrdom. Bruno of Querfurt described this triple good again when he referred to Otto's death at the age of twenty-three: "He longed to do better, and God's ardent desire for the three highest goods, any one of which is sufficient unto salvation: the monastic habit [monastery], the solitary life [hermitage] and martyrdom."[41]

> It is important to realize from the outset that this monastic program set forth by Emperor Otto III was Otto and Bruno's program, not Romuald's.

36. Belisle, *Primitive*, 420.

37. Cf. Cacciamani, *Le fondazioni*, 5–33; Giuseppe Pallazzini, "S. Romualdo e le sue fondazioni tra i monti del Cagliese, *Studia Picena* 18 (1948) 61–76; Celestino Pierucci, "La piu antica storia di Fonte Avellana," *Benedictina* 1–2 (1973) 121–39, Celestino Pierucci, *La riforma*, 39–59.

38. Cf. Anselmo Giabbani, ed., *Camaldolesi; Le Figure più Espressive dell'ordine viste da S. Pier Damiani, Dante, Petrarca, ecc.* (Camaldoli, 1944) 211–14.

39. Belisle, *Primitive*, 421.

40. Cf. *V5F*, 95.

41. *V5F*, 111.

That fact does not mean that it did not become Romuald's program in time—it certainly became Romualdian, as such—but as far as conception is concerned, the idea is more Ottonian and certainly Brunonian. It is particularly crucial to remember this fact when viewing the third component of the triple good: evangelization-martyrdom.[42]

In his book on primitive Camaldolese eremitical life, Anselmo Giabbani[43] interprets this triple good variously. The cœnobium (monastery) is the formative ground for monastic training and discipline, but also the place for the infirmary and the hospitality accorded to guests. The hermitage is the place for contemplative joy, voluntary ascesis and immersion into the liturgy. The relationship between cœnobium and hermitage when they are situated together (as at Camaldoli) could be seen as a monastic progression from the former to the latter when the time is right—a model found in John Cassian. "Giabbani interprets evangelization/mission (the third good) in a number of ways: the voluntary martyrdom of Romualdian and Camaldolese reclusion, that is, the voluntary martyrdom that comes the way of Athanasius' *Vita Antoni*; second, the ministry of preaching and participation in the active Church life, particularly in terms of monks called upon to be bishops and cardinals; and third, active missionary life."[44] The majority of Romualdian foundations did not follow this cœnobium/hermitage model as at Camaldoli. There were more than one model at work in the Romualdian world of monasteries, hermitages and cells.

Other scholars[45] maintain that viewing the cœnobium as the first stage (via Cassian's schema) is likely the elaboration of Bruno. "Bruno himself was related to the emperor and was familiar with impressive imperial abbeys, as well as being a member himself of a cenobitic monastery in Rome (Saints Alexis and Boniface) before becoming Romuald's disciple."[46] Viewing the cœnobium as a preliminary step to the hermitage within Romuald's reform was quite possibly Bruno's combination of Romualdian

42. Belisle, *Primitive*, 422.

43. Anselmo Giabbani, *L'Eremo: Vita e Spiritualità Eremitica nel Monachismo Camaldolese Primitivo* (Brescia, Morcelliana, 1945).

44. Belisle, *Primitive*, 422.

45. Cf. H. G. Voigt, *Brun von Querfurt, Mönch, Eremit, Erzbischof der Heiden und Märtyrer* (Stuttgart, 1907); Walter Franke, *Romuald von Camaldoli und seine Reformatatigkeit zur Zeit Ottos III* (Berlin, Ebering, 1913); Tabacco, *Romualdo*; Jean Leclercq, "San Romualdo e il Monachesimo Missionario; Momenti e Figure di Storia Monastica Italiana," ed. V. Cattana, *Italia Benedettina* 16 (Cesena, CSBI, 1993); Jerzy Kloczowski, "L'Érémitisme dans les territoires slaves occidentaux," *L'Eremitismo in Occidente Nei Secoli XI e XII* (Milan, SEVEP, 1965); Roberto Fornaciari, "Monachesimo—Missione—Martirio; Bruno-Bonifacio di Querfurt dall'Eremo del Pereo a Kiev," diss., Gregorianum, 1994.

46. Belisle, *Primitive*, 423.

eremitical life with his own personal Saxon religiosity and Teutonic mo-
tives. "As much as he undoubtedly loved and admired Saint Romuald, there
is a side to Bruno-Boniface that never quite reconciles itself to the Romualdian world. Leclercq, Tabacco, and others allude to this situation.[47] Kloczowski stresses that Bruno "remains however always tied to Germany and
the Empire."[48] The Pereo[49] cœnobium was Otto's idea, in addition to the
mission to Poland—springing from his own monastic aspirations.

> Otto thought that he could somehow provide the monks at Pereo at least two
> of the three goods until he himself could renounce the imperial crown and
> realize his own idea for monastic mission/evangelization. His proposal for
> two superiors at Pereo provided an abbot who would deal with the practical
> details of living monastic life (*abbas corporum*) and an abbot who would care
> for the spiritual needs of the monks in the capacity of spiritual master (*abbas
> animarum*)—designating Romuald himself as the latter abbot.[50]

In any case, Otto's Pereo experiment was a disaster. Romuald did reform cenobitical monasteries when they asked him to do so, but he normally channeled his energies into eremitical pursuits. "Such might not
have been Bruno's goal or Otto's idea, but it was Romuald's emphasis—
even if history would transform those Romualdian decades into Camaldolese centuries."[51] Giabbani indicates that this cœnobium/hermitage
combination became the constitutional mainstay of Camaldolese monastic history. This ideal has surely been the case for Camaldoli itself, but for
most of Camaldolese history, the various foundations have been either one
or the other. The Romualdian orbit was more concerned with eremitical
experience, though not exclusively so. After Romuald's death, later Romualdian and Camaldolese history would encompass both the eremitical
and cenobitical spiritualities more inclusively.

Considering the personality of Romuald, the Romualdian movement's approach to reform on a small scale and the particular apostolic dimensions to that vision (conditioned by Otto and Bruno), Romualdian
spirituality's success was due, in no small part, to the bonds of love expressed within the movement. "Tabacco demonstrates convincingly how
important personal relationships of advanced spiritual intimacy and love
were to Romuald's reform movement. Considering their small-scale approach to monastic reform, strong fraternal bonds strengthened Romuald
and his followers, and helped to form and define the direction of their

47. Ibid, 424.
48. Kloczowski, *L'Érémitisme*, 345.
49. Cf. *V5F*, 95–97.
50. Belisle, *Primitive*, 423.
51. Ibid.

movement."[52] Romualdian love of God was intense and needed to be shared. The followers of Romuald were known for the love they shared.

> The spirituality that underpinned the Romualdian world was contemplative, Benedictine, monastic spirituality. But Romualdian (and early Camaldolese spirituality) had experienced certain historical factors that conditioned its unique character. That uniqueness stemmed from its small-scale approach to monastic witness centered on the Word of God in solitude—particularly eremitical solitude—and was characterized by an intense *koinonia* based on the monks' love of God, which had to be shared with one another and the world.[53]

4. Camaldolese History

Camaldoli and Fonte Avellana became the two power bases for the Romualdian reform movement during those decades and early centuries after Romuald's death. In 1076 Pope Gregory VII (r. 1073–85) established Fonte Avellana and its dependencies as a congregation. Called the "Congregation of the Dove" by some, officially it became known as the "Avellanita Congregation" or "Congregation of the Holy Cross of Fonte Avellana." Camaldoli became the head of the Camaldolese Congregation under Pope Paschal II (r. 1099–1118), whose bulls *Ad hoc nos* (1105) and *Gratias Deo* (1113) erected the congregation as an autonomous union of monasteries and hermitages under Camaldoli.[54] By 1113, Camaldoli had accrued an impressive list of monasteries, hermitages, churches, and dependencies to form its new congregation. The twelfth century proved a time for still more phenomenal growth as various bishops and popes donated churches and monasteries to the fledgling congregation. The second half of this century was a conflictive period for Camaldoli as it staved off episcopal interests on the part of Arezzo's bishops and asserted its status of exemption, under the Holy See's protection. This apostolic support was a key proponent to Camaldoli's success during these early centuries.

Another major period of growth occurred in the thirteenth century when still more foundations were brought into the congregation—in 1227, for example, when Pope Gregory IX (r. 1227–41) confirmed new acquisitions. Pope Innocent IV (r. 1243–54) allowed Camaldoli to accept

---

52. Ibid., 426.
53. Ibid., 429.
54. Cf. Giuseppe Vedovato, *Camaldoli,* 65–76 and Cécile Caby, *De L'Érémitisme Rural au Monachisme Urbain; Les Camaldules en Italie à la Fin du Moyen Âge,* Bibliothèque des Écoles Françaises D'Athènes et de Rome (École Française de Rome, 1999) 79–82 for lists of monasteries, churches, hermitages, and dependencies.

other monastic congregations into its own. Naturally, an ongoing process of development within the life of the congregation paralleled its outward expansion. A series of constitutions were established which moved from initially describing the simple life at Camaldoli under Rudolf IV[55] to elaborating and consolidating customs for an entire congregation under Martin III.[56] Gerard II[57] first published two series of constitutions (1278) that reinforced customs regarding the eremitical life among Camaldolese. But at the General Chapter of 1279 in Soci,[58] Gerard added a fourth book to Martin's extant three books *de Moribus* regarding the general organization of the congregation, including the establishment of minimum requirements for life in a hermitage. Candidates would now have to be at least twenty-five years old and have experienced at least three years of cenobitic life in the congregation. At the 1328 General Chapter in Bologna still another Prior General, Bonaventure of Fano, would add yet a fifth book to Martin's original three and Gerard's one, thus comprising the five books of *de Moribus*.[59]

Like any other religious congregation or order, the Camaldolese underwent a series of ups and downs, growth and decline, refinements and reformations. As the congregation grew in size, it encompassed increasingly more urban foundations. Gradually Camaldoli's influence within the congregation lessened. As caretaker of Romuald's vision during the eleventh century and motherhouse of a fledgling congregation of the twelfth century, Camaldoli would become a revered hermitage whose power would pass to other houses—even cenobitical houses—whose superiors would be elected Priors General. Other urban hermitages such as St. Matthias of Murano (Venice) and Holy Mary of the Angels (Florence) would become powerful centers of government and influence. Other cenobitical monasteries, St. Michael of Murano and St. Hippolytus of Faenza, would know the same power and prestige. As people moved from rural life into the cities and urban existence, so the Camaldolese Congregation gradually focused its energy in that same direction.

In 1338 the Congregation organized itself into nine groups of houses, each with its own studentate.[60] The fifteenth and early sixteenth centuries were crowned with Renaissance studies, great intellectual endeavors and

---

55. Johanne-Benedicto Mittarelli, *Annales Camaldulenses Ordinis Sancti Benedicti . . .* 9 vols. (Venetiae, 1755–73) III, App., cols. 512–51. Hereafter *Annales Camaldulenses*.

56. Ibid., VI, App., cols. 1–65.

57. Ibid., VI, App., cols. 240–55.

58. Cf. Caby, *De L'Érémitisme*, 123.

59. *Annales Camaldulenses* VI, App., cols. 272–87.

60. These studentates were located in Classe, Polesine, Urano, Pisa [2], Siena, Camaldoli, Volterra, and Murano.

artistic pursuits. Western civilization took a great step forward. Under Prior General Ambrose Traversari, St. Mary of the Angels in Florence became a center for humanist pursuits. The monks opened a college for the youth of Florence where the Letters and Sciences flourished alongside the Arts. This monastery had already become known for its arts (painting, miniature painting, weaving of tapestries, drawing, metalwork, embroidery, transcription of manuscripts, illumination of manuscripts) and its artists (Lorenzo Monaco, Jacopo Dei Francesche, Silvestro Dei Gherarducci, and Simone Camaldolese). These latter three were accomplished miniaturists whose work, writes Kanter, "so completely dominated the production of illuminated manuscripts in Florence in the last quarter of the fourteenth century—as did that of their Camaldolese successor, Lorenzo Monaco, in the first quarter of the fifteenth century—that the concept of a '*scuola degli Angeli*,' understood not as referring to a particular scriptorium but as a term of convenience loosely defining a Florentine miniaturist style over a period of more than fifty years, is not entirely inappropriate."[61] There was not so much an art school, as such, as what the Renaissance art scholar Miklos Boskovits called a "Camaldolese miniaturist center."[62]

Traversari began a school for boys at Fonte Buono (the monastery at Camaldoli) under the direction of Mariotto Allegri. Camaldoli became another Camaldolese center for humanist dialogue. St. Michael of Murano also ran a reputable school and developed a fine library from the fifteenth century onwards. Most manuscripts came from the Venetian monasteries as well as the holdings of famous Venetian scholars and churchmen, but many also came from the area around Siena and Mount St. Catherine's Monastery in the Sinai. These manuscripts were in Greek, Latin, French, Italian, and various Eastern languages. In all, John-Benedict Mittarelli's eventual codex catalogue of manuscripts at St. Michael of Murano numbered 1,425 pages!

But Renaissance and humanist times were also a period of general monastic decadence. Traversari initiated reforms within the congregation, while Priors General Mariotto Allegri and Peter Delfino, as well as Paul Giustiniani pursued similar avenues of reform. At the end of the fourteenth century, the Camaldolese were a real "patchwork" of communities very different from one another, as Caby[63] perceives in her work. This lack of unity in organization, control and customs, only presaged further fragmentation.

61. Laurence B. Kanter, ed., *Painting and Illumination in Early Renaissance Florence 1300-1450* (New York, The Metropolitan Museum of Art, 1994) 10.

62. Cf. Miklos Boskovits, "Su Don Silvestro, Don Simone e la *Scuola degli Angeli*," *Paragone* 265 (1972) 35–61.

63. Caby, *De L'Érémitisme*, 527.

In 1446 St. Michael of Murano became the head of a newly formed autonomous Camaldolese congregation with nine chief monasteries.[64] By this time, Camaldoli was somewhat on the margin of things, with the Hermits of Tuscany counter-balancing Murano on the Camaldolese scale. Tensions existed between the two groups, mirroring the ongoing political tensions between Florence and Venice. An unfortunate mix of the religious and political spheres finds Venetian soldiers attacking the monastery of Camaldoli itself in 1498! Pope Leo X (r. 1513–21) with the bull *Etsi a summo* (1513) approved a reunion of all Camaldolese houses, separated into seventeen different groups. This union would last a shaky century, but not without further disruptions and surprising developments.

Paul Giustiniani (1476–1528) had joined Camaldoli in 1510, clothed as a novice on Christmas. Problems regarding monastic observances existed at the time and, although Prior General Peter Delfino had tried to regularize the observance among the houses during the early years of his ministry, his efforts were to little avail. Some houses wanted to assume the reform customs of the Santa Giustina movement begun by Barbo, particularly those houses in the Veneto. Delfino found himself helplessly ineffective between those who wanted to reinstate the full rigorous observance of former times and those who wanted to move into a progressive reform mode. Antipathy between Camaldolese hermits and cenobites was generally at a very high level.

When Giustiniani's good friend John de Medici became Leo X (r. 1513–21), he enabled Giustiniani and Peter Quirini (a compatriot of Giustiniani's who had joined Camaldoli in 1512) to legislate reformation of the Camaldolese Congregation at the 1514 General Chapter in Florence. During the fifteenth century, the General Chapter became the real power in Camaldolese life, and this 1514 Chapter early in the century witnessed the resignation of Delfino, the last life-term General of the Congregation. Giustiniani was elected superior at the hermitage of Camaldoli in 1516, received from Leo X all of Camaldoli's ancient privileges in 1518, and published the *Regula Vitae Eremiticae* there in 1520. Malcontent still prospered at Camaldoli and, although he was reelected superior at the hermitage, Giustiniani finally departed Camaldoli with Leo's blessing and gathered like-minded disciples around him to form the Company of Hermits of St.

---

64. The nine houses: St. Michael of Murano, Holy Mary of the Angels in Florence, St. Benedict of Florence, St. Matthias of Murano, Holy Mary Delle Carceri of Este, St. Savino of Pisa, La Rosa of Siena, Holy Angels of Bologna, and St. John of Giudecca. Cf. Alberico Pagnani, *Storia dei Benedettini Camaldolesi; Cenobiti, Eremiti, Monachi ed Oblati* (Sassoferrato, 1949) 125–6; Vittorino Meneghin, *S. Michele in Isola de Venezia*, I (Venezia, Stamperia di Venezia, 1962).

Romuald.[65] The Company soon became an autonomous eremitical congregation, though that had not been Giustiniani's original intention, and later took the title "Camaldolese Hermits of Monte Corona." An attempt to reunify Camaldoli and Monte Corona failed in 1540, as did the period of attempted reunion ordered by Pope Urban VIII (r. 1623–44) in 1634—a period of thirty-three years, the last twenty of which were characterized by mutual distrust, defiance and disdain. Pope Clement IX (r. 1667–69) dissolved this attempted union of Camaldolese in 1667.

On December 10, 1569, Pope Pius V (r. 1566–72) issued the bull *Quantum animus noster* which suppressed the Avellanita Congregation and bestowed the former Romualdian hermitage and then Avellanita cœnobium[66] of Fonte Avellana along with its dependencies upon the Camaldolese Congregation. In 1601 the eremitical Piedmontese Congregation[67] began, at the behest and patronage of Carl Emanuel I, Duke of Savoy. Alexander Ceva, a monk of Camaldoli who had been named superior of a monastery near Turin, collaborated with the duke to begin this unique eremitical group[68] which quickly acquired autonomy and modeled itself on the Monte Corona customs rather than those of Tuscany. This was the wealthiest of the Camaldolese groups, supported by the court and many wealthy benefactors. Still another eremitical congregation formed in France around the figure of Boniface d'Antoine (+1673), a member of the Piedmontese Congregation. Though tied to this congregation and adopting the constitutions and customs of Monte Corona, this French Congregation[69] of Camaldolese Hermits remained a basically autonomous congregation— thanks in no small part to its physical distance from the Italian groups. If the Piedmontese were the wealthiest congregation, the French were by far the poorest, enjoying a reputation for extreme austerity.[70]

65. In 1526 the congregation assumed the name "Congregation of Camaldolese Hermits of Monte Corona." Cf. Pagnani, *Storia*, 130; Placido Lugano, *La Congregazione Camaldolese degli Eremiti di Montecorona* (Frascati, Sacro Eremo Tuscolano, 1908).

66. Pope John XXII (r. 1316–34) suppressed Fonte Avellana as a hermitage and erected it as a cœnobium in February 1325.

67. This aggregate was officially called the Confraternity of the Holy Annunciation of Villafranca Piedmonte.

68. Main houses: Holy Savior of Turin, Belmonte, Selva Maggiore and Lanzo. Short-lived house: St. Tecla of Genoa.

69. Main houses: Our Lady of Consolation, Val-Jésus, Grosbois, La Rochelle, St. Gilles of Besse, Sarthe, Our Lady de Sapet, Holy Savior of Rogat and l'Île-Chauvet. Short-lived houses: Brieure, Mont-Valerian and Senart.

70. Their poverty forced the French to open cells to rich benefactors who could die in the hermitage in exchange for monetary recompense. Some notable *donati*: a chancellor of the king, a Transylvanian prince, judge, lawyer, bishop, two ambassadors, and the king's armor-bearer.

Since the 1513 union between Camaldoli and Murano had ceased when the Hermits of Tuscany withdrew in 1616, the Camaldolese Congregation officially broke into eremitical and cenobitical branches. With the addition of the French, the Camaldolese now became a collection of five autonomous congregations—all separate, all calling themselves Camaldolese, all eremitical except Murano.[71] If the sixteenth century of Camaldolese history had highlighted the power of the General Chapter, the seventeenth century now displayed the disheartening factiousness of Romuald's family! The short-lived union attempted by Urban VIII quickly began to erode due to bickering over various customs[72] among the houses and traditions. When Clement IX dissolved the trial union, another door of opportunity closed. Still one further attempt at reunion among the hermits was broached, but Tuscany barred this path to unity.

Although the seventeenth century proved a time for disunity, it was also a time for Camaldolese growth. The cenobitic congregation moved into a re- markably observant and prosperous period—as many as forty-six monaster- ies in four geographical provinces (i.e., Tuscany, Venice, Marches, and Romagna) that produced notable scholars, teachers, writers, and scientists. Their houses became centers of culture on Murano, in Florence, Rome, and Ravenna. The hermits of Monte Corona experienced incredible growth and expansion. In 1669 there were 356 Coronesi in eighteen houses.[73] By 1767 they had grown to 554 hermits in five provinces (Papal States, Veneto, Naples, Poland/Lithuania, Germany-Austria-Hungary-Slovakia).[74] At their apex dur- ing this time, the Hermits of Tuscany had 575 choir monks and conversi.[75]

But the winds of political change were moving. Revolutionary forces in France suppressed the French Camaldolese in 1770, putting the last prior of Val Jésus to the guillotine in the process. The Piedmontese Camal- dolese followed suit in 1801. Various Camaldolese houses were marked for suppression in Italy during these troubling decades of the late eighteenth century until 1810, when all the religious orders were suppressed in Italy during the Napoleonic occupation. Certain restorations were made in

71. Hermits of Tuscany, Cenobites of St. Michael of Murano, Monte Corona, Pied- montese and French congregations.

72. For example, the Piedmontese Congregation was angered by the request that the prior of Turin would have to surrender his pontifical regalia! This same issue would prevent a later attempt at union between Monte Corona and Piedmont, prior to the religious sup- pressions of the late eighteenth and early nineteenth centuries.

73. Cf. Giuseppe M. Croce, "I Camaldolesi nel Settecento: tra la 'rusticitas' degli eremiti e l'erudizione dei cenobiti," *Settecento Monastico Italiano* (Cesena, Badia S. Maria del Monte, 1990).

74. Ibid.

75. Ibid.

1814, and pockets of Camaldolese gathered to resume the regular life. But the nineteenth century proved a century of suppression for Camaldolese history, despite the fact that this same period produced a Camaldolese pope, Gregory XVI (r. 1831–46)! Between 1855 and 1873 all the Camaldolese houses would again be suppressed under the Italian Republic's religious suppressions. Most houses were never recovered during the rebuilding and reacquisition period of the twentieth century.

When the monks of Camaldoli were expelled in 1866, the majority of hermits moved to a small villa[76] a few kilometers away, at Prataglia, where they tried to maintain their monastic rhythms of life together, sustaining themselves through benefactions, their own meager government allowance and later, the running of a *collegio*. The first three alumni of this school were clothed as Camaldolese in 1891. The government allowed the monks back at Camaldoli in a "caretaker" role and the congregation slowly revived, as did the cenobitic and Monte Corona congregations. Prior to World War I, Camaldoli opened a foundation in Brazil while the cenobites started one in Texas. Concerned that regular observance be established and eremitical life promoted, the Holy See ordered an apostolic visitation of all three congregations in 1912.

In 1927, hopes of insuring congregational life in South America, should Italian politics once again suppress religious houses, were dashed when the Brazil foundation had to be terminated for various reasons. In 1935 Pope Pius XI (r. 1922–39) issued *Inter religiosos* which suppressed the floundering cenobitic congregation, closing the houses in Faenza, Volterra, Florence, Perugia and Texas. Fonte Avellana and the houses in Rome, Fabriano and Sassoferrato were given to Camaldoli's congregation. The cenobites were given the options of incorporation into the Tuscan Hermits, incardination into diocesan structures or laicization. After the Holy See ordered an extraordinary Chapter for Camaldoli, Anselm Giabbani and Benedict Calati were sent to Fonte Avellana as prior and master of students, respectively, since all Camaldolese student monks would now be sent there for formation. Giabbani and Calati enkindled fresh interest in the Camaldolese primary sources and spirituality, publishing studies and promoting preliminary work on a reform of the Camaldolese Constitutions. Also during this time, Camaldoli became a center for political and social action, for the theological training of laity in the Italian Church, and for programs in youth and cultural studies. Msgr. Montini (later Pope Paul VI) was involved with the programs for Catholic laity, notably FUCI.[77]

76. Carlo Scimoni, a benefactor of the community, offered the use of this villa, which they named St. Alberigo.

77. Federazione Universitari Cattolici Italiani—for the theological formation of laity.

After World War II, Giabbani was elected Prior General and various publications on Camaldolese history and spirituality began to appear. A new set of constitutions was approved. Camaldoli sponsored an American foundation in California in 1957, while the other Camaldolese congregation still extant, the Monte Corona Congregation, made foundations in Ohio (1959) and Colombia (1963). After Aliprando Catani's six-year ministry as Prior General during which the Tuscan Hermits joined the fuller Benedictine Confederation (1966), Benedict Calati was elected Prior General in 1969. During his tenure, the Camaldolese Benedictines opened foundations in India and Brazil, continued the programs at Camaldoli itself, and fostered ecumenical dialogue in all its houses. The current Camaldolese Constitutions were approved in 1985. After eighteen years of Calati's stewardship, the current Prior General, Emanuele Bargellini, was elected in 1987, continuing the work of his predecessors who brought the congregation to its healthy status and prospect—corporately and spiritually.

5. Camaldolese Spirituality

Foundationally, Camaldolese spirituality down the centuries mirrored its spiritual roots in the Romualdian world: monastic, Benedictine, contemplative spirituality. Within the monastic tradition, Camaldolese spirituality is intimately connected with the word of God. Monastics experience themselves as called by the word; they dwell with that word, being both formed and challenged by the word in the process. Monastic spirituality presupposes the biblical ground as the very foundation beneath its structure: centering on the biblical portrayal of salvation history, being especially drawn to the sapiential voice within God's Word, the way of Wisdom. It honors the importance of *lectio divina* in all its varied forms for the monastic life, valuing highly the desert tradition of monastic literature— very biblical in nature—as well as the lived experience of monastic brothers and sisters throughout the Christian centuries. Monastic spirituality moves into liturgy where it takes symbolical expression in a mature form: celebrating life and salvation history, intensifying the baptismal commitment, and enabling participation in lived, ordinary mysticism.

Camaldolese spirituality is monastic, but more precisely, Benedictine monastic spirituality. Looking to the *Rule of St. Benedict* as their traditional monastic guide, Camaldolese are concerned that life be an ongoing participation in the life of Christ. This approach to life[78] assumes an intimate

---

78. Cf. Camaldolese Congregation of the Order of Saint Benedict, *Constitutions and Declarations . . .* (Camaldoli, 1985) no. 147, 1.

relationship with Christ, whereby life itself becomes a commentary on God's Word, a living witness to salvation history's unfolding, and the extension of baptism's call. The Benedictine way approaches life itself as sacred, and the vow of *Conversatio morum* is its daily dynamic of participation. Stability focuses and localizes that participation while obedience, as *imitatio Christi*, puts flesh and blood on the bones of religious life. Given the *Rule*'s flexibility to the conditions of time and space, the virtue of *discretio* (called "mother" of monastic virtues) is allowed to flourish in a truly Spirited life.

Camaldolese Benedictine monastic spirituality is also intentionally contemplative. "The Camaldolese Congregation consists of hermitages and monasteries. The hermitage is the characteristic element of the congregation and as such orients the spiritual life of all its members. In both hermitage and monastery the monks attend to the contemplative life above all else."[79] But contemplation does not mean vegetation. Even in the Romualdian world, contemplation and action both clamored for attention. Romuald's own life could be a character study in the action/contemplation dialectic, while Peter Damian's ecclesiastical experience put to the test his own feelings about the issue. Although the Camaldolese family has discussed this topic down the centuries—often merely agreeing to disagree—the experience and grace of wisdom is inclusive on the issue. Action is complementary to contemplation. And Camaldolese spirituality, although primarily contemplative in focus, is not exclusively so. Calati[80] has elucidated this fact vis-à-vis Rudolf of Camaldoli and Peter Damian in a number of works. And Camaldolese tradition confirms the time-tested principle of the unity between action and contemplation. Nevertheless, within the context of the Benedictine world, the Camaldolese have consistently placed more emphasis on the contemplative dimension of the mix in their spirituality.

Naturally, Camaldolese spirituality did not develop in a vacuum over the centuries of its history. The Camaldolese approach to monastic life was consistently conditioned by history, by the times, by tradition, by reform, by grace. The *devotio moderna* movement of the late medieval period, for instance, proved highly influential in the spiritual climate of the fourteenth and fifteenth centuries, not only among the laity (for it was, indeed, a

---

79. Camaldolese OSB, *Constitutions*, nos. 3 and 4.

80. Cf. Benedetto Calati, *Sapienza Monastica saggi di storia, spiritualità e problemi monastici* (Roma, Studia Anselmiana, 1994); Benedetto Calati, "Spiritualità monastica," *Vita Monastica* XIII (1959) 3–48; Benedetto Calati, "Vita attiva e vita contemplative . . . la tradizione patristica nella primitiva legislazione camaldolese," *Camaldoli* 6 (1952) 10–24, 83–90; 7 (1953) 48–57; 8 (1954) 66–77; Benedetto Calati, *Comunione e libertà; il monachesimo di S. Pier Damiano (sec. XI)* (Camaldoli, Edizioni Camaldoli, 1995).

movement aimed at the spiritual rejuvenation of that laity), but also among the members of religious orders. Though it began in the Netherlands and spread quickly into pre-Reformation Germany, the institutionalized side of the movement did not move further abroad. Still, the spirit of this movement affected the greater Church. Although in retrospect, many modern "isms" claim to have found some of their historical roots in the *devotio,* one assertion that can be made about this movement's own roots is that they can be found in traditional monastic spirituality. Is it any wonder that Bernard of Clairvaux, his fellow Cistercian writers and many medieval Carthusians were beloved by the *devotio*'s adherents? Inner devotion, the individual's efforts, the interior life, the spiritual dimension of manual labor, the imitation of Christ, freedom in the Holy Spirit, conversion—all are common themes shared by both medieval monastic writers and the proponents of *devotio moderna.* These themes found their way into the minds and hearts of countless Christians everywhere, including Camaldolese.

Another major line of renewal in the fifteenth-century Church was Christian Humanism which found one of its most eloquent proponents in Ambrose Traversari, Prior General of the Camaldolese Congregation. "True master of Christian Hellenism,"[81] Traversari translated extensive portions of Basil, John Chrysostom, Paul, Jerome, John Climacus, and many others. Humanism promoted a "learned piety" which saw a rebirth in the study of Scripture and patristic writings. Reformer and papal legate on behalf of ecumenical work with the Eastern Church, Traversari promoted unity within plurality—a concept he saw expressed concretely within the Camaldolese tradition by the union of the active and contemplative dimensions. He promoted dialogue on the ecclesiastical front by his participation in Church unity negotiations, as well as on the home front by forming humanist discussion groups at both Holy Mary of the Angels in Florence and at Camaldoli. As both an able administrator and a deeply spiritual reformer, Traversari influenced Camaldolese spirituality. Other Camaldolese Christian humanists who followed in his footsteps remained faithful to this spiritual quest—monks like Mariotto Allegri and Peter Delfino, as well as other humanists who interpreted things a bit differently, notably Paul Giustiniani and Peter Quirini. In its own unique wedding of hermitage and cœnobium, Benedictine Camaldolese spirituality continued to embrace the monastic values of communion and community, at a time when individualism ran rampant.

---

81. Cf. A Corsano, *Per la storia del rinascimento religioso in Italia: dal Traversari a G.F. Pico* (Napoli, Perrella, 1935).

When Traversari was asked to devote himself to ecumenical work with the Eastern Church, he did so wholeheartedly because he loved that Church: its history and tradition, its treasures of faith and spirituality. Traversari stood in good company; Romuald himself was born in tenth-century Ravenna, a city very much within the Byzantine sphere of influence at that time. And Romuald's personal openness to Otto III's mission to the East and the idea of evangelical work among non-Christians gave precedence for Camaldolese ecumenical endeavors.

Today the Camaldolese Benedictines are involved in ecumenism and interfaith dialogue on a number of fronts. Camaldoli has become a center for dialogue, particularly Jewish-Christian and Orthodox-Catholic relations. Saccidananda Ashram (Shantivanam) in South India is, by its very nature, an ecumenical crossroads and sacred place of dialogue. Incarnation Monastery in Berkeley, California, has been involved in Anglican-Catholic dialogue for nearly two decades; in fact, the monastery began as an experimental Anglican-Catholic foundation sharing common monastic spaces. New Camaldoli Hermitage in Big Sur, California, has sponsored interreligious work through the "Four Winds Council" (Buddhist-Christian and Native American-Christian relations) and the "Camaldolese Institute for East-West Dialogue" (intermonastic dialogue). All Camaldolese houses are encouraged to provide hospitality to Christians and non-Christians alike. "If a believer of another faith asks to spend a longer period of time in the community, the prior shall carefully consider the request with the conventual chapter; let the monks remember that ecumenism is today an especially monastic way of responding to the Lord's call to preach the gospel (cf. Mark 16,15; *V5F* 2)."[82] Camaldolese guesthouses have become sanctuaries of spirituality for seekers of all faiths. Robert Hale writes of the Camaldolese spirit that "has a universal openness, affirmed by the present constitutions of the Congregation of Camaldoli regarding spiritual ecumenism, also in its widest scope (n. 125). The Vatican has also commended this ministry to the Camaldolese. But this openness extends out from the specific center of Christ and the particular Benedictine Camaldolese heritage that gives rootedness to such dialogue."[83]

There is a strong thread running through Camaldolese Benedictine history and spirituality that ties together the particulars of time and space, forming a durable seam of love. Romualdian spirituality was built on loving relationships that overflowed into witness—even the witness of missionary work and martyrdom. During the first Camaldolese millennium,

82. Camaldolese, *Constitutions*, no. 125.
83. Robert Hale, "Camaldolese Spirituality," *The New Dictionary of Catholic Spirituality*, ed. Michael Downey (Collegeville, The Liturgical Press, 1993) 107.

that love was challenged and tested. But Camaldolese spirituality has embraced real unity within its diversity, a unity that is real insofar as it is preserved in love. For in its own charismatic and prophetic way, to quote one of its most highly esteemed proponents, Don Benedict Calati,[84] Camaldolese Benedictine spirituality subsists in the "primacy of love."

84. Cf. Calati, *Sapienza*, 241–79.

Part Two
Sustaining the Spirit

An Image of the Praying Church: Camaldolese Liturgical Spirituality

Cyprian Consiglio

There is a story told about Robert Hale when he assumed his role as the new prior of New Camaldoli. He began a presentation to the assembled brethren shortly after his election by placing on the desk before him the Bible, the *Documents of Vatican II*, the *Rule of St. Benedict*, and the Camaldolese *Constitutions*, and announced that these would be the four elements on which life at New Camaldoli under his ministry as prior would be based. I cannot think of a better way to begin this attempt at describing the Camaldolese approach to liturgy than by recalling this same image. This, too, is the way Camaldolese approach the liturgy of the Church: as encounter with the Word, as Roman Catholics of the Vatican II renewal, as Benedictines, and as Camaldolese—each of these elements focusing us more and more.[1]

1. Ecclesiology: General Theology of the Opus Dei/Monastic Liturgy

We begin by standing on solid ground, i.e., the renewal of Vatican II. The People of God, and liturgists in particular, not only embraced the renovations and innovations called for by *Sacrosanctum Concilium*, which were challenging in and of themselves; led by the Spirit of *aggiornamento*, they went even beyond the original practical suggestions of the council. The People of God were ready to own their public prayer again; the Church was ready to ease up on the strident clinging to tradition in the name of Counter-Reformation; the Church was ready to open the doors to the world; the People of God were ready to sing a new song to the Lord!

---

1. The author is liturgist and choirmaster at New Camaldoli Hermitage in Big Sur, California, and so this chapter will have a specifically American, at that, "Californian," bent as well.

The Benedictine world, while itself being a slow-moving vessel weighed down with its own charter as the bearer of traditions, was both a prophetic voice within the liturgical movement beginning in the late nineteenth century, mainly through careful scholarly work, and a careful observer, awaiting patiently its own renewal, in some instances anticipating the reforms of Vatican II. Though we perhaps still await a complete articulation of the theology of monastic liturgy in light of Vatican II, the Benedictine Confederation embraced the principles laid down by the council. After the promulgation of the revised Liturgy of the Hours for the Roman Rite in 1970, with its accompanying *General Instruction of the Liturgy of the Hours*, (which Burkhardt Neunheuser, o.s.b., speaking not only his own sentiments, calls a "masterpiece of liturgical theology"[2]), the Benedictine Confederation was ready to speak for itself as well, and did so in the *Thesaurus Liturgiae Horarum Monasticae*, with its "Directory for the Celebration of the Work of God" and "Directive Norms for the Celebration of the Monastic Liturgy of the Hours."

Why was it necessary to restate what had already been stated so well? Monastic liturgical tradition, particularly regarding the Divine Office, has always run parallel with the Roman liturgical tradition. While other religious, and indeed "secular" clergy, were mandated to pray the Divine Office, it is the monastic order that has always had its "own" Office, its own *Antiphonale* (and *Graduale*) and *Breviarium Monasticum*. While eventually all other orders grew to depend on the Roman Rite after Trent, acknowledging, of course, the cross fertilization since the time of Benedict himself between the so-called basilican tradition and the monastic, the monastic orders, short of their own rite, have always maintained at least their own style and usage. Further, as Anne Field points out, it's a question of ecclesiology, really. The *General Instruction* is concerned with the canonical prayer of the Church, whose ecclesial character is "most clearly seen when the bishop, joined by his priests and clergy, leads in this liturgy the local church in which Christ's one holy, Catholic and apostolic church is truly present and operative."[3] Monasticism, on the other hand, is essentially a lay institution that does not belong to the hierarchical Church structure.

> The ecclesial dimension of monastic liturgy . . . does not derive from the fact that it is celebrated in union with the bishop and the clergy or in the official name of the Church, but from the fact that the monastic community itself, assembled to celebrate the Work of God . . . constitutes the Church at prayer.[4]

2. Anne Field, ed. *Directory for the Celebration of the Work of God* (Riverdale, Md., Exordium Books, 1981) 10; hereafter *DWG*.

3. *General Instruction for the Liturgy of the Hours* in *Liturgy of the Hours*, vol. 1 (New York, Catholic Book Publishing, 1975) no. 20; hereafter *GILH*.

4. *DWG*, p. 5, no. 2, p. 19.

From this follows one of the subtle characteristics of specifically monastic liturgy: we do not celebrate, for example, the Office "'by delegation of' or 'in the name of the Church.' The community itself, by the very act of coming together, constitutes 'the Church at prayer;'"[5] the monastic community is "an image of the praying Church."[6]

> The *General Instruction* states that particularly contemplative communities represent in a special way the Church at prayer; they are a fuller sign of the Church as it continuously praises God with one voice, and they fulfill the duty of "working," above all by prayer, "to build up and increase the whole mystical Body of Christ," and for the good of the local churches.[7]

Not enough can ever be said, though, about the fact that it is Christ who is the celebrant here, who is the priest, and who is the worshipper. By virtue of our baptism, we exercise our role as a priestly people by sharing in Christ's priesthood, indeed as priests of all creation.

This is what makes us an image of the praying Church: our unity in the priesthood of Christ. Bargellini wrote in 1975 that the document on the Liturgy of the Hours reclaims this background in order to indicate the sense and the function that communal prayer has in the Church—communal prayer as a condition and a mode of existence in which every single member, and all together the ecclesial body, is "animated from that unique and same Spirit that makes of the existence of each Christian a praying cry; and of all the members a communion."[8] Our communal liturgies, therefore, are truly our "strong moments" as community, times of "special power and efficacy;"[9] and indeed "the central element around which the life of the monastery is structured."[10] In the liturgy we express not only who we are, but also who we wish to become, hope to become, expect to become. In a stronger sense yet, in the liturgy we also *become* who we are. As the *General Instruction* articulates about postures and actions, so our very gathering is a "sign of the unity . . . [which] both expresses and fosters the inner spirit and purpose of those who take part in it."[11] Our gathering not only expresses our unity; the very act of gathering wants to bring about such unity. And we shall only see God in the "Work of God" (Opus

---

5. Ibid.

6 . Ibid., p. 7.

7. *GILH*, p. 24.

8. Emanuele Bargellini, "Liturgia delle Ore: Pregare nel Ritmo del Tempo" *Vita Monastica* 123 (1975) 280.

9. *DWG*, no. 8, p. 24.

10. Ibid., no. 1, p. 19; no. 12, p. 28.

11. *General Instruction on the Roman Missal* in *The Sacramentary* (New York, Catholic Book Publishing, 1974) II.II.20; hereafter *GIRM*.

Dei) "if we are joined with our brothers or sisters in genuine communion. Then 'God will abide in us (1 Jn 4.12).'"[12] Indeed the *Directory* specifies that this is another of the characteristic elements of monastic spirituality, that the common celebration of the Liturgy of the Hours must carry with it a spirituality of communion.

The genius of the Romualdian reform and the Camaldolese tradition to this day is the combination of the greater emphasis on solitude while retaining its foundation in Benedictine monasticism, so much so that even the hermitage is situated between the cenobitical and anchoritic ways of life, seeking to create a wise balance of solitude and life in common by keeping the best elements of both. In both Camaldolese hermitages and cœnobia, communal liturgy is seen as "supreme expression of communion among the members of the community."[13] Hence, the liturgical life of a monastery is the most important thing we do as a community. Still, because of our accent on solitude,[14] there is for us perhaps more than for other Benedictines an added tension in the dynamic between private and common prayer.

2. Liturgy and Private Prayer

> The communal moment does not exhaust all the experience of the prayer of the Christian. There will also be the moment in which it is better to close oneself in one's room and pray to the Father without words (cf. Mt. 6.6), but this will also be prayer in the Church and with the Church. It is the fundamental law of solidarity of one with others in Christ in the interior of salvation's mystery.[15]

As a matter of fact, it is specifically in the hermitage where a monk is enabled, even expected, to have the ability to immerse oneself in the liturgy of the Church and have "deeper immersion into the liturgical celebrations of the life of Christ."[16] Liturgy is, by its nature, public—defined as "public work done for the service of others." It seems important to point out that there is no explicit conflict between liturgical and private prayer; both form a harmonious unity. There remains, though, a kind of underlying tension between public prayer and private prayer, often unspoken. Some of

12. *DWG*, no. 15, p. 31.
13. *DWG*, no. 8, p. 25.
14. The Camaldolese *Constitutions* state that even cenobitical life should have not only simplicity and austerity, but also solitude. Cf. Camaldolese, *Constitutions* I.6.
15. Bargellini, *Liturgia*, 282.
16. Peter-Damian Belisle, "Primitive Romualdian/Camaldolese Spirituality" *Cistercian Studies Quarterly* 31:4 (1966) 422, citing Giabbani.

it grew out of the *devotio moderna*, which laid such great stress on the individual's inner life. Certainly until the liturgical reforms of Vatican II, devotionalism was preferred by many devout Catholics, including vowed religious and monks, because active participation in the liturgy was limited, if it existed at all, due to the language barrier and general lack of active participatory elements, for instance.

Another danger in the eremitical life is to consider liturgy as not all that important, so beauty and care about the liturgy are likewise unimportant. This tension seems to stem back to the general tension between the active life and the contemplative life: liturgy as more active and spontaneous; personal prayer as more contemplative. The earliest Egyptian monks, for instance, did not place great stress on liturgical prayer, though even they gathered. For Evagrius of Pontus, psalmody is the work of the active (as opposed to contemplative) life,[17] and wordless prayer in the heart, without images or words, even beyond thought, flows from active prayer, and is the normal fulfillment of active or liturgical prayer. In his "Commentary on the Our Father," John Cassian says liturgical prayer bursts forth in a wordless and ineffable elevation of the mind and heart to what he calls "fiery prayer"—*oratio ignita*—where the mind is "illumined by an infusion of heavenly light, and not by narrow human words."[18] This fiery prayer is the normal fruition that bursts forth, by God's grace, when vocal prayer is well made. Here is the classic monastic belief which Cassian passes on to Benedict, that secret and contemplative prayer should be inspired by liturgical prayer and be the normal crown of that prayer, even though for Benedict, liturgy was certainly seen as the highest form of contemplation. But does liturgical prayer lead us to contemplative prayer or does contemplative prayer lead us to liturgy? Is "fiery prayer" somehow dependent on liturgical prayer? In a sense, it does not really matter because they cannot be separated. Thomas Merton argues that monastic prayer cuts through this distinction.

> [T]hough liturgical prayer is by its nature more "active," it may at any moment be illuminated by contemplative grace. And though private prayer may tend by its nature to greater personal spontaneity, it may also be accidentally more arid and laborious than communal worship, which is in any case particularly blessed by the presence of Christ in the mystery of the worshipping community . . . The doctrine of the early Benedictine centuries

17. This, of course, uses the word in its earlier, broader sense: "active" not being merely apostolic, but any activity, even ascetical, such as psalmody, fasting, vigils.

18. John Cassian, *The Conferences*, trans. Boniface Ramsey (New York, Newman Press, 1997) 345–46.

shows us that the opposition between "official public prayer" and "spontaneous prayer" is largely a modern fiction. . .[19]

It is exactly the objective element of the liturgy that is the safeguard and the springboard for our personal prayer. Liturgy is also subjective in that "encounter with God does not happen to a nameless crowd, but to beloved and conscious human persons."[20] The ideal is a balance between private and public prayer.

> A monk's personal participation in the liturgy and his practice of *lectio divina* are reflected in his interior prayer, flowing up from the depths of the soul under the impulse of the Holy Spirit.[21]

Our *Constitutions* go on to urge monks to model their prayer on the mystery of Christ by "following the Church on her journey through the annual liturgical cycle" and by upholding Sunday as the weekly celebration of the Lord's Passover. In this way liturgy becomes the objective standard, the source of spirituality. Devotions (and strictly speaking, anything outside Eucharist and Liturgy of the Hours is a devotion) are not discouraged; but in keeping with *Sacrosanctum Concilium* they must always be brought into harmony with the liturgy, find inspiration in it and lead up to it. In this view, all private practices from yoga and zazen to rosary and Stations of the Cross, must find their source and summit in the communal liturgical life of the Church.

Vagaggini writes that the novice should be shown how to make participation in the communal celebration of the Eucharist and Divine Office

> the center of his spiritual life, to which all the rest is ordered and . . . from which all the rest derives: ascesis, prayer and private meditation, study, apostolate. Neither should one omit making the novice understand that active participation in the communal liturgy . . . is the connatural place also for the mystical encounter with God.[22]

Christian prayer is born for communion with God, and created from the Spirit in the body of Christ, so cannot be seen as something issuing from an autonomous source. And praying together is not a purely functional fact. "It is a sacramental sign that realizes and expresses the mystery of the Church, the communion of children in dialogue with the Father and

---

19. Thomas Merton, *The Climate of Monastic Prayer* (Spencer, Mass., Cistercian Publications, 1969) 85.

20. *DWG*, no. 21, p. 37.

21. Camaldolese, *Constitutions* III, 79.

22. Cipriano Vagaggini, "Liturgia e questione monastica," *Vita Monastica* 12 (55) (1958) 170.

among themselves."[23] It is always prayer in communion, because from it each person receives the capacity to call God "Father."

3. Historical Notes

Romuald came out of the Cluniac tradition, with all its liturgical splendor, his first monastery being St. Apollinare in Classe. The Cluniac tradition, of course, was *laus perennis*, the unending round of vocal prayer. While the Cluniac liturgy could be considered a "disgraceful aberration from the austere simplicity of the Rule,"[24] still Peter Damian has high praise for Cluny. We are careful not to say that Romuald's reform was a re-action against the excesses of Cluniac observance, only a reaction against corruption within the system.

What was Romuald's vision of the liturgy? We can only guess. Lawrence describes the Romualdian monastery as a "cenobitical commu-nity following the *Rule of St. Benedict* with an austere simplicity."[25] We know that the earliest hermit monks were known as the "sensible monks who lived under a Rule;" and the Rule certainly called for the celebration of common offices. As mentioned earlier, even the hermitages were not seen as places where one might be relieved of the burden of communal liturgy, but where one might immerse even more deeply into the mystery of Christ as revealed through the liturgy. Can we safely assume then that this applies to the liturgy as well: sensible and austere? We are in this tra-dition, not precisely as vehemently anti-Cluniac as Bernard, but as monks seeking to move away from splendor and prosperity to live a life of sim-plicity and austerity.

While we have little evidence of the liturgical life at Camaldoli in the first years, Patricia McNulty[26] gives some indication of the life at Fonte Avellana in its early days. Eleventh-century Fonte Avellana consisted of a church (the crypt of which still remains), a cloister, scriptorium and other offices, and close to the church, the cells in which some of the brethren lived in pairs. Speculation is that farther out, scattered on the high slopes, must have stood the cells of those who lived a life of strict reclusion. The recluses only left their cells to join in common worship on Sundays and the great feasts. There were four groups: professed brethren, at least some of whom were priests, who lived as recluses in the distant cells; professed

23. Bargellini, *Liturgia*, 280f.
24. C. H. Lawrence, *Medieval Monasticism* (New York, Longman, 1989) 101.
25. Ibid., 153.
26. St. Peter Damian, *Selected Writings on the Spiritual Life*, trans. Patricia McNulty (London, Faber and Faber, 1959), Introduction.

brethren who, if their duties demanded, lived in the cells close to the church; novices, each of whom was placed under the tutelage of one of the brethren who instructed him in spiritual discipline and was responsible for his welfare; and lay brothers who performed most of the manual labor.

The hermits only kept whatever books were necessary, including a psalter, a breviary and texts from the scriptorium. Their day was spent in manual labor, reading, private prayer, and recitation of the Divine Office. In addition to the canonical hours, their practice was to recite an entire second psalter for the faithful and, as much as possible, yet another one for the faithful departed. The brethren who lived two to a cell led a life similar to the recluses except they sang the canonical hours in choir. Peter Damian was effusive in his praise of the canonical hours; he wrote that they "are like seven baptismal fonts set up in the bosom of the Church,"[27] and that when the monks hasten to church to chant and pray, they are like a formation of soldiers, "particularly at the night hours when the brethren, roused from their sleep as by the sound of a trumpet, form ranks and in orderly battle array, march together, inspired to readiness for the divine combat."[28]

The practices of the Avellanita hermits raise two interesting points. First, even a recluse was bound to observe the canonical hours, not just any form of prayer he chose. The monks of Fonte Avellana could very well have been spending up to six hours a day praying the "official prayer of the Church" with the additional practice of the extra psalter (perhaps a link to the desert tradition, but not an uncommon practice in Cluniac houses as well). Secondly, one might ask why the public prayer was prayed privately? In his "The Book of 'The Lord Be With You,'" Peter Damian treated this and similar issues, giving us one of the most beautiful images in our tradition: "The Church of Christ is united in all her parts by such a bond of love that her several members form a single body and in each one the whole Church is present." So, even a monk in his cell is somehow the whole Church, and praying the Office as the whole Church![29]

> And so whatever belongs to the whole applies in some measure to the part; so that there is no absurdity in one man saying by himself anything which the body of the Church as a whole may utter, and in the same way many may fittingly give voice to that which is properly said by one person.[30]

27. S. Petrus Damianus, "De horis canonicis" PL 145: 223, quoted in Maurus Wolter's *The Principles of Monasticism*.

28. S. Petrus Damianus, "De significatione horarum" PL 145: 316, ibid.

29. This apologetic serves also as Peter Damian's justification for the celebration of "private masses," what one of our monks calls an "eloquent defense of a dubious practice." Still . . .

30. St. Peter Damian, "The Book of 'The Lord Be With You'" in McNulty, *Selected*, 59.

In sum, their father reformer left the early Romualdian monks under the guidance of the *Rule of St. Benedict*. One comes to appreciate the wisdom of our rootedness in that tradition, which affords us the possibility of leading "a contemplative life of real solitude and simplicity, without formalism and without rigid, inflexible prescriptions of minor detail" while, by virtue of our Benedictine roots, fully protecting us "by spiritual control and by religious obedience."[31] This is how we remain rooted, especially through our communal liturgy, in the Church, through Scripture and tradition: all of which give contemplation and solitude a focus, and keep us from drifting into solipsism or idiosyncratic spiritualities, whether to the "left" or the "right."

4. Constant Prayer and Sanctification of the Day

> Time is a holy creature with which the liturgy puts one in meaningful touch . . . Time's sacredness is not imposed by liturgical worship. Liturgical worship discovers that sacredness and summons the assembly to take part in it.[32]

We must never lose sight of the Liturgy of the Hours' raison d'être: a way of prayer that grew out of the desire not simply to sanctify every hour of the day, but to pray at all times, or perhaps, taking our cue from Kavanaugh, to recognize the sacredness of time. Some of the earliest Christian writers such as Clement of Alexandria were cautious about setting aside certain fixed moments of the day dedicated to prayer, since the goal was to pray constantly! We do not even refer to an "Office" for the Egyptian hermits; they only at times did communally what they would have been doing individually. At the other extreme, Cluny tried to praise God every moment of the day, albeit liturgically.

Without losing sight of the injunction to constant prayer, under the reform of Vatican II, the key moments have been restored to their proper time and given their proper stress. Vatican II sought to restore a certain graduated solemnity, as it were, to ensure that no matter what else occurred in the day, Lauds and Vespers were given their prime import over the other hours of the day. The *Directory* reaffirms this for Benedictines: "the pre-eminence of these two hours arises from the fact that they are 'memorials,' the one of the resurrection, the other of the death of our Lord Jesus Christ," and therefore they are analogous with and share in the

31. Thomas Merton, *The Silent Life* (New York, Noonday Press, 1957) 153–54.
32. Aidan Kavanaugh, *Elements of Rite: A Handbook of Liturgical Style* (Collegeville, The Liturgical Press, 1990) 24.

pre-eminence of the Eucharist, with which they constitute "a spiritual triad." The Roman Office also reaffirms the importance of the hour of Matins, but adjusts it to be an Office of Readings that can be prayed at any hour of the day. The *Directory* likewise states that, while Lauds and Vespers are the two principal hours, "in monastic tradition Vigils are also of great importance," but stresses the retention of its character as a night Office by maintaining the name "Vigils" that gives a certain eschatological meaning to the Office.[33]

If it is true that ritual is "ideology in action," then what better way to describe the Camaldolese approach to liturgy than to look at an ordinary monastic liturgical day? Our community here in Big Sur celebrates communally in keeping with the stress of the *Directory*: early morning Vigils, Lauds, Eucharist at midday, and Vespers.[34]

The hours especially have a certain cosmic aspect to them as they are recited at key moments of the day: night, dawn and sunset. The longer a person lives this life, the more each of the hours takes on a very definite quality. Vigils, for instance, is perhaps the most meditative of all the Offices. As the *Directory* describes it, "The celebration of Vigils is distinguished not by its external solemnity, but by its own special character, which is that of contemplative, peaceful and prolonged prayer."[35] We mostly recite it in a sober fashion, which, with its two long readings and solo recitations of some psalms, proves quite reflective—really a communal meditation on the Word. It is significant that a number of monks remain in the darkened rotunda after Vigils, keeping watch around the empty altar, preparing the altar of the heart for the coming of the risen Lord, a long drink of silence before "joy comes with dawn" and the greeting of the Risen One. Vigils taps into the anticipation or longing of the human heart for the Light of lights, the morning star rising in our hearts. Shawn Carruth writes that whereas Lauds and Vespers belong to the whole Church, Vigils are the characteristic hours of the monastic Office because the night

33. *DWG*, no. 26, 43.

34. Because we accent solitude in the cell, the monks in America were relieved early on of the obligation to pray the Little Hours in common at all, so the tradition of doing so here is all but forgotten. We celebrate a communal midday prayer once a month on community recreation days, during the Easter Triduum and on rare occasions of special gatherings, but generally the midday hour is given to Eucharist. Some of our Italian houses employ midday prayer as their "Office of Readings" in place of Vigils, especially houses where students live, in keeping with the Roman tradition. Here in Big Sur, monks in formation are taught about the tradition of the Little Hours and are presented with a variety of ways to set aside certain times of the day, especially exhorting them to pray privately whatever psalms may not be part of the monastic communal cursus.

35. *DWG*, no. 26, p. 43.

is full of difficulty and ambiguity, yet also of resolution. . . . Night is a time to reflect on God's work, a time of visions and dreams . . . "Night vision" is the vision of the world as God sees it, as God would have it. Our monastic "incessance" is unceasing prayer, the kind of prayer symbolized in the concept of vigil.[36]

Lauds then always remembers and offers praise for the resurrection and captures the breaking forth of light dispelling the darkness of sin and death. It is sung throughout, and is centered on the first proclamation of the Gospel of the day.

The *Directory* stresses that the Liturgy of the Hours has an intimate link with the Eucharist, indeed that it is a "preparation for and a prolongation of the Eucharistic celebration," but also by virtue of the fact that both the Eucharist and the Liturgies of the Hours are memorials.

> Since the Work of God is in fact a prayer memorial of the history of salvation and shares this character with the Eucharist, it is justifiably called, like the Eucharist, a "spiritual sacrifice." . . . The Work of God, like the sacrifice of the altar, is intended to be eucharistic, that is to say an offering of thanksgiving and praise to God for the wonderful things he has done in his love for us and for which we contemplate in the mystery of his divine plan.[37]

This "memorial" must be sensed in its most profound liturgical sense, a remembering that "makes present." Every celebration of the eucharistic mystery is an *anamnesis*, an "efficacious memorial rite," not only of the death but also of the resurrected Lord, writes Vagaggini, urging him to quote John Chrysostom: "The Paschal mystery has no greater intensity than that which is presently celebrated (in the Mass). It is one and the same. The grace of the Spirit is the same. It is always Easter!"[38] This is liturgical memorial: *that which is remembered is present!* The memorial here is not simply commemoration. It is a sacred sign implying a continuity, a "mysterious permanence of the great divine actions."[39]

Here in Big Sur we normally celebrate Eucharist at midday, giving temporal evidence to the "spiritual triad" that the *Directory* calls for, of Lauds, Eucharist, and Vespers. We have already begun preparing ourselves for the Eucharist at first light as we bow to or sit around the empty altar, waiting in joyful hope. Certainly on Sundays, feast days and solemnities, the readings of Vigils have been preparing us for the Gospel of the day, as a patristic commentary is read for our second reading and the Gospel is

---

36. Shawn Carruth, quoted in Monastic Liturgy Forum 9 (1) (Summer 1997).

37. *DWG*, no. 13, pp. 28–9.

38. Vagaggini, *Theological*, 271.

39. Louis Bouyer, *Eucharist* (Notre Dame Press, 1968) 84.

solemnly proclaimed after the singing of the Te Deum; and on ferial days as well, the Gospel at Lauds already directs our prayers toward the pre-eminent moment of the liturgical day, the Eucharist.

Finally as the sun sets and the work of the day is done, we give thanks at Vespers for the grace of the day, for God's continual presence with us, and for preparing us for the descent of night. After Vespers, according to ancient custom, the community chants a hymn to Mary. This gesture prepares us to enter into the night silence where we ponder the word of God, and hopefully like Mary, allow it to take flesh in us. Once again there is an optional time of communal silent meditation, this time with the Blessed Sacrament present in a modest monstrance. More monks and guests as well attend this evening meditation, and the symbolism is rich: as we began the morning in silence, our hearts an empty altar, so we have spent the day attending to the Word becoming flesh in us, ultimately calling us to respond—for God's Word always demands a response.

Occasionally on Sunday evening we celebrate a communal Compline, but normally the monastic compound noticeably takes on a tone of quiet each evening after Vespers, leading into the "grand silence" from 9 P.M. until the opening words and gesture of Vigils when we trace the Sign of the Cross on our lips once again and sing: "O Lord, open my lips and my mouth shall proclaim your praise." And so, "the daily round, the common task" begins again.

The *Directory* exhorts monastic communities to recognize the Work of God as the summit and source of the monastic day. Toward that end, in Big Sur we rarely omit celebrating any of the hours, and only combine liturgies two or three times a month—on Recreation Days when the celebration of Eucharist is delicately combined with Lauds, and on Community Quiet Days when it is celebrated in the context of Vespers. On other rare occasions, the regular celebration of certain offices is supplanted by some other form of communal prayer: a communal penance service in place of Vespers on Wednesday of Holy Week; a New Year's Eve Vigil from 9 P.M. to midnight, beginning with Compline and ending with Vigils of Mary Mother of God; an evening Interfaith Prayer Service combining silent meditation with chants and readings from other religious traditions. But all told, the actual lived life of the community bears witness to what is most important. As one guest said, "When the bell rings, there's no doubt where you're supposed to be!"

5. *Lex orandi, lex credendi*: Liturgy As Formator

Vatican II already stressed the general importance of the study of sacred liturgy for those in religious formation. It is common wisdom that in monastic life it is the life itself that is the main formator, the daily existential reality, and the demands of the normal pattern of our day. This applies especially to our liturgical life. If our liturgies are indeed the strong moments of our day, the most important communal events, then we can assume they are also the strongest formative elements of the communal life. Not only as encounter with the Word, but also as the shaper of one's spirituality and the source and summit of one's prayer, because, we would argue, the monk's spirituality is nothing if it is not liturgical.

We would stop short of saying liturgy is didactic, but certainly it is formative. Liturgy forms and fosters, slowly, day after day, an understanding of God and of Church, through encounters with God and Church. *Lex orandi, lex credendi* we are taught, or, in full form *Lex supplicandi legem statuat credendi*: the law of believing is subordinated to the law of worship. One's very faith is formed by the God encountered in liturgy. The image of God we promote in our liturgies, and the image of Church, especially that of the "local church," the monastic community, we foster in our liturgical assembly, are the God and Church we are asking our monks to embrace. In our liturgy we are fostering an encounter with the divine; we are incarnating a concept of ecclesial community. So, little things matter. God is indeed in the details that tell the real story and form "liturgical spirituality." There is no communal activity that takes as much a share of the monk's day, and offers such a rich fare for the open heart. For houses such as our American ones, who are not heavily academic groups, the liturgy becomes even more important, not only as the structure for the very life but also as the prime "stuff" of formation.

Vagaggini says it is a matter of "slowly forming the religious psychology and sensibility of the young according to . . . liturgical piety."[40] This is especially true for the novitiate when the monk should be introduced to liturgical spirituality "as a complete form of the ascetical life," and participation in the liturgical life "the center of his spiritual life, around which all else is ordered and . . . from which all the rest derives: ascesis, prayer and private meditation," the "connatural place for the mystical encounter with God."[41] Furthermore, this "liturgical formation" of monastics should last all of life because the liturgy should be for the monk a complete and never-ending form of spirituality. Liturgical spirituality pervades all the other

---

40. Vagaggini, *Liturgia*, 170.
41. Ibid.

disciplines. No question should ever be considered exhausted before having shown its connection with the liturgical life of the Church.

6. Liturgy As Listening, Encounter with the Word

There is, of course, a traditional distinction between monastic liturgy and cathedral (basilican or parochial) liturgy. The distinction is not pressed quite so finely today. Guiver says that monasticism itself "has become so diversified that the borderlines are almost completely smudged."[42] But a distinction can be made, perhaps, between an evangelical liturgical style that attempts to attract and engage an assembly, and a contemplative one that assumes a certain commitment and demands a greater attentiveness. The former concentrates more on ceremonials and variety while the latter is characterized by greater sobriety, to name one element. But perhaps the subtlest distinction, and the most telling, is that the former focuses more on *addressing* God in praise or supplication, while the latter focuses on *listening to* God, on "contemplative praise." So the Office especially is seen in the contemplative tradition as a Liturgy of the Word. In the desert tradition, the psalms were read to the assembled monks by one of the group, while in some cases those listening continued with their work. It was only after the psalm was finished that the monks would stand, with arms outstretched or prostrate on the ground, and offer prayer. The psalms were not seen as prayers addressed to God as such, but God addressing the assembled faithful.

At some point between the desert tradition and the time of St. Benedict this character seems to have changed (from being understood as the word of God addressed to humanity to the homage of humanity to God). But this may be what the *Directory* (and *General Instruction*) is trying to recover in stressing that the essential structure of the Liturgy of the Hours is that of a dialogue, and even more by insisting that "sacred silence" should get its rightful place in the liturgy "to help them to hear all that the Holy Spirit wishes to say in their hearts and to unite their personal prayer more closely with the Word of God."[43] It is certainly our approach as Camaldolese.

This applies not only to the Liturgies of the Hours, but to the Liturgy of Eucharist as well (and every other sacrament!) which in its very choreography teaches us that the very act of gathering around the table is done

---

42. He goes on to explain that not only "many religious are more apostolic than some parish priests," but as well "(t)here are some Christians 'in the world' whose lives are in many respects monastic." Our oblate chaplains would certainly testify that this is true! George Guiver, *Company of Voices: Daily Prayer and the People of God* (New York, Pueblo, 1988) 187.

43. *DWG*, no. 4, 5, p. 21; *GILH* 202.

as a response to the Word, in thanksgiving for the *mirabilia Dei*, the wonders of God.

A marvelous new image emerges from this understanding; for instance, when a soloist reads the second and fourth psalms at Vigils, we are obviously doing as the desert monks did before us. But even when we are chanting or reciting back and forth across the choir, we are listening to our brothers and sisters proclaiming the Word of God to us! A visiting Zen abbot thought it strange that chanting psalms was the monk's main practice. One of our monks politely offered the counter view that our main communal practice was *listening* to the psalms. The pauses and silences are very important, very much a part of the entire prayer. In some sense, we only chant the psalms so we can be in silence afterwards and pray. The psalm leads to prayer, as in the Eucharistic Liturgy the proclaimed word of God leads to thanks and praise, to raising the cup and breaking the bread!

Primacy, of course, has always been given to the psalter, most especially in the Offices when five or six psalms and canticles are chanted or proclaimed. The psalms were important already in the earliest monastic traditions, the *Rule of St. Benedict*, and in the *Brief Rule* of St. Romuald. Romuald had his own enlightenment experience and received the gift of tears while reading the verse from Psalm 31: "I will instruct you and teach you the way you should go. I will give you counsel with my eye upon you." For Romuald, as for the ancients before him, it is Christ himself who is hidden in the psalms; so it is Christ we must find in the psalms and thus realize we are in God's presence.

In addition to psalmody, as one of our monks likes to say, "we are swimming in Scripture here!" Since liturgy is the birthplace of Scripture, it is the natural ambience to hear it proclaimed and exposed. The biblical readings are at the heart of each hour of the Office; in a sense, they "complete the promise of the psalms." They are also the pivotal moment of the Eucharist. The Gospel reading for the Eucharist is read at Lauds in order to emphasize its centrality for the day (so, in a sense, even our morning prayer is pointing us toward another liturgy). For ongoing *lectio*, a monk is taught that his main reading for the day should be that same Gospel with its accompanying scriptural readings of the day. As preparation for the coming Sunday Eucharist, we often gather to break open the Sunday readings in our Wednesday evening group *lectio*, which we call *collatio*.

7. Hospitality and Inclusivity

Liturgy is also an act of hospitality. The *Directory* instructs us that monastic liturgy should be open to "all who desire to take part in it" and calls for an openness by which "people coming from outside are welcomed in the midst of the praying community."[44] Vagaggini refers to a monastery's liturgy as its apostolate. He says the efficacy of retreats in a monastic setting

> depends at least half on the liturgical monastic atmosphere of the monastery. . . . For a monastery there is no apostolate more suitable than that which consists of opening the doors wide to those who want to make retreats among us.[45]

Practically speaking, every effort is made for participation on the part of the whole assembly in terms of liturgical books and explanations, and there is never great separation between monks and guests, either at Office or Eucharist.

We Camaldolese stand in a wonderful position to explore inculturation, another kind of inclusivity, specifically in regards to monastic/contemplative liturgy. We have communities not only in Europe and the United States, but in Brazil, India, and Africa as well. We also share a charism of interreligious dialogue and benefit from the great pioneering work of Bede Griffiths in the use of sacral elements from various traditions in the ashram at Shantivanam. The last two international Camaldolese meetings have been marvelous examples of the weaving of cultural expressions, especially musical ones. At Big Sur we are also firmly committed to the inclusivity of women: we maintain a high level of sensitivity to inclusive language; when our women monastics visit, they are given preference in being welcomed into choir.

Lastly, our sense of liturgy as intercession is strong, inclusive of our local community and the needs of the world, echoing that which is so beautifully articulated in the *General Instruction* that, besides the praise of God, we express in the liturgy the prayers and desires of all the faithful. It is humorously pointed out that the general intercessions are like the daily news. But how heartening it is to see our bulletin board filled with prayer intentions, and to know that we are carrying the needs and intentions of the body with us. What greater gift to offer?

8. Conclusion

These, then, are the primary themes of Camaldolese liturgical spirituality. The monastic community at prayer is an image of this praying Church, as priest, body, bride, mother. Constant and persevering prayer belong to the very essence of what it means to be a monk. There is no better

44. *DWG*, no. 22, p. 39.
45. Vagaggini, *Liturgia*, 171–72.

way for us to express ourselves as community than in prayer, just as no better way to become community exists than by prayer, and no better way for us to pray than with the Church's prayer. This is not only the source and summit of monastic spirituality and our formator, but also the connatural place for our mystical encounter with God. It is also our apostolate, our ministry to the Church. The monastic community that gives such stress to common prayer can bring this mode of "being Church" back to its proper level of attention, and repropose it to the whole Christian community, to "reclaim the primacy of prayer in the life of the Christian community."[46]

---

46. Bargellini, *Liturgia*, 287–88.

Lectio Divina and Monastic Theology in Camaldolese Life

Alessandro Barban

1. *Lectio Divina* As Monastic Practice

Lectio divina is a "spiritual exercise," a way of living, thinking and praying that involves one's whole being and spiritual progress in human life.[1] Spiritual "exercise" in the monastic tradition is not a spiritual "retreat," but the spiritual orientation that transforms my being every day. In this light, monastic life is an ongoing spiritual exercise. *Lectio divina*, then, is a way of being that deeply changes how one lives. It is the traditional center of monastic life. Why the center? A useful approach to answer this question is to ask another: "Why have we come here to live in the monastery?"

This question, writes Merton,

> is one which we should ask ourselves again and again in the course of our monastic life. . . . It is a question which confronts us with a new meaning and a new urgency, as we go on in life. . . . The question is one which must never be evaded. If we face it seriously we will strengthen our vocation. . . . The monk who ceases to ask himself "Why have you come here?" has perhaps ceased to be a monk. What are some of the answers we give to the question: "Why have you come here?" We reply "To save my soul," "To lead a life of prayer," "To do penance for my sins," "To give myself to God," "To love God." These are good enough answers. They are religious answers.[2]

But it is clear that these religious answers are not the "theological answer."

"It makes much more sense to say, as St. Benedict says, that we come to the monastery to *seek God*, than to say we come seeking (our) spiritual

---

1. Cf. P. Hadot, *Exercices spirituels et philosophie antique* (Paris, Études Augustiniennes, 1987).

2. Thomas Merton, *Basic Principles of Monastic Spirituality* (The Abbey of Our Lady of Gethsemani, 1957) 5–6.

perfection"[3] or our personal salvation. And so, to say "Why have you come here?" is the same as saying "What does it mean—to seek God?" How do you know you are seeking God, or not? Our faith-response must be: *through* Christ, *with* Christ, *in* Christ.

If we look to Emmaus, we are those disciples walking along, thinking we know the road and our goal. We have known Jesus Christ, but then we are unable to recognize him. It is Christ who draws near us, who seeks us out and enters into our lives. *Through* Christ's hidden presence in our lives, we walk our road. We understand the cross, but we have not yet comprehended its event.

We discover that Jesus Christ is *with* us. We are not yet with him, but he is with us. He is so through the Scriptures, a presence "like a burning fire." Then he is with us when he breaks bread for us. Only the grace of the Word and the gift of the eucharistic bread open our human eyes to the contemplation of the risen Lord. Only then do we recognize Christ and really begin to *see* our road and our goal. Meeting the Lord, we begin a conversion, an interior spiritual transformation, and we are no longer alone, but give ourselves to a community. We begin to discover the joy of the Christian community and to recognize Jesus in our brothers and sisters.

St. Paul writes, "I now live, not I, but Christ living in me" (Gal 2:20). He experiences his entire person transfigured by Christ's presence. Christ is in him and he is *in* Christ. Paul also writes, "because we have Christ's Spirit dwelling within us, we can call out in sonship with Christ" (Gal 4:6; cf. Rom 8:14-17). His faith-experience is a living reciprocity between Christ and himself. In other words, it is what promises in John 14:23: "Who loves me will obey my teaching. My Father will love him, and my Father and I will come to and live with him." What is the paradigm of this "love?" It is the same deep reciprocity of love between the Father and Son that spreads in a radiant circle, embracing us.

The commandment to love one another is not different from remaining in Christ's love. We live within the same reciprocity of love that exists between Father and Son, and within their radiant circle. The spiritual perspective of John's Gospel is totally theological: if we love one another (i.e., if we respond with loving obedience to his commandment) we remain in the love of Christ. But the love of Christ is within the reciprocity of love with the Father, so we participate in the loving circle of the Trinity because in God, the bond of love that unites Father and Son is the Holy Spirit. We can say with Augustine: "the Father is the loving, the Son is the beloved, and the Holy Spirit is the love." An important consequence follows:

3. Ibid., 6.

in the inner trinitarian life the love of Father and Son is not closed in upon itself. The Holy Spirit completes the circle of the divine life; however, it is not a closed circle, but an open one.

Thus we arrive at the real heart of our monastic vocation. We are monks to seek God, but *through, with* and *in* Christ. Our monastic life is a life in Christ, a life by which we remain in his love, sharing his relationship with the Father, and participating in the spiritual circle of love that is the Holy Spirit. Christ is our life. He is the deep meaning of our existence and monastic life. Nothing in the monastery makes any sense if we forget this central truth. But who is this Jesus Christ? Our response to this question is the spiritual life, a life animated by the Spirit. Monastic life is "spiritual" not because monks pray so much or perform asceticisms, but only because they seek the Father in Christ through the Holy Spirit. Therein lie the roots of monastic contemplation. As von Balthasar writes,

> Contemplation is made possible, insofar as it is prepared by God—by the Father who . . . chooses and accepts us as his sons; by the Son, who makes known to us the Father, and gives himself to us in his self-giving unto death and the Eucharistic mystery; by the Holy Spirit, who brings and makes known to our souls the divine life.[4]

Lectio divina is the center of monastic life because it is how we seek the Father through, with, and in his Word by the Holy Spirit. It is that daily exercise of prayer that opens our hearts to receive God's Word in loving movement of the Holy Spirit. *Lectio* is fundamentally an exercise of receptivity—a practice of silence, concentration and prayer that allows us to remain in Christ's love. For this reason, *lectio divina* is the one thing necessary in monastic life. It gives significance and shape to our search for God. Why else does monastic tradition remind us continually in Psalm 95, "If today you hear his voice, harden not your hearts!" Jesus himself said, "My mother and brothers are those who hear the Word of God and do it" (Luke 8:21). But what does this "hear" mean, if not "comprehend"? This is the work of theology: to comprehend the mystery of the Christian faith. And every Christian is called to be a theologian, that is, to endeavor to penetrate God's mystery. For this reason, without theology we cannot do *lectio divina* well.

2. Theology in Monastic Perspective

One hears the lament that a terrible dichotomy exists between theology and life, between theology and spirituality. Theology is often accused

4. H. Urs von Balthasar, *Prayer* (London, Chapman, 1961) 66.

of being barren theology.[5] Many Christians—and sometimes monks—say that theology is difficult and abstract, and not all that important for the spiritual life. However, theology is very important, even fundamental and essential to monastic life. Theology is the main requisite for entering into and embodying Christian wisdom. We read the Scriptures, but without theology, we understand only the letter and do not enter into the spirit of the gospel of Jesus Christ. We read the mystics, but without theology, we do not understand the profundity of their spiritual insights and enter into mystical experience. We have authentic moments of silence, meditation and prayer, but without theological exercise, our life will not become doxological, permeated by prayer and thanksgiving. Theology is the way to enter into God's mystery.[6]

Christian theology has a method, but it would be better to say that it *is* a method. Theological method opens a road for us; it is a path that leads us on the way. In this perspective, Christian theology is a daily spiritual exercise: a way of living and thinking, because I live as I think, and think as I live. There is a deep reciprocity between life and thought. Theology daily presents to us the hidden path of the Spirit. And it is important to know and study the methods present in the history of Christian theology.[7]

The theological method of the Fathers does not divide the mystery dualistically between life and thought, contemplation and praxis. Their vision proceeds from particular to general, from kataphatic to apophatic, and, above all, from knowledge to wisdom. Their theology is mystagogical and sapiential: the essential paradigm is the *life* of Christian faith. In later Scholastic theology, the main paradigm becomes the *science* of Christian faith and its method is conceptual, abstract and distant from the spiritual life. The human being becomes the center of the universe, the subject of knowledge that is empirical and scientific, while all reality (including God) becomes the object of science.

Not until Vatican Council II and the great theologians of the twentieth century (Barth, De Lubac, Congar, Rahner, von Balthasar, Moltmann, Pannenberg, Jüngel) do we have a new theological method with a new paradigm of theological knowledge.[8] Theology returns to the consideration of the theological paradigm of the Fathers, but it develops a dialogical method that is more existential and transcendental.

---

5. J. O'Donnell, *The Mystery of the Triune God* (London, Sheed & Ward, 1988) vii.

6. Cf. B.J.F. Lonergan, *Method in Theology* (New York, Herder and Herder, 1972).

7. Cf. C. Vagaggini, "Teologia" *Nuovo Dizionario di Teologia* (Roma, Edizioni Paoline, 1982).

8. Cf. H. Küng/D. Tracy, *Paradigm Change in Theology* (New York, Crossroad, 1990); D. Tracy, *Plurality and Ambiguity: Hermeneutics, Religion, Hope* (Chicago, Univ. Press, 1994).

The method of monastic theology is dialogical because it moves from the chaos of human existence to the cosmos of a transcendental horizon across the poles of reality.[9] It makes present the harmony of mystery in creation. Modern monastic theology is not one-sided or dualistic, but tries to understand the differences present between the poles of reality. It thinks over the "between" of the polarity's mystery. In other words, monastic theology presents itself as a dynamic process that seems to have the structure of love, of that grateful union within the person. Why love? Because love is a dialogical unity that respects the polarity's mystery and the being's difference.[10] I would say the method of theology carries out a loving knowledge, where understanding is a comprehension of myself, of the other, and of the mystery of our communion in diversity. Theological method is a path that explores the hidden regions of the Spirit, of the Mystery that embraces us.

Theological knowledge is not only an intellectual understanding but also a relational comprehension. Here comprehension is a spiritual unity between subject and object, between you and me. But we cannot comprehend one another without an affinity where we recognize each other. I cannot know the other unless I self-communicate to the other my own self-comprehension. I come to know the other through my self-knowledge and I am known by the other's comprehension. It is a circle of reciprocity.

Theological knowledge is a symbolical comprehension because the theological gaze contemplates the symbol hidden in daily life. This symbol is the profundity of the Sacred Mystery, of the Spirit's action that embraces everything with a delivering love. In this sense, theological comprehension becomes wisdom because only wisdom sees the symbolic horizon of every human being. It also becomes mystical when it experiences the symbolic mystery of the divine presence. Mystical wisdom's external coordinates are time and experience, while its internal coordinates are method and comprehension. But together—time, experience, theological method and comprehension—constitute an open meadow where wisdom comes to dwell. Wisdom is a gift of the Spirit. Only mystical wisdom, given by the Spirit of God, recognizes and *sees* the work of the same Spirit—the upbuilding of the kingdom of God. The presence of the Spirit is a "silent word" within us and among us. We hear the sound it makes, remaining in amazement at the Spirit's creative freedom.

Theological method opens for us a road to comprehension. Theological comprehension opens us to the self-communication of God who comprehends us. Finally, there is mystical wisdom, a gift of the Spirit, that

---

9. Cf. J. Leclercq, *Esperienza spirituale e teologia* (Milano, Jaca, 1990).

10. Cf. E. Jüngel, *God as the Mystery of the World* (Edinburgh, T. and T. Clark, 1983) and the theological works of von Balthasar.

is the joy of seeing "primordial communion" unite and differentiate everything: you and me, us and the world, the world and God. Beyond all differences (identity, character, culture, language, sex, education, etc.) we share a common living "background": where we laugh and cry; where we know days of solitude and desperation but also days of happiness and communion; where we experience health and illness, life and death; where we contemplate the beauty of nature and confront disquieting questions in our mind. Mystical wisdom sees the unity of divine wisdom beyond creation's polarity. It gazes at the "background" that comprehends all—that "primordial communion," the realm of the Trinity where, in loving freedom, Father gives himself to Son in the unity of the Holy Spirit.

Mystical wisdom is the joy of a global cosmic vision. It is an "ordered" gaze that perceives, by intuition, all things—bringing them to light. It contemplates the true loving power of God, the strength of reconciliation and love's order.

We return to the questions, "What does seeking God mean?" "How do we know if we are seeking God, or not?" Monastic theology answers that God is not an object we can seek and know; instead, God seeks and comprehends us in Jesus Christ. We pretend to understand God's Word instead of letting the event of God's Word comprehend us. God's Word is not speech *about* the love of God for us, but is itself the completion of this love, the Word-event. We must not imagine that, in a chaotic age like ours, our function is to preserve the ancient attitudes and customs of our spiritual tradition or to keep alive in the world the memory of God. We must keep ourselves alive by contact with the living God. And we are only truly alive if we remain in Christ's love and remain open to the loving freedom of the Spirit. Theology is that way of living and thinking that reminds me *who* God is: a community of love and freedom. *Lectio divina* is the spiritual practice of prayer that lets me be a monk, i.e., live the "theological" life, centered in God: pure faith, hope in God's kingdom, and love in the Holy Spirit.

3. *Lectio Divina* As "Prayed Word"

It is very difficult to translate *lectio divina* into English and the other modern languages. It is not only a problem of translation, but also a question of interpretation. I can meditate on a book or poem, but this practice is not *lectio* according to the traditional meaning of the expression. *Lectio divina* requires a slow, in-depth and pregnant reading that opens up to listening. It is a "heard" reading of God's word. But even the word "reading," strictly speaking, insufficiently explains this contact with the Scriptures. *Lectio divina* is not only a reading, but also an assimilation that, together with reading, requires a rumination (*ruminatio*) upon God's word. The monastic practice of rumination moves from the personal reading of the gospel of the day and the liturgical listening to that text at Lauds and Eucharist to its repetition from memory throughout the day. We could call it *meditatio,* but meditation is only a moment of *lectio* and cannot exhaust its spiritual sense. Rumination consists in keeping the word alive within us by its repetition. So we begin to know God, to abide in God's love. This kind of knowledge is a comprehension of participation, union, and love.

In other words, *lectio divina* is not only a method of reading but also an experience of God. If we receive the Word of Jesus Christ, we remain in his love and abide in the Father. The relationship between Father and Son comprises the bond of love (*vinculum amoris*) of the Holy Spirit. So we can see the Holy Spirit as the divine ecstasy of love in God. In this sense, *lectio* is *divina* because, listening to God's Word, we remain in Christ's love and participate in the trinitarian life. We can also consider this trinitarian relationship as an "eternal prayer" of worship and love. So, I think of *lectio divina* as "prayed Word" that allows us to enter into God's "prayer," i.e., the divine liturgy of love in the Trinity. The ultimate goal of *lectio* is praise that culminates in silent adoration before Sacred Mystery. Here, God is recognized, worshiped, and loved. Because its goal is this kind of praise and adoration, I consider *lectio* the center of monastic spirituality.

St. Augustine writes, "Pray to understand the Scriptures."[11] Isaac the Syrian adds, "Do not approach the mysterious words of the Scriptures without prayer, without asking God's help. Say, 'O Lord, give me the gift to receive the power that is in the gospel.' You must think of prayer as the key that unlocks the truth of the Scriptures."[12] St. Cyprian also gives a maxim for biblical reading: "Either pray assiduously or read; either speak to God or listen to him."[13] In other words, without prayer we can neither read the Scriptures nor hear God's Word. Prayer is the support and the background of *lectio,* but is also its final goal.

St. Jerome synthesizes this movement of prayer and *lectio* in a famous expression, "*Lectio* follows prayer and prayer, *lectio.*"[14] Thus *lectio* leads us

11. St. Augustine, *De doctrina christiana* (CCL 32) 116.

12. This text is cited in L. Leloir, *Désert et communion* (Abbaye de Bellefontaine, 1978) 281, n. 39.

13. "*Sit tibi vel oratio assidua vel lectio; nunc Deo loquere nunc Deus tecum*" S. Ciprianus, Ep. 1.15 (Migne, PL IV) 226.

14. "*Orationi lectio, lectioni succedat oratio*" San Girolamo, Lettera CVII a Leta: "Come educare la figlia Paola," *Le Lettere,* III (Roma, 1961. See also D. Gorge, "Saint Jérome et la lecture sacrée dans le milieu ascétique romain" *La Lectio Divina, Des origines du cénobitisme à saint Benoît et Cassiodore,* I (Paris: Picard, 1925) and I. Gargano, "Cultura e spiritualità nella tradizione monastica," *Cultura e spiritualità nella tradizione monastica* (Roma, Studia Anselmiana, 1990).

to prayer because it comes from prayer. Within the practice of *lectio* there is a dynamic movement of *oratio/lectio/oratio*. Prayer supports our *lectio*, but *lectio* itself is the key that unlocks the "spiritual sense" of God's Word.[15] It is from this "spiritual sense" of God's Word that this "new" prayer comes. This prayer is "new" because, though it is our response to the Word, it would not be possible without the action of the Spirit within us.

Paradoxically, our receptivity to God's Word is both an act of our freedom and the enabling action of the Holy Spirit within us. The Spirit guides us to pray to Jesus Christ, so that we can comprehend his Word. The Spirit also gives us the "spiritual intuition" of *lectio*. It is always God's Spirit who prays within us a "new" prayer of thanksgiving and praise: it is contemplative prayer. St. Paul says, "The Spirit explores everything, even the depths of God's own nature" (1 Cor 2:10). So, it is up to the Spirit to open our way to the depths of divine life. The possibility for contemplation lies not only in God's openness to us, but also in our openness to God. Our ability to receive God's Word as something alive within us is due to the Spirit's action. We can see how *lectio* exists within a trinitarian circle: the Word becomes alive within us by the Spirit; this Word of life becomes a visible expression in God's icon, Jesus Christ; Christ is the manifestation of the Father's love.

Our monastic vocation is to serve and worship God through a contemplative life that reveals the trinitarian love of God. For this reason, *lectio divina* is not a technique of interpretation or meditation of the Scriptures, but the very *heart* of monastic spirituality. Our own asceticism must be built on God's Word. The monastery is a school of the Lord's service because it is where we learn to *hear* our Lord Jesus Christ. Silence, ongoing conversion and solitude are meant for listening. They are conditions of possibility for our spiritual growth.

In monastic life it is necessary to have, in addition to the vocation itself, a deep sense of God's love from the Scriptures. For this reason, monastic contemplation is a life transfigured by God's Word. To read, to meditate, and to repeat the gospel throughout the day: this has been the center of daily ascetical practice for generations of monks down the monastic centuries. In this contemplative light, we can understand the famous coupling of fasting and vigilance. Fasting in the monastic tradition is understood as a support for the practice of vigils.

---

15. "Fundamentally, there are two senses in the Scriptures: one is literal, the other is spiritual. . . . The Spirit is in the letter such as the honey is in honeycomb. A Christian receives the letter and the Spirit as a double coat." H. De Lubac, *Exégèse médiévale; les quatre sens de l'Écriture*, 4 vols. (Paris, Aubier, 1964).

Camaldolese practice for fasting expects the monk to eat something every day, according to personal needs, but to eat only what is necessary— like the Israelites with their manna in the desert (Exod 16). The spiritual significance of the allusion is to live only by God's grace, one day at a time. To live by God's grace in the monastic hermeneutic is to live by the Word— promise of God. To live by God's Word, then, means to open our heart every morning to receive this "food" that does not come from the earth. Scripture says, "[humanity] does not live on bread alone, but on every word coming from God's mouth" (Deut 8:3; Matt 4:4). So, we are able to stay awake, i.e., to be vigilant (Matt 24:42). In this context, being vigilant means being attentive to God's Word and to ourselves: to God's Word, because the gospel is our spiritual polar star; to ourselves, because we are concerned with the purification of our heart. Thus fasting is meant for vigilance, keeping vigil is meant for being attentive to God's Word, and being attentive is meant to foster purity of heart. Clearly, fasting and vigilance are not sufficient unto themselves for the practice of *lectio divina*. Spiritual attentiveness and purity of heart are also necessary to enter deeply into the life of Scripture.

In order to foster a relationship of friendship, knowledge and spiritual affinity with God's Word at Camaldoli, the postulancy begins with the consignment of the Bible to every postulant. On that occasion the prior invites the new candidates to monastic life to begin their spiritual path with, and under, God's Word. They begin with the gospels, especially the gospel which the liturgy offers us daily. And with that gospel, it is very important during our periods of silence and personal prayer to repeat some psalms that we have prayed in the Liturgy of Hours. Why the psalms? I can find myself in the psalms. Through the psalms I can praise God with trust and hope, but I can also give free rein to my darker thoughts that might otherwise lie in wait within my heart. Above all, the psalms sing my own thirst for God, the joys and sufferings of my search for God. The psalms are a support for our prayer and *lectio divina*.

But *lectio* begins by reading the gospel in the cell; and we must learn to read it. Monastic tradition prefers reading aloud so we can lend our voice to the Word. In this sense, our reading becomes listening. I should not read the gospel like I read another book or newspaper. When we monks read the Scriptures, our goal is only to hear God's Word. And to hear, I must first listen to the Word. So, the first exercise of *lectio* is the proclamation of the gospel. We read the text at least three or four times, with attentiveness and concentration, accompanied by lengthy, deep pauses of silence. God's Word is a gift that does not come to confirm my thoughts or life, but to convert them.

And so, *lectio*'s first exercise is to read aloud the gospel in a context of silence, concentration and prayer, and to repeat this reading a number of times (perhaps with different translations) in order to hear attentively the living Word of our Lord Jesus Christ. We will begin to experience an initial spiritual intuition. After reading and above all, hearing the text, we must pay attention to its structure. A parable is quite different from the narration of a miracle or a speech of Christ. And every text has its own context we must see in its concrete biblical redaction because each writer develops a theology in a personal literary style.

All of this spiritual exercise in reading, repetition and hearing makes sense if we discover the *center* of the text. What is this center? In *lectio* we do not search for the textually central spot, but that spiritual center that gives the text a contemplative sense. Such a center can be a sentence, a verb or series of verbs, a teaching, etc. In other words, this center is not always the exegetical center. It is the *heart* of the text for me, right now, in my present spiritual path. That center we discover in our *lectio* is a gift of the Spirit, a spiritual intuition that comes from God, not from our intellect. In the beginning, it is not always easy to uncover the spiritual center of a text. But we must never forget Jesus' words, "Ask, and it will be given you; seek, and you will find; knock, and the door will be opened" (Matt 7:7).

How can we check our spiritual intuition? Here are three methods of confirmation: the Scriptures themselves, the liturgy, and the community. Every text has other biblical passages that can aid comprehension of our intuition. The Fathers said that Scripture explains Scripture. After the wisdom of Scripture comes the "school" of the liturgy. The liturgical gospel— the text of our *lectio*—is always introduced by the alleluia verse, a key to the liturgical interpretation along with the accompanying readings of the day, the opening prayer, preface, and communion antiphon. The liturgy is the "school" of our faith and our mystagogical growth in God's presence. Then, to solve more difficult Scripture passages, monastic tradition encourages occasional colloquies with a spiritual guide, with older seasoned monks, and with the abbot. There is also the tradition of *collatio*, a practice still current in our houses. *Collatio* is the communal experience of *lectio*, important for two reasons: we can check the spiritual intuition of our personal *lectio* and we can hear and receive the action of the Holy Spirit through our fellow monks.

In the Christian monastic tradition, *meditatio* is not primarily a technique for emptying the soul. Meditation is an exercise in attentiveness, purification, and concentration, but its primary goal is the fullness or maturation of God's Word within us. According to the most ancient tradition, meditation is biblical. And in *lectio divina*, three important "moments" constitute *meditatio*: the ant's work, the bee's work, and discernment.

The ant's work is to harvest the food. Our food is God's Word. How can we harvest our spiritual food in the Bible? The Fathers use the image of "hammering." I mentioned that *lectio*'s first step is to discover the text's spiritual center in order to receive its contemplative sense. That center is the keystone of our text. The hammering of this keystone produces many sparks that call to mind other texts. We harvest our food where our memory ceases, but the important thing is to hammer that keystone, the spiritual center of the text. One who is more familiar with Scripture will have the advantage of recalling a greater number of texts.

We must not only harvest our food, but also work with it like a bee. Each bee produces honey from the nectar and pollen collected from flowers. As another example we can use the analogy between an artist and the artwork. A sculptor must first find the material, and then work with it. But for the ancients, a work of art was virtually present within the material; it was only necessary for the artist to unveil the art within. In other words, the monk's work is to meditate, i.e., to reveal the hidden sense of Scripture, to produce the honey of evangelical wisdom. Monastic tradition calls this second step of meditation *ruminatio*. The repetition of God's Word means the capacity to digest the Scriptures. After the harvest work, we assimilate God's Word within us.

God's Word entering our lives begins a work of discernment, of purification, of *krisis*—transformation and conversion. Whereas with *lectio* we read Scripture, during *meditatio* God's Word "reads" us. This can prove a painful process. This presence and action of the Word within us is often so smarting we are tempted to escape its scrutiny. But if only we remain in the crucible of meditation, we receive the gift of "new" prayer.

If God's Word begins to "read" us, a new relationship with the Lord will commence because our prayer will be not only the fruit of our intentions, but will also become an answer to the Spirit's cry within us. This is a "new" prayer. In prayer we often bring to the Lord a false image of ourselves, that self we would *prefer* to be rather than the self we actually *are*. If we dare to abide in God as we are, God's burning light will purify our darkness. And after this purification comes the promise of a radiant union. There is a progression in our prayer: from the concrete place of the monastic cell and a prayer of the lips to the "cell" of the heart and a prayer of contrition, purification, and petition, and then to the "nuptial cell" and the prayer of thanksgiving and silent praise. The life of prayer is not static. *Oratio* is a journey from the lips to the purification of heart, to the loving/waiting of the sentinel in Psalm 130 who watches for the dawn. This is the attitude of the Christian contemplative. *Contemplatio* is the fourth step of *lectio divina*.

The term "contemplation" has held many meanings in the history of spirituality. Even today, many distinguish between contemplation and praxis, between contemplative life and apostolic life, between contemplative religious orders and active religious congregations. Hence the belief that the Christian "contemplative" is one outside human history given to prayer, while the "active" Christian is addicted to a practical realization of the Christian faith in the world! Such a spiritual view engenders an unfortunate consequence of having "contemplatives" as an elite in the Church, while the majority of believers cannot know the gift of contemplation. This tension between contemplation and action has not only been a mistaken interpretation of the spiritual life and the Church's apostolicity (all Christians are called to be contemplatives and missionaries of Christ's gospel), but also a concrete risk of departmentalizing the Church into a hierarchy of holiness and vocation (moving from hermits and monastics to modern religious orders, to priests, to nuns, to sisters, and finally to the laity) and creating a theological "schizophrenia" between faith and spirituality, liturgy and Christian life.

Such an interpretation of "contemplation" runs the risk of dividing the unity of the Christian Mystery. All believers are called—according to their personal vocations—to celebrate the paschal mystery of Christ in the liturgy, to be contemplatives in their spiritual life, and to bear witness to Jesus Christ's resurrection. In this light, contemplation is not a gift of the Spirit offered to just a few believers. The Spirit wants to give it to all, and in different ways. Contemplation is the process of a believer's divinization made possible by the trinitarian God. The Greek term for contemplation—*theoria*—is found only once in the New Testament: "When the crowd gathered for the spectacle (*theoria*) saw what had occurred, they went home, beating their breasts" (Luke 23:48). This verse seems marginal, but it is very important. *Theoria* comes from the Greek *thea*—meaning "sight" and *orao*—meaning "to see." Etymologically, *theoria* means "to see a sight," or better, "to see in sight," i.e., "to enter into sight." In the Christian faith only the crucified Christ is the place/space for contemplation!

And if Luke calls the cross the "spectacle" of Love's revelation, John understands spiritually the Mystery of Christian contemplation. In fact, John's entire gospel is either an introduction to the spiritual life, especially the Christian experience of contemplation, or a narrative theology of the Word-made-flesh. In Christ crucified, every believer contemplates heaven opened up (i.e., God's loving self-communication) and the event of a new creation because Christ is that place/space of the unity between heaven and earth, between the revelation of the trinitarian God and the vocation of the new humanity. From this perspective, the cross of Jesus Christ is the center of Christian contemplation. Believers can see within the event of the crucified God their own existence, the life of every human being, history in the past, present and future, and the ultimate meaning of the world because there the eyes of faith contemplate the gift of love.

The culmination of our experience of Jesus is a contemplative realization of his cross, or of the paschal mystery. We must understand Jesus' own words in this sense, "Anyone who loves his life loses it; anyone who hates his life in this world will have eternal life. Whoever serves me must follow me, and my servant will be with me where I am. My Father will honor one who serves me" (John 12:25-26). When John writes, "They will look at the one whom they have pierced" (John 19:37; Cf. Zech 12:10), he clearly intends that we interpret the verb "to look at" in the Johannine sense of "to see and comprehend." But here the comprehension of the Christian Mystery is a real participation in the gifts of the pierced Christ: water and blood. The Church has, in fact, always contemplated them as symbols of baptism and Eucharist because they are sacraments of the paschal mystery that celebrate our rebirth, our transfiguration, and our vocation. The origin of contemplation is the birth of a new creature in the death and resurrection of Jesus Christ—the divinization of the whole human being at the eucharistic banquet and the full realization of our life in the vocation the Lord has given us.

4. Concluding Remarks

Every day we monks live important spiritual practices, such as stability, attentiveness or mindfulness, meditation, silence, prayer, obedience, purity of heart, simplicity, openness, and many others. But *lectio divina* is the center of our monastic life. Monastic practices are not simply things to do. They are dimensions of the Spirit. If we cannot live these dimensions, we are not really monks. Sometimes we live them to lesser degree because we experience moments of temptation and sin, but if we cannot live them in an ongoing life of conversion and prayer, then we are not monks.

Again, monastic practices are dimensions of the Spirit, not moral or devotional exercises. They are a magnetic field in which we seek God and are found by God, where we experience strong temptations, where we know our own poverty and fragility, where we even sometimes sin. But in humility and grace, we are able to remain in this field of transfiguration. We Camaldolese know what temptation and sin are, as well as forgiveness and God's compassion, because we have personally experienced them. We are still here in the monastery where we persevere in our spiritual life. I conclude with a text by Georges Friedmann that seems a good modern interpretation of ancient monastic practice:

To undertake one's own flight every day. At least a moment—it can be brief, but it must be intense. Every day a "spiritual practice" alone, or with another who also wants to grow. Spiritual practices. To go beyond duration. Endeavor to strip oneself of one's passions, one's vanity, the desire for internal noise surrounding one's name (that every now and then smarts like a chronic disease). Flight from detraction. To lay down one's piety and one's hatred. To love all of humanity free. Eternalize oneself, surpassing oneself.[16]

16. G. Friedmann, *La Puissance et la Sagesse* (Paris, 1970) 359.

Monastic Wisdom
The Western Tradition

Bruno Barnhart

Monastic life is a way of living the mystery of Christ. Monastic *wisdom* can be understood as the contemplative dimension of this monastic life. Wisdom knows and lives the mystery as *mystery*: that is, as a fullness of life, light and energy which, as it is known, infinitely exceeds the knowing. The mystery of Christ, as known and lived in the early Church, has separated into different strands through the centuries. Monastic life, in its coherent simplicity, binds and holds these strands of the mystery together at the center—at a level deeper than our understanding—as does the Eucharist.

The solitude that distinguishes the Camaldolese Benedictine tradition nourishes and expresses that contemplative interiority within which the Word opens its spectrum of interior meanings—exemplified in the classical schemes of the "senses of Scripture." The interior pluralism of the Camaldolese vocation—signified by the "three goods" of community, solitude and the *evangelium paganorum*—represents at once the fullness of the one mystery and its unfolding into successive stages of interiority and of spiritual fruitfulness. The dimensions of this monastic tradition that appear in the chapters of the present book express the various threads or facets of this one mystery. "Monastic wisdom" is, inseparably, the life and consciousness comprehending within itself this unity and this diversity.

1. Introduction

> Listen carefully, my son, to the master's instructions, and attend to them with the ear of your heart. This is advice from a father who loves you; welcome it, and faithfully put it into practice. The labor of obedience will bring you back to him from whom you had drifted through the sloth of disobedience.[1]

1. Timothy Fry, ed., *RB 1980: The Rule of St. Benedict* (Collegeville, The Liturgical Press, 1980) 157.

These opening words of the *Rule*, in their simplicity, carry much more within them than their author could have consciously intended. This is the overture to a millennial Western tradition of monastic *wisdom*, and the field of implication of these words will live and widen through the centuries. The wisdom of Benedict, however, is not primarily a "theological" or literary wisdom, but rather that of a way of life in which a person learns to become an embodiment of the divine Word.

Condensed within these few words is a world of biblical resonances, evoking the whole mystery of salvation; yet everything is implicit. Striking straight to the heart of the Christ-mystery, Benedict's words open a plenitude of reflections that only gradually emerge into the monk's consciousness in his daily meditation. Veiled within this field of resonances glows the Mystery of God incarnate, a divine fullness communicated through faith and baptismal initiation, new birth as a child of God. The prodigal son who, lost in the distant "land of unlikeness," comes to himself, rises and sets out upon the journey of return to his father's house is Adam, is everyone, is myself. This cloud of allusions surrounding the luminous mystery, is typical of a literature of wisdom, particularly of this biblical wisdom of the monks.

Life according to the *Rule of St. Benedict* is cruciform in structure. The central vertical column of divine filiation is represented by the figure of the abbot, whose voice is heard already in the opening words of the *Rule*. The horizontal dimension of Benedictine life is the *koinonia*, the community: this is a monastic life of persons dwelling together. The monastic community, articulated in these two dimensions, becomes—like the Church itself— a "sacrament" of the unitive gift that is the heart of the New Testament. This living body of wisdom and communion will be the matrix of a culture and theology of monastic wisdom.

2. Monastic Wisdom

A knowing in unknowing characterizes the monastic wisdom, the *docta ignorantia* of young Benedict, who was to become father of the monks of the West. He left Rome and the life of a student for the wilderness "wisely ignorant and rudely wise," we are told by his biographer, Gregory the Great. And because this knowing is in unknowing, it is unlimited "beginner's mind." Yet there is a kind of consciousness, of understanding and of expression that corresponds to the unspeakable mystery. We recognize it in the *Tao Te Ching* or the *Bhagavad Gita* or the *Lotus Sutra*. We know it in the prologue of John's Gospel. This is "wisdom": wisdom consciousness, wisdom teaching and literature, a wisdom or sapiential culture.

I propose a working definition of this wisdom as *participatory* consciousness (or understanding or communication). It is a knowing through and in union, rather than "objectively," and it lacks the clarity that depends upon separation of subject and object. We might call it *unitive* consciousness, for it knows things first of all in their unity (within themselves, with one another) rather than in their distinctness. Beyond knowing things, finally, it simply "knows"; this is the interior light, consciousness itself, without a second, without an object of consciousness.

The *Rule of St. Benedict* itself, in comparison with much of the literature of the eastern monasticism that preceded it, has little of the flavor—or the special, savory language—of a "contemplative" writing. The *Rule* should be seen, however, as belonging to the great Christian wisdom tradition. The old monks, with all their limitations, possessed something precious that has become a rarity in today's world. Perhaps the best word for it is *simplicity*. As in the better examples of every monastic tradition, what we find in these monks is a single-heartedness, an integrity that seems to embody the ultimate oneness of God. It is a quality that flees examination, can hardly be described, and is found in admixture with every kind of defect. Within the beauty we discern in their architecture or their cyclical chant or in the very inwardness of their regular, nearly invisible lives, there is a gentle luminosity that touches the deepest levels of our own being. In rediscovering the wisdom of these monks, we discover—perhaps for the first time—seeds deep within the ground of our own soul that contain within themselves yet unrealized potencies. There are potencies of union but also of new creation: energies for the future.

We are speaking of wisdom as a kind of consciousness, experience, understanding, expression, a theology and a culture. It has already been suggested, however, that Christian wisdom in the most authentic sense is deeper than consciousness. It is a life of faith and love, of what we may call *fontality*, that terminates in a complete self-giving in the manner of Jesus Christ. Paul points to this wisdom beyond wisdom. "When I came to you, brethren, I did not come proclaiming to you the testimony of God in lofty words or wisdom. For I decided to know nothing among you except Jesus Christ and him crucified (1 Cor 2:1-2; cf. 1 Cor 13:2, 8-13).

As we speak of the monastic wisdom that is accessible to us in the Benedictine literary tradition, we should keep in mind this ultimate, vital and substantial wisdom in the hearts of centuries of monastics, that is not directly within the reach of our study. Monastic culture with its theology is an epiphenomenon, a secondary expression of this substantial wisdom.

There are various levels and dimensions in this knowing. But at the same time it is one: indeed, its basic characteristic is oneness. Throughout—

and beneath—the wisdom literature, we perceive a single quality that begets a multitude of metaphors. It is a depth dimension, and it may be better if we refrain from attempting to define whether this depth is psychological, ontological or spiritual: depth *simpliciter*. We might, then, call it the vertical dimension. This is what we perceive in the biblical narratives of the creation of the world, of Moses' initiation at the burning bush, or in the stories of Jesus' baptism, transfiguration or crucifixion. It is as if an *axis mundi*, a tree of life had become manifest, of such density and power of being, such pure authority, that the world obediently disposes itself around this center.

We might propose a "depth coefficient" in thought and literature, a measure of the degree to which reflection and expression exceed the flat epistemology of casual prose, of science or everyday journalism. It is this quality—if we may call it so—that characterizes the monastic writing that really engages us, that begins to break through the enclosure of our own habitual consciousness. We find this also in much of the writing of a contemporary Western monk, such as Thomas Merton or Bede Griffiths.

As we look back in history for the point of emergence of a Christian wisdom, it is only in the New Testament that we find a definitive starting point. Monastic wisdom as well finds its root and plenary source here, and particularly in the Pauline and Johannine writings. In Jesus Christ "are hid all the treasures of wisdom and knowledge" (Col 2:3). This fullness is communicated to those who, through faith and baptism, are "in Christ." John tells us that the divine Wisdom, or Word, become incarnate in Jesus Christ, has communicated the fullness of divinity to those who have received him: "And from his fullness have we all received, grace upon grace" (John 1:16).

This is a consciousness and a knowledge that is integral with *faith*. This knowing is related to the *scriptural Word*. Scripture has furnished the symbolic vocabulary, the language and the nutritive ground of this knowing. Historically, Christian wisdom theology has been expressed largely in commentaries on the biblical writings of both testaments. This consciousness and understanding is centered in Christ, in the *mystery of Christ*, which is its interpretive light or eye. It is a knowing which is already abundantly evident within the *New Testament* itself.

This knowing is a fruit of the baptismal anointing with the Holy Spirit, through which the Christ-mystery becomes a living presence within the individual person. It is a knowing illuminated by the divine Spirit. It is a delightful knowing, an intuition, knowledge, and understanding inseparable from affirmation and from joy. It is a loving knowing. Essentially participatory, this is an experiential (rather than merely objective) knowing. The culmination of this knowing is a mystical or contemplative union with God.

One may speak of this knowing as progressive consciousness of the "new Self" received in baptism. This knowing is integral with life. It has a circular relation with one's active or exterior life, such that the knowing animates the living and at the same time is a fruit of the living. This knowing, therefore, generates a spirituality that is centered in the interiorized mystery of Christ. Paul writes repeatedly of the importance of understanding the gifts or the gift one has received. The sapiential or contemplative knowing is furthered by prayer, by reflection and by silent meditation. The patristic-monastic wisdom is multidimensional; traditionally this plurality of levels of meaning has been represented in the "four senses of Scripture."

3. The Continuity of Biblical Wisdom

St. Athanasius' classic biography of Antony of Egypt, "father of monks," tells us how his vocation to the monastic way was catalyzed by the successive hearing of two gospel texts at the Sunday liturgy: "If you will be perfect, go sell all that you have, and give it to the poor; and come, follow me and you shall have treasure in heaven" (Matt 19:21); "Be not solicitous for the morrow" (Matt 6:34).[2] When pressed by the monks for guidance, he began, "The Scriptures are really sufficient for our instruction . . ."[3]

Major sections of the *Rule of St. Benedict* have the appearance of a tissue of scriptural quotations and allusions.[4] A contemporary edition of the *Rule* lists 132 references to the Old Testament and 189 references to the New Testament.[5] It is clear—from other sources as well—that these monks dwell in a biblical culture, that their lives are filled with the imagery and words of the Scripture and the Bible furnishes the language in which they express their own spiritual experience. Since monastic wisdom is grounded in the New Testament and in baptismal initiation, we may be surprised both by the continual reference to Old Testament texts and by the lack of explicit mention of baptism in the *Rule*.

We are struck by the extraordinary authority conceded to the biblical word, by the time and attention devoted to the reading of the word. The *Rule of St. Benedict* prescribes a total of from two to three hours each day to be devoted to *lectio divina*, the personal, meditative reading of the Scriptures. This continual reading of the Scripture in the context of monastic

2. St. Athanasius, *The Life of Saint Antony*, Robert T. Meyer, trans. (New York, Newman, 1950) 19–20.

3. Ibid, 33.

4. Cf. Prologue, ch. 7.

5. *RB 1980*, 587–93.

life quite naturally—indeed inevitably—produced a theology. "Monastic theology," surprisingly, has only recently been rediscovered as an autonomous tradition. This monastic theology is a further development of the patristic theology of East and West in the first five centuries. The monks, however, develop by preference certain potentialities of the patristic tradition.

Jean Leclercq has distinguished two currents[6] within this theology. The "black monks"—the main Benedictine tradition—developed a more objective theology of the history of salvation. This centering of their theological reflection upon the "objective mystery" is in line with the mainstream tradition of the Church Fathers. On the other hand, the "white monks"—mainly Cistercians, of a more contemplative bent—evolved a theology concentrated upon the spiritual life, experience, and development of the individual. This is an *interiorizing* of the Word. This line of development comes to constitute something new, a peculiarly Western monastic theology.

The monks expressed their experience of the Word in terms of the "four senses of Scripture," a scheme which they had inherited from the Greek Church Fathers. In addition to the literal or historical meaning of the text, these commentators distinguish not only the typological or "allegorical" interpretation in terms of Christ and the Church, but also a "personal" (moral or tropological) and a "final" (eschatological or mystical) level of meaning in the biblical word. This graduated or layered structure is typical of medieval conceptions of the spiritual world. In a parallel scheme, Guigo II the Carthusian imagined union with the word as proceeding in four stages, called in the original Latin *lectio, meditatio, oratio,* and *contemplatio* (or reading, reflection, prayer and silent contemplation). *Lectio* is a slow and meditative reading of the Scriptures. *Meditatio* is the silent rumination, the turning over of the word in the mind and heart, which opens its inner fullness. *Oratio* is the word become prayer, pouring forth from the heart. *Contemplatio* is a resting within the word beyond the movement of thought, the delightful stillness of union.

4. Monastic Theology

Medieval monastic theology reaches its culmination in the twelfth-century springtime of the Cistercian Benedictine reform, with Bernard of Clairvaux, William of St. Thierry, Aelred of Rievaulx, Guerric of Igny, Isaac of Stella. This is a Christian vision from an anthropological point of view:

6. Jean Leclercq, *The Love of Learning and the Desire for God* (New York, Fordham, 1961) ch. IX.

the human person once again becomes the central focus of theology, and with a new sense of the personal subject. Its distinguishing characteristic—more than in the monastic writing of earlier centuries—is *experience*: it is a theology emanating from the personal experience of the monk. If this emphatically contemplative thought differs from the more speculative and objective thought of the "black monks," it differs much more clearly from the "pre-scholastic" theology of the universities and urban schools of the time. Jean Leclercq and many others have pondered over this difference. If the central feature of the school theology is disputation, or the *quaestio*, the mark of the monastic reflection is an expression of personal spiritual experience.

The difference is a clear one; we may become convinced that it manifests a deep structure of reality. The distinction is analogous to that between prose and poetry, if the two terms are taken as polar opposites: as the language of objective statement and a language of personal experience. The question, however, leads deeper into the heart of what we have called a wisdom consciousness. This personal experience manifests *participation*. Only through participation does the Mystery yield to a deeper knowing. Participation in the Christ Mystery through faith and baptism, as we have seen, constitutes a new person, a new Self. The spiritual experience that characterizes this monastic theology can be understood nonobjectively, nondualistically, as the manifestation of this new Self in consciousness. This new Self is a *unitive* Self, one with the Word, one with Christ, one with God, and thus one with the Mystery in which all things are one. The unitive Self may offer itself as a hermeneutic key for understanding this monastic theology of the twelfth century. It will bring light to the central themes and structures of this theology. Listen to Bernard, contrasting the two ways of theology:

> It is not disputation, it is sanctity, which comprehends if the incomprehensible can, after a certain fashion, be understood at all. And what is this fashion? If you are a saint, you have already understood, you know; if you are not, become one and you will learn through your own experience.[7]

Experience, then, is an expression of being; what you feel—and know in the feeling of it—depends upon what you are. Can we say that this experience is itself the knowledge of what you are? We may recall that in the early Church, the "saints" were the baptized rather than a particular category of the baptized. To experience is to know that which cannot be understood in the ordinary (external or "objective," dualistic) way, "the incomprehensible."

7. Bernard of Clairvaux, *On Consideration* 5.30, quoted in Leclercq, *The Love*, 269.

To have this experience is to know *that which you are* in Christ. You may not be able to articulate this knowledge in words.

It is from the Eastern patristic tradition that these twelfth-century writers bring forth two strands of thought to bridge the chasm between humanity and God. First, they develop from the Genesis creation account a metaphysical view of divine union through the human person's participation in God as *image and likeness* of God, in which contemplative experience deepens with progressive likeness. Secondly, they adopt the Eastern fathers' spiritual and personal interpretation of the biblical *Song of Songs* in the light of John's Prologue. The divine Word, become a human person in Jesus Christ, is Bridegroom of the soul. In these two currents there is ample space for both a sapiential and an affective development. In William of St. Thierry, a third unitive feature appears: his conception of the Holy Spirit as the *divine unity* itself. William's teaching often shines with the luminosity of true spiritual experience, and reflects as well the practical experience of one who has observed the spiritual journeys of others—as well as his own—for many years. The way on which they have walked, he testifies, has often taken them where they wanted to go: into the *unitas spiritus*.

5. The Momentum of History: Differentiation

The monastic vocation is a call to rebirth, to the "beginning"; implicitly a call into the wilderness of the baptismal event. The monastic impulse is an attraction to the Source and to the original creative moment. "For it is the God who said, 'Let light shine out of darkness,' who has shone in our hearts to give the light of the knowledge of the glory of God in the face of Christ" (2 Cor 4:6). Within the person, at this central point, a plenitude of undetermined creative energy may be encountered. Moments of monastic renewal in history can be discerned, in retrospect, as points of origin for enormous religious and social movements. Thomas Merton presents the fourth-century Egyptian Desert Fathers in this perspective of radical creativity.

> The Desert Fathers did, in fact, meet the "problems of their time" in the sense that *they* were among the few who were ahead of their time, and opened the way for the development of a new man and a new society. They represent what modern social philosophers (Jaspers, Mumford) call the emergence of the "axial man," the forerunner of the modern personalist man.[8]

When this orientation to the beginning, or to the "center" is expressed in the cultural and institutional forms of monasticism, however, these forms almost invariably—and quite naturally, given the inertial tendency

8. Thomas Merton, *The Wisdom of the Desert* (New York, New Directions, 1960) 4.

of form itself—are conservative rather than forward-looking. We find a tremendous tension, therefore, between the creative dynamism of the beginning, the "nuclear awakening," and the almost entirely repetitive and conservative external forms in which the monastic charism becomes embodied. This is true both of institutional and of cultural and theological expressions. Here again the monastic community appears to be a microcosm of the Church.

The medieval monks dwelt not only within a cloister of stone, but within a biblical/theological cloister as well. Their mental horizons were very much defined by the possibilities of thought and expression that they found in the Scriptures, as interpreted by the patristic theologians, and above all by St. Augustine. We may begin to suspect that we are looking at an early stage of a historical process and that this confinement within the biblical word cannot continue forever. And indeed that is what we find as we continue to follow this history. Eventually we shall have to ask ourselves what the implications of this historical development may be for our own relation to the word today.

Medieval monastic consciousness—notwithstanding an inherited dualism—was characterized by a *unitive* quality. The other side of this, which emerges as we look at medieval monasticism in a larger context of history, is *undifferentiation*—in every sense of the word. When, from the thirteenth century onward, religious orders would arise with more specific orientations—following Francis, Dominic, and then Ignatius—these orders seem to sprout like branches from the single root of monasticism. The image of a root or the single massive trunk of an oak tree is deeply suggestive. Monastic life, with its interiorizing spirituality, attempted to plunge deeply into the "ground" of reality, of the human person and of the biblical word. By turning away from the world and returning to this ground—a return to some metaphysical beginning, as it were—monastics had always sought to merge with God, with the One.

Recall once again the opening words of Benedict's *Rule*, but now from a different perspective. The master directs the monk to a way of return: "The labor of obedience will bring you back to him from whom you had drifted through the sloth of disobedience."[9] *Return*: the way is back to the beginning rather than forward toward something new. One feels a tension with the forward thrust of the New Testament, with the Good News proclaimed by Jesus. The way is back into the undifferentiated rather than forward in the way of differentiation that is the way of history itself and of the normal development of the person. This theme of "return" is a constant in monastic literature. It is a central theme in the Old Testament. The

9. *RB 1980*, 157.

medieval monk, remaining confined within the cloister of the biblical word, and committed to a way of "return," may seem to remain a child in a world which is parentally defined and governed. The monk's way is that of obedience, of humility, and of unremitting self-renunciation. Any movement toward freedom and autonomy, toward an expansive self-realization or the emergence of personal creativity would be disapproved as an expression of self-will.

From a modern point of view, therefore, the monastic period may seem to be a prepersonal phase of history. The monastic life, with its cyclical regularity and liturgical rhythms, may be seen merely as a culture of repetition. The monastic literature, indeed, is characterized more by imitation than by creativity. The moments when the homily or commentary is enkindled by personal experience, when we feel that the author has broken free of the cultural container and found something new emerging from within, are frequent only in the work of exceptional saints like Bernard. Even then, the whole thrust of the discourse is usually toward the surrender rather than the realization of the person.

The monk, in pursuing the "beginning," may reject any forward-looking perspective. In opting for the "undifferentiated," he may condemn any movement toward differentiation. It is natural, then, that in a historical era of differentiation, monastics will assume a posture of resistance. The monastic wisdom of the West flourishes and declines somewhere between the vanishing of a sense of the historical Christ-mystery in the Western Church and the emergence of a sense of the person in the Western world. On the one hand, the dimensions of the Christ-event—especially its historical dynamism—have been contracted as Christian consciousness became enclosed within the medieval Western Catholic container. On the other hand, the differentiation of the individual person that has become the distinctive characteristic of the modern West was only beginning to appear, e.g., in the personalizing spirituality of the Cistercian masters at the end of the "monastic age." Soon after, "wisdom" would surrender its place to "science" in the Western theological world.

Theology: wisdom or science? The question would emerge very concretely and visibly in the twelfth century, when the human person began to discover himself or herself with a new autonomy. At the same time—and as the leading edge of this personal self-discovery—there emerged a new autonomy of human reason with respect to the authority not only of tradition but also of Scripture itself. The public dramatization of this conflict took place in the controversy between Abelard, appearing in the role of the bold individualist and rationalist innovator, and St. Bernard of Clairvaux, expressing the traditional monastic theology at its best.

The medieval monks, at the threshold of a new world of differentiated spheres of culture, of an autonomous human person, of creative innovation, conserved the essentials of a Christian life of faith—the scriptural word, liturgy, communal life, prayer and work—as within the nucleus of a cell. The "old wisdom" would then lie neglected and virtually dormant for long centuries as the new growth proliferated both inside and outside the Church. A rebirth of the Christian sapiential tradition would come within reach only when the Church itself took a dramatic new turn in the middle of the twentieth century. Monasticism would be confronted with the challenge of realizing its unitive charism anew in a world of free and differentiated "subjects."

6. Rebirth of Monastic Wisdom

The long sapiential parenthesis would show signs of coming to an end when the era of rampant rationalism itself manifested signs of exhaustion. Dissatisfaction with the linearity and depthlessness of empirical reason alone, the depredations of a technological culture, widespread social and psychological disintegration and the growing awareness of an interior famine, called forth alternative ways of knowing from every side. Gradually, even while the obsessive containment persisted, Western humanity began to have dreams. The image of oneself as a purely rational consciousness and the corresponding image of a perfectly rational world began to dissipate. This mind and world without illusion were another illusion! Color and depth begin to return to the world, feeling and wonder are repatriated. The sober linearity begins to give way to a contoured, moving surface in every sector of culture. Philosophy, psychology, art, even science itself rediscover an iridescent boundary of wonder. In the moist liminal twilight, Gnostic schools proliferate once again like mushrooms. Market stalls and bins abound with wisdoms of every quality and price.

During the first half of the twentieth century, a constellation of scholarly movements within the Catholic Church worked to excavate the old sapiential tradition. Biblical movement, liturgical movement, patristic movement, each digging within its own patch and bringing forth ancient treasures, collaborated in uncovering the single root, the Mystery. This work began to bear fruit in the documents of Vatican Council II. While the perspective remained largely objective, external, the Mystery began to emerge as a visible form at the heart of early Christianity.

At the same time, the council recognized the emergent values of human freedom and creativity, the positive value of the other religious traditions, and a forward and positive progression in history. Religious orders—Benedictine monastic communities included—were given a double mandate for their renewal: both the recovery of their sources, in the light of the gospel, and the revisioning of their way of life in the light of the world and the human person of today. These pronouncements of the council, taken together, direct monastic men and women not only to the recovery of the "old wisdom" but to the discovery—or creation—of a *new Christian wisdom* that is at once vitally rooted in the gospel and attuned to the movement of the Spirit today.

When Western monastics begin to look for clues to the renewal of their sapiential tradition today, it is first to the *Eastern* horizon that they are drawn. Eastern Christianity presents them with an integral wisdom tradition, essentially the "old wisdom" lived through the centuries. Still farther East, the great Asian traditions of Hinduism, Buddhism, and Taoism challenge them to a personal discovery of the very roots of their Christian and monastic vocation, and to a unitive self-realization. Meanwhile, around them, the modern Western world calls them forward to a creative actualization of the person.

Several generations of monks—scholars and contemplatives—have labored during the twentieth century toward the rebirth of a Christian and monastic sapiential tradition. Odo Casel played a fundamental role in the rediscovery of the Christ-mystery in its centrality and power, and in the recognition of the sapiential depth and richness of the liturgical tradition. Columba Marmion, another transition figure, began to bring forth a participatory vision of this Christ Mystery from the legacy of post-Reformation scholasticism. Anselm Stolz helped bring monks within reach of a theology and spirituality properly their own, with roots in the New Testament and patristic tradition. Damasus Winzen helped to make accessible once again a sapiential approach to the Scriptures.

Cyprian Vagaggini, Benedictine monk and theologian who became a Camaldolese, brought into relief the sapiential tradition of patristic and medieval times in contrast to the later theologies, characterizing it in his monumental work on the liturgy. Later he would see a broad return to the sapiential way emerging in the work of a number of twentieth-century Christian theologians. Jean Leclercq, in addition to his extensive work in making the medieval sapiential writers accessible through editing, translation, and interpretation, focused explicitly on this wisdom tradition and brought it into clear visibility in contrast to other and later ways of theology. Leclercq succeeded in making the fragrance and flavor of monastic wisdom present for people of today.

A number of monks of the Benedictine tradition worked specifically at the recovery of a Christian *contemplative* wisdom. Well known are Thomas Merton, Abhishiktananda (Henri Le Saux), John Main, Bede Griffiths, and Thomas Keating. Each of these men was influenced by the Asian traditions—Hinduism or Buddhism—in his sapiential quest. Let us look briefly at the work of Merton and Griffiths.

Thomas Merton exemplifies clearly the co-existence and interaction of these two poles: the monastic charism with its demands, and the self-awareness of a differentiated person of the twentieth-century West. Merton consistently exhibits a combination of interiority and innovation, of inner light and creative fire. In his writings, he was continually occupied with the quest for contemplation, for that deepening of consciousness that is an experience of union with God. And yet at the same time we observe in him— more and more clearly as he finds himself—a restless creative spirit, an impatience with outworn ways and entrenched structures, a wild independence of the unquestioned presuppositions and the sleepy consensus of the multitude. The depth and the "newness" are evident in the same person, and they appear to be complementary, to nourish one another. If on the one hand Merton is obsessed with the contemplative experience and its pursuit, he is capable on the other hand of the most radically innovative writing. It is in his obscure and very personal poetry (and "antipoetry") that we find this latter, subversive activity most perfectly manifested.

Finding wisdom in the writings of Chuang-Tzu from third-century B.C.E. China, Merton found it as well in the fiction of William Faulkner. He moves easily between an ancient contemplative wisdom with which he is very much at home, and a new wisdom that combines contemplation and creativity, interiority and a personal participation in contemporary realities—whether issues of peace and justice or the creative cultural ferment. Without theorizing much about it, he offers us the example of a person stretched between the terms of our question. He confronts us also with an issue that may well descend into the depths of our quest for a new wisdom: the place of woman, of the feminine, of *Sophia* in the sapiential world of our time.

Bede Griffiths went to India after many years in an English monastery, to find "the other half of my soul." For almost forty years he worked at the "marriage of East and West," and particularly the relationship—spiritual and theological—between Hinduism and Christianity. Immersed within an Asian culture as Merton was unable to be, he differed from Merton also in his project of a personal theological synthesis. Merton had remained, throughout his many books, primarily a spiritual writer rather than a theologian or religious philosopher. Griffiths found, at the core of all the great religious traditions, a universal wisdom or "perennial philosophy." Central to this universal vision is the unitive principle, nonduality or *advaita* (expressed also in the Hindu concepts of *Atman* and *Brahman*).

Secondly, the vision is structured according to a tripartite scheme: all reality consists of the three inseparable and interpenetrating worlds of body, soul, and spirit. Griffiths sought and found these two principles also within the Christian tradition. He saw the principle of nonduality expressed primarily in the Gospel of John, where Jesus reveals that the relationship of love and communion between Father and Son will be communicated to the believer. Bede Griffiths' work is a first, bold sketch of a "new vision of reality" that integrates the religious traditions of Christianity and the East with insights of contemporary science. It calls for a further step of integration with that Christ-mystery which is emerging into the light in our time.

7. The Treasure in the Field

Jesus said, "The kingdom of heaven is like treasure hidden in a field, which a man found and covered up; then in his joy he goes and sells all that he has and buys that field" (Matt 13:44). The treasure, discovered, is quickly buried once again in the ground. This parable somehow expresses the central paradox that we have found in viewing the Christian monastic life and its wisdom in the light of the baptismal fullness disclosed by the New Testament writings. From a slightly different angle, we find at the heart of those writings the gift of the Spirit inseparably joined with the law of the Cross.[10] Monastic wisdom cannot, finally, be other than that word of the Cross that is simultaneously the gift of the divine Spirit.

Monastic life is the working of that field. It is a way of acquiring what one already possesses, of becoming that which one already is. The hermit Seraphim of Sarov, to the question, "What is the meaning of life?" responded quickly, "the acquisition of the Holy Spirit."[11] The Holy Spirit, we know, is already received in baptism. The monk's apparent renunciation of the very gift of the new person and its freedom is in view of realizing this gift, this new self, more purely and fully. This "Buddhist" rejection of immediate dividends for the sake of the hidden principal is intrinsic to Christian monasticism as well. The intuition is valid, but its living out is surrounded by pitfalls. It is too easy for the apparent renunciation of the gift to become an actual rejection of the gift, too easy—as in the counterparable—for the talent to be buried, with best intentions.

Jesus himself both teaches and exemplifies this way of *descent*; it is close to the heart of his message. The monk is the person who continues

10. Cf. 1 Cor 1–2 and Mark 8–9.
11. Franklin Jones, ed., *The Spiritual Instructions of Saint Seraphim of Sarov* (Los Angeles, Dawn House Press, 1973) 42.

to dig deeper into the dense earth of the heart, where the paschal mystery is to be consummated. Isolated from an awareness of the plenary gift of baptism, however, this way may promptly lead one back from gospel to law, from grace to slavery, from spirit to letter and even from a human to subhuman life. Without Jesus' baptism with the Holy Spirit, the wilderness remains outside the gospel. The way prepared in function of realization of the human person can become a road to depersonalization. At its best, the monastic way leads to a genuine transformation, a progressively deepening life of faith, a growth in love and a fuller actualization of the person—the "new creation." The expressions of this experience and this transformation reveal the treasure beneath the often colorless surface of monastic life.

Literature is not life; it is both grander and infinitely less than life. Reviewing theological and spiritual literature in the light of the gospel, we may begin to feel a kind of "stone of Daniel"—a disconcerting mountain growing under our feet and overturning all the theoretical constructions. Is it possible that the best theological and spiritual formulations of the Christ-reality are hopelessly awry? That the one Stone of Incarnation, one with our bodies, quietly eludes all our analyses and syntheses? That in developing our theological vision each of us is helpless to do more than to build, with blind human ego, one more tower? Is it possible that the gospel really is so revolutionary that, asserting itself once again, it shakes off culture and theological constructions like cobwebs? The suspicion (implicit differently in Buddhism and in Protestantism) is both frightening and exciting, and very likely valid. The monk–theologians, building away from the ground with their spiritual ladders and towers, will not have been much more successful than the other theological builders. It is their lives—and the light and fire communicated in their lives and their words—that will endure.

8. The Challenge

Monasticism has been traditionally associated with the "old Christian wisdom" of patristic and medieval times. Monasticism and the old wisdom went into recession together in the West at the end of the Middle Ages. We have begun to speak of the need for a rebirth of Christian wisdom in new forms, for the birth of a *new wisdom*. What does this imperative imply for western monasticism today? The question may best be considered, I think, in relation to the situation of the Church itself in this era of Vatican II. As the Church breaks free of its rigid cultural shell—almost unchanged since the time of the Counter-Reformation—it rediscovers its identity and essential elements, within, "at the center." At the same moment, it begins to break out of the container to encounter the world and humanity with simplicity and freshness, with a new, confident affirmation.

Western monasticism, likewise, is invited to break free of its cultural container to rediscover its inner identity and wellspring, and at the same time to discover a new relationship with everything around it: Church and world, humanity and cosmos. According to the mind of the council, this means to return to its authentic sources and to come into relationship with the movement of the Spirit in the world today—also in new, strange, and unfamiliar places and modalities. Put briefly, monasticism, if it is to bring forth a new wisdom, must open itself beyond itself. It must open to the length and breadth, the height and depth, of the gospel and Christ-mystery, of the human person, and of the experience of human persons in the world today.

In the era of Vatican II, the Church turns away from a closed and defensive self-obsessiveness to attend to the person, to humanity, and the world. Monasticism must, in its own way, go through this same conversion. It is something like a mutation in consciousness, a leap from one phase of growth, overprolonged, to another, with new and wider horizons. Monasticism today needs not only to understand itself in terms of the realization of the *Atman*, or unitive Person (this itself, for Western monasticism, is a fresh discovery), but also of the differentiated, free and creative person, rooted in this same unitive center or ground. Perhaps the key to a new monastic wisdom is in this realization of both the inward and outward person. Monasticism will no longer thrive as a culture of conservation and of repetition. To rediscover itself from within is to know itself as a wellspring of newness and creativity.

The opening of Christian monasticism beyond itself and the rediscovery of its own identity may proceed concurrently. This takes place clearly, for example, in the encounter with the Asian contemplative traditions in which Christian monastics discover the essential relationship of their vocation to their unitive center. At the heart of its charism and its wisdom, monasticism is rediscovering this *unitive* principle. It is important that this principle now be known and accepted in its purity and autonomy, rather than subordinated to the "word"-related structures of theology and institution. The same can be said of the feminine principle.

A new wisdom today will integrate the rational-critical mind, while at the same time situating it firmly within its limits. It will find the place of the feminine principle, and its relationship to the divine Spirit. Along with this we can hope for a new and deeper understanding of sexuality and its relationship to spirituality. In defining itself by a renunciation of the world, monasticism has often lost a vital connection with body, earth, and cosmos. A new wisdom will seek to recover this bodily dimension and the sacramentality that is so intimately bound up with the vitality of Christianity.

Monasticism is on the way to discovering anew its place within the Church. This implies both a stronger sense of the autonomy and essential freedom of the monastic charism, and a deeper understanding of the relation of monastic life to the Christ-mystery. As we rediscover the relationship of the monastic vocation to baptism, we may come to understand the monastery—like the wilderness of the Baptist in which Mark's Gospel begins—as a place of *initiation*. Monastic life, dedicated to interiority, comes to be seen in the context of the Christ-event as the place of the *arche*, the "beginning" (Mark 1:1; John 1:1; cf. 1 John 1:1). In the experience of God that is the beginning and the heart of monastic life, the human person—a new creation—is born again and again. A new monastic wisdom will be, first and foremost, the knowledge of this beginning, both in its divine depth and in its creative dynamism. This wisdom will embrace, as well, the *way* in which a person grows from this new birth to the fullness that has been traditionally named purity of heart—an embodied fullness of love that we may also call Eucharist.

Today, in a Christianity often polarized by the twin reductionisms of fundamentalist and scientistic interpretation of Scripture, the wisdom tradition—which has been intrinsic to the monastic tradition—has a special importance. It carries within it a living participation in the Christ-mystery that is the heart and eye of biblical understanding and interpretation.

Camaldolese Benedictine monasticism originates in the time of the undivided Church, and carries within it, whether in seed or in blossom, the fullness of the Mystery known and lived in the New Testament and early Christianity. This sense of the fullness of the Mystery reemerges today, in a fresh encounter of "East and West." Camaldolese Benedictine monastics are called to make the Mystery present in its fullness in today's world. Essential to this is the recovery of the separated strands of the Christian wisdom tradition: the frayed threads of the Word.

Part Three
Configurations of a Charism

The Threefold Good:
Romualdian Charism and Monastic Tradition

Joseph Wong

At the conclusion of the first millennium of Camaldolese history and the beginning of a new epoch, it is opportune for the Camaldolese family to seek spiritual renewal through a deeper understanding of their charism. According to the double criterion indicated by Vatican Council II, the renewal of religious institutions should be based on a return to the sources, as adapted to the present day situation. The aim of this chapter is to reflect on the basic elements of the Romualdian/Camaldolese charism through the early sources. *The Life of the Five Brothers* by Bruno of Querfurt offers an important complement to Peter Damian's *The Life of Blessed Romuald.*[1] The expression "threefold good" (*triplex bonum*), originating in Bruno's treatise, found its way into the Camaldolese *Constitutions* in 1993.[2] The General Chapter of 1999 adopted the symbol of threefold good as a concise expression of the Romualdian charism and Camaldolese identity.[3]

After a brief reflection on the complementary character of the bipolar structure of cœnobium/hermitage in Camaldolese tradition, this chapter will study the threefold good in *The Life of the Five Brothers* within the wider context of monastic tradition. Thus, "cœnobium" is seen in the tradition of monastic friendship. "Golden solitude" is compared to the cultivation of *hesychia* in the desert tradition. "Preaching the gospel" or "martyrdom" is lined to the themes of *peregrinatio* and "martyrdom of love" in monastic spirituality.

1. Both are contained in Thomas Matus, *The Mystery of Romuald and the Five Brothers* (Big Sur, Hermitage Books, 1994).
2. Camaldolese Congregation OSB, *Constitutions and Declarations*, no. 3.
3. Cf. Emanuele Bargellini, "L'identità camaldolese davanti al nuovo millennio" *Camaldoli ieri e oggi. L'identità camaldolese nel nuovo millennio* (Camaldoli, Edizioni Camaldoli, 2000) 9; Joseph Wong, "Identità camaldolese e formazione: il *triplex bonum*" Ibid., 29–54.

1. Communion and Solitude: Complementary Polarities

The classical text of the threefold good, or "threefold advantage" (*tripla commoda*), is found where Bruno gives an account of Otto III's project of choosing some of the more fervent disciples of Romuald as missionaries to Poland. There they were to build a *monasterium* in Christian territory near an area where pagans dwelt, secluded and surrounded by woods:

> This would offer a threefold advantage: the cœnobium, which is what novices want; golden solitude, for those who are mature and who thirst for the living God; and the preaching of the gospel to the pagans, for those who long to be freed from this life in order to be with Christ.[4]

Bruno continues, "Meanwhile, so that we might enjoy the first two advantages—since the third was not available here—as soon as we had established a hermitage Otto decided to build a cœnobium."[5]

An attentive reading of the text quoted above will reveal a problem in interpreting the meaning of the threefold advantage. The first paragraph seems to indicate that the threefold advantage is to be pursued in the same setting, that is, in a *monasterium* built in a secluded place bordering on Christian and pagan territories in Poland.[6] There the monks could enjoy the threefold good of community life, solitude, and preaching of the gospel. In the second paragraph, however, the first two advantages are linked to different external settings. As Romuald's disciples were already enjoying the advantage of solitude at the hermitage in Pereo, the emperor wanted to build a monastery nearby so that beginners might experience the advantage of community life.

Bruno gives another listing of the threefold advantage as "three highest goods" (*tria maxima bona*): "He [Otto] longed to do better, and God's mercy strengthened his feeble will, enkindling in him an ardent desire for the three highest goods, any one of which is sufficient unto salvation: the monastic habit, the hermitage, and martyrdom."[7] Combining the two texts, we find two different terms for each of the three goods: "cœnobium" and "monastic

---

4. Matus, *Mystery*, 95. I have changed the English expression for the first good "community life" into "cœnobium," which is the literal translation of the Latin text.

5. Ibid., 96.

6. The term "monastery" is used again after Benedict and John had arrived in Poland where Duke Boleslaw "built them a monastery." Cf. Matus, *Mystery*, 106. The scene of their martyrdom that describes a common dormitory further confirms the fact that the Brothers were living in a cœnobium in Poland. Cf. Matus, *Mystery*, 132–36.

7. Matus, *Mystery*, 111. To render the Latin *heremum*, I have substituted "hermitage" for the expression "solitary life" as found in Matus' translation.

habit," i.e., monastic life; "hermitage" and "solitude"; and *evangelium paganorum* and *martyrium*. It becomes clear that, in Bruno's mind, the first two goods refer to external locations, as well as different aspects of monastic life. The third good, however, is not confined to an external setting, but can be pursued in a monastery, hermitage, or even outside institutional structures, as in the case of an itinerant monk/hermit. It is important to bear in mind the polyvalent significance of the threefold good.[8]

There is another important difference between the two texts. Whereas the first one presents the threefold good in the fashion of an ascending ladder, the second text eliminates the idea of subordination by presenting the three aspects of monastic life as "three highest goods," each of which is "sufficient unto salvation." The idea of cenobitical and solitary life as two complementary aspects of the monastic life was probably derived from Bruno's own experience as a monk at SS Alexius and Boniface Monastery in Rome, which adopted not only the *Rule of St. Benedict* but also that of St. Basil, who upheld the primary importance of cenobitical life.[9] In the case of Pereo, the idea of joining cœnobium to hermitage in one place had been Otto's. However, Pereo was not an isolated instance. Later some other Romualdian foundations adopted the same model: Valdicastro, Sitria, Biforco and Furlo.[10] Romuald himself had lived with other anchorites at Cuxa for a number of years,[11] where he learned the ancient Palestinian model of *laura*, representing solitude in communion, which he later adopted for his reform program of the eremitical life.[12]

2. The Threefold Good in *The Life of the Five Brothers* and Monastic Tradition

A. *"Privilege of Love" and Monastic Friendship*

The first good refers to the communal aspect of monastic life that consists, above all, in the fraternal relationships so important prior to entering into deep relationship with God or facing spiritual combat in solitude. The

8. Cf. Benedetto Calati, *Sapienza monastica. Saggi di storia, spiritualità e problemi monastici* (Roma, St. Anselmo, 1994) 530–37.

9. Matus, *Mystery*, 214. This monastery hosted monks of Latin and Greek rites. Cf. p. 90.

10. Cf. Anselmo Giabbani, *L'Eremo. Vita e spiritualità eremitica nel monachesimo camaldolese primitivo* (Brescia, Morcelliana, 1945) 36–37; Giovanni Tabacco, *Spiritualità e cultura nel Medioevo* (Napoli, Liguori, 1993) 225f., 235f.

11. Matus, *Mystery*, 180–83.

12. Cf. Emanuele Bargellini, "Camaldoli tra Oriente e Occidente," *Monaci e missione*, A.c. Farrugia e Gargano (Verrucchio, Pazzini, 1999) 33–34. For the *laura* structure of the hermitage at Pereo see introductory note in Matus, *Mystery*, 95.

normal setting for training in communal life is the monastery, where greater emphasis exists on the communal aspects of monastic life. But the first good is not limited to the cœnobium or novices. In *The Life of the Five Brothers*, fraternal love or friendship is the distinguishing mark of Romuald's disciples, whether in a cœnobium or at the hermitage. The entire book can be viewed as a memoir of the fraternal relationships among these disciples, as well as between them and Romuald.

The expression chosen by Bruno to describe his friendship with Benedict was "privilege of love." Romuald entrusted Bruno to the care of Benedict, the chief protagonist of the *Life*. The two shared a common cell at the Pereo hermitage. Bruno wrote, "It was my privilege to be the object of his love and to hear him call me, 'my brother.'"[13] Their bond of friendship was based on the special goal that they pursued together in their monastic life: to preach the gospel in a pagan land and to shed their blood for Christ. Bruno kept insisting that Benedict set out for Poland to preach the gospel, while he himself would follow later because, as a counselor and close friend to the young emperor Otto, Bruno felt he had to stay behind and wait for Otto to make his final decision to embrace the monastic life.[14] Persuaded by Bruno's words, Benedict began to thirst for martyrdom and accepted the idea of leaving for Poland to bear witness to Christ in a pagan land.

While Bruno called Benedict "the other half of my soul," Benedict, for his part, declared, "We two ought to be one."[15] Theirs was a spiritual friendship with genuine human warmth. This aspect was especially evident when they bade each other farewell the night before Benedict's departure:

> I cannot speak of our last evening together without tears in my eyes. Night was near, and in the waning light I began to traverse the heavens with Benedict. My sorrow was all the greater because of the great love that united us— and yet, miserable man that I am, I confess that I remember our last conversation together as a happy occasion.[16]

They were sad because of separation, but joyful for coming close to their goal.

Thus Benedict and John, another disciple of Romuald, departed for their mission in Poland, leaving Bruno behind to assist the emperor and to obtain the official papal letter for preaching the gospel in non-Christian

13. Matus, *Mystery*, 98. Cf. Tabacco, *Spiritualità*, 167–94.

14. Ibid., 98–101.

15. Ibid., 100.

16. Ibid., 104. Bruno continues: "We continued to bid each other farewell, embracing and exchanging the holy kiss. As we walked and talked, in the manner of friends who are seeing each other for the last time, I kept telling him, 'Dearest brother . . . I beg you, for the sake of our common hope of Jesus Christ, the Son of the Virgin, never forget that I shall always be with you, and you with me.'"

territories. Duke Boleslaw, ruler of the Poles, warmly received the two monks and built them a monastery. There Benedict and John, with two Polish novices, started a new monastic presence in preparation for their missionary activities, while waiting for the arrival of Bruno with the papal letter. In the anguish of their prolonged waiting, Benedict and John supported each other with a close friendship reminiscent of that between Benedict and Bruno:

> The two holy brothers lived in perfect harmony. Whatever one of them wanted, the other—even against his own preference—wanted as well, whether it was a question of the cell or of work, of clothing or livelihood or prayer. If one of them expressed a desire, the other took care not to disagree with him, for the sake of brotherly love and to avoid all self-will. Together they loved God above every other good. Together they lived an orderly monastic life and gave themselves to prayer with a pure heart.[17]

This text that recalls the "good zeal" recommended by the *Rule of St. Benedict* (*RB* 72) is important because it reveals the renunciations necessary for maintaining harmony in the everyday common life, and especially during times of difficulty. The authentic friendship between the disciples of Romuald is the fruit of an asceticism that implies detachment from self-will and respect for others' wishes. This same fraternal friendship—the "privilege of love"—that bonded Bruno with Benedict, and Benedict with John, also joined Romuald's disciples with their beloved master. It offers an excellent model for monastic friendship. In his book on monastic friendship, Brian P. McGuire shows that monastic friendship, which reached its golden period in what he calls the "age of friendship" in the twelfth century, has a history reaching back to fourth-century monasticism.[18] Immediately preceding the "age of friendship," the author presents two other periods leading up to it: "the eclipse of monastic friendship" (ca. 850–1050) and "reform and renewal" (ca. 1050–1120). It is interesting to note that Romuald and his disciples belonged to the end of the "eclipse" period that would usher in a period of "renewal," with new impetus toward monastic friendship.

Seen in this context, *The Life of the Five Brothers* occupies an important place in the renewal of the experience of monastic friendship. Historically speaking, Bruno's treatise can be situated within the larger movement of the "Ottonian synthesis of political friendship with a monastic tone."[19] In point of fact, Bruno also wrote a second version of the life

17. Ibid., 128.
18. See Brian P. McGuire, *Friendship and Community: The Monastic Experience, 350–1250* (Kalamazoo, Cistercian, 1988) 231–95.
19. Ibid., 146–56.

of St. Adalbert of Prague,[20] who enjoyed an intimate bond of friendship with Otto III. Adalbert, like Bruno after him, was a monk at SS Alexius and Boniface.

Otto became acquainted with Adalbert at Rome in 996 and made him an "intimate" (*familiarem*). During that period, they seem to have been together almost all the time.[21] John Canaparius and Bruno both describe the love between the older man and the young prince, spiritual father and son, in terms of friendship. In their case, friendship is based on admiration of spiritual quality and the zeal for the kingdom of God. After the departure and martyrdom of Adalbert, a similar bond of friendship was formed between Otto and Romuald, who was hoping to help the young emperor to embrace the monastic life.

The bond of friendship among Romuald's disciples is based on their spiritual pursuit after a common goal: the monastic ideal in general and the specific desire to preach the gospel in a pagan land, and to endure martyrdom for the sake of Christ. As friend, or as Gregory the Great put it, as "guardian of the soul" for one another,[22] they felt the need to communicate this ideal to each other and sustain one another in the common endeavor, especially in difficulty.

B. "Golden Solitude" and Hesychia in Desert Tradition

Although St. Romuald reformed and founded hermitages as well as monasteries throughout his reform activities, his preferences undoubtedly leaned toward hermitages. His special contribution consisted in gathering individual hermits into small groups and giving them a rule to follow. It happened that hermits living in isolation, for lack of guidance, almost always ended up with excesses in their ascetical practices. For this reason Romuald was called "Father of reasonable hermits who live under a rule."[23] Evidently the rule Romuald proposed was the *Rule of St. Benedict*. Fortunately, however, Bruno also left us with a *Brief Rule* that John received from Romuald as guidance for his life. One can find the ideal of "golden solitude" well condensed in this *Brief Rule*:

---

20. Bruno of Querfurt, *S. Adalberti Pragensis episcopi et martyris vita altera*, Monumenta Poloniae Historica, t. 4 (Warsaw, 1969).

21. John Canaparius, *Vita S. Adalberti episcopi et martyris*, Monumenta Poloniae Historica, t. 4 (Warsaw, 1968) 591.

22. Gregory the Great, *Forty Gospel Homilies* (Kalamazoo, Cistercian, 1990) 215. The translation renders *custos animi* as "soul-keeper."

23. Matus, *Mystery*, 88.

Sit in your cell as in paradise. Put the whole world behind you and forget it. Watch your thoughts like a good fisherman watching for fish. The path you must follow is in the Psalms—never leave it. If you have just come to the monastery, and in spite of your good will you cannot accomplish what you want, then take every opportunity you can to sing the Psalms in your heart and to understand them with your mind. And if your mind wanders as you read, do not give up; hurry back and apply your mind to the words once more. Realize above all that you are in God's presence, and stand there with the attitude of one who stands before the emperor.

Empty yourself completely and sit waiting, content with the grace of God, like the chick who tastes nothing and eats nothing but what his mother brings him.[24]

This *Brief Rule* is to be studied together with chapter 31 of *The Life of Blessed Romuald*, where Peter Damian narrates the episode of Romuald receiving the gift of tears, spiritual knowledge, and mystical prayer.[25] The *Brief Rule* and chapter 31, I believe, firmly situate Romuald and disciples in the ancient tradition of "hesychast" spirituality. Hesychasm[26] should be understood in its primitive sense, which had its origin in the desert fathers and reached its high point in the spirituality of Sinai, especially in the writings of John Climacus and Hesychius of Sinai. My intention is to present a commentary of the *Brief Rule* and chapter 31 in the context of desert spirituality, especially through the writings of John Climacus and Cassian. Whereas we are told that Romuald read the *Lives of the Fathers* and followed the teachings of the *Conferences* by Cassian,[27] I do not claim that Romuald had read John Climacus' writings. However, as *The Ladder of Divine Ascent*, written by Climacus, was the novitiate manual for eastern monks, Romuald likely knew about Climacus' spiritual teaching indirectly through contact with monks of the Greek tradition.[28]

The Greek term *hesychia* means a state of silence, stillness, or tranquility, as a result of the cessation of external trouble and internal agitation. Cassian's "purity of heart" contains the aspect of "tranquility of mind"[29] and thus, the idea of *hesychia*. The term also means solitude or retreat. Hermits

24. Ibid., 158.

25. Ibid., 222–23.

26. Cf. "Hesychasme," *Dictionnaire de Spiritualité*, t. 7 (Paris, Beauchesne, 1968) 381–99; Kallistos Ware, "Silence in Prayer: The Meaning of Hesychia," *One Yet Two: Monastic Tradition East and West*. Ed. Basil Pennington (Kalamazoo, Cistercican, 1976) 22–47.

27. Matus, *Mystery*, 185, 87.

28. Around the figure of St. Nilus, for example, the influence of Basilian monasticism reached Rome, especially through the monasteries of SS Alexius and Boniface and Grottoferrata; cf. Gregorio Penco, *Storia del monachesimo in Italia* (Milano, Jaca, 1983) 207f.

29. John Cassian, *The Conferences* (New York, Paulist, 1997) 46.

and cenobites alike seek hesychia as an essential monastic value, but in the earliest sources, the term "hesychast" usually denoted a monk living in solitude, or hermit.[30]

The beginning of Romuald's *Brief Rule*, "Sit in your cell," is typical advice given to hesychasts. Abba Moses gives a similar injunction: "Go, sit in your cell, and your cell will teach you everything."[31] Abba Rufus explains the meaning of *hesychia*: "*Hesychia* means to remain sitting in one's cell with fear and knowledge of God, holding far off the remembrance of wrongs suffered and pride of spirit."[32] The link between *hesychia* and the cell is also clearly stated by Antony the Great: "Just as fish die if they stay too long out of water, so the monks who loiter outside their cells or pass their time with men of the world lose the intensity of *hesychia*."[33] Then, the idea of the cell as "paradise" can be traced back to Jerome: "As long as you remain in your country, you should take your cell as paradise."[34] In the desert tradition, the cell is considered a place of repose, a house of prayer, and the dwelling place of God.[35]

The *Brief Rule* continues: "Put the whole world behind you and forget it." Hesychast spirituality distinguishes between exterior and interior *hesychia*. Whereas exterior *hesychia* refers to a remote and quiet place, interior *hesychia* means the inner stillness of the hesychast. External solitude is the favorable condition for cultivating inner stillness. Thus, it is not enough to remain in one's own cell; it is more important to cultivate the interior cell of the heart. For this reason John Climacus exhorts the hesychast to close a threefold door: "Close the door of your cell to your body, the door of your tongue to talk, and the gate within to evil spirits."[36]

Interior *hesychia* can be disturbed by attachment to people or things of the world, or by concern with worldly affairs. The *Brief Rule*'s categorical injunction of forgetting the whole world clearly belongs to the same spiritual tradition. Forgetting the external world means that, while staying in the cell, a monk should avoid wandering in the world with his mind but remain centered on himself. This inward understanding of *hesychia* is emphasized in the classical description of the hesychast given by John Climacus: "The hesychast is one who strives to confine his incorporeal being within his bodily house."[37]

30. Ware, "Meaning," 23.
31. Benedicta Ward, *Sayings of the Desert Fathers* (Kalamazoo, Cistercian, 1975) 139.
32. Ibid., 210.
33. Ibid., 3.
34. St. Hieronymus, "Ad Rusticum monachum," PL 22, 1076.
35. Ware, "Meaning," 25.
36. John Climacus, *The Ladder of Divine Ascent* (New York, Paulist, 1982) 263.
37. Ibid., 262.

The *Brief Rule* continues: "Watch your thought like a good fisherman watching for fish." To attain interior *hesychia* and freedom from concern, the desert tradition offers two other key concepts: vigilance (*nepsis*) and attention (*prosoche*). According to John Climacus, vigilance is the distinctive attitude of the friend of *hesychia*, which is "always on the watch at the doors of the heart, killing or driving off invading notions."[38] Climacus has already employed the metaphor of fisherman when speaking of vigilance: "The vigilant monk is a fisher of thoughts, and in the quiet of the night he can easily observe and catch them."[39] The objects of vigilance, both for Romuald and Climacus, are thoughts (*logismoi*), meaning passions or vices. In this regard, Climacus shows creative dependence on the classical treatment of the eight "thoughts" in Evagrius.[40]

Hesychia, or inner silence, is not an end in itself: it is cultivated as a means for a noble goal—contemplation or unceasing prayer. In the monastic tradition, prayer and contemplation have their origin as response to the word of God. For this reason, after giving the instruction for vigilance over one's thoughts, the *Brief Rule* introduces the main task of a monk while sitting in the cell: "The path (*una via*) you must follow is in the Psalms; never leave it."[41] The *one* way is in the Psalms. As the Fathers, Athanasius and Cassian in particular, view the Psalter as a condensation of the entire Bible, this *one* way refers to the Bible as a whole and especially to the book of Psalms as its compendium.[42]

The *Brief Rule* continues with instructions about the way of the Psalms, presenting a unified view of reading, meditating, and praying the Psalms. They are different moments of a single activity, during which one can freely move from one to the other without following a strict order of sequence. Even if the word itself is not found here, the idea of "meditation" (*melete*) in its ancient monastic meaning of repeatedly reciting a certain text to understand better the meaning and commit it to memory is surely contained in this passage.[43]

As it appears in the *Brief Rule*, the invitation to follow the path of the Psalms only comes after the exhortation to forget worldly concerns and

38. Ibid.
39. Ibid., 196.
40. Evagrius Ponticus, *The Praktikos and Chapters on Prayer* (Kalamazoo, Cistercian, 1981) 16–26; John Climacus, *Ladder*, 64–66.
41. Matus, *Mystery*, 158.
42. Athanasius, *The Life of Antony* and *The Letter to Marcellinus* (New York, Paulist, 1980) 101–06. For Cassian, not only does the Bible find its condensation in the Psalms, the latter are further condensed in the opening verse of Psalm 69; Cf. Cassian, *Conferences*, 378–83.
43. Cf. Irenée Hausherr, *The Name of Jesus* (Kalamazoo, Cistercian, 1978) 172–80.

keep vigilance over one's thought, i.e., cultivate inner silence. In their turn, constant reading and meditation are proposed as means for guarding the attention of a wandering mind. Thus, inner silence and constant meditation are the two essential elements of spirituality of the cell, and are indispensable to each other. In this regard, one finds a similar approach in Cassian. For him, it is impossible to concentrate on spiritual reading without cultivating inner silence.[44] On the other hand, according to Cassian, assiduous reading and meditation offer the most effective means for avoiding harmful thoughts, by nurturing holy memories and sentiments.[45] The necessity of combining the two aspects—silence and meditation—is beautifully formulated in the *Eremitical Rules* of Blessed Rudolf, fourth prior of the Hermitage of Camaldoli.[46]

If we follow the classical division of the two stages of spiritual life— *praktike/theoria* (ascetical practice and contemplation)—the way of the Psalms is present in both stages as their bridge. Constant reading and meditation lead to *hesychia*, or purity of heart, and open the door to contemplation—what Cassian calls "spiritual knowledge" or deeper understanding of Scripture. He refers to reading and meditation as ascetical practice[47] that, at the same time, bear the fruit of spiritual knowledge.[48] Cassian highlights the close links among asceticism, assiduous reading and meditation, and spiritual knowledge, or contemplation.[49] These elements are inseparably connected and should be practiced throughout one's monastic journey.

The *Brief Rule* contains a synthesis of these various elements of the spiritual life. The "way of the Psalms" presupposes an asceticism through vigilance over one's thoughts and, in its turn, prepares the way for contemplation. However, as the *Brief Rule* is given to beginners, it rightly exhorts the disciple to wait patiently for God's grace. To gain a glimpse of the special grace promised in the *Brief Rule*, we need to turn to *The Life of Blessed Romuald*. In chapter 31, Peter Damian describes the episode when Romuald received the gift of tears of compunction for the first time. *Compunctio* here goes beyond its usual meaning of penitential sorrow to mean

44. Cassian, *Conferences*, 512.

45. Ibid., 57, 514f.

46. Blessed Rudolf, *Eremiticae Regulae*, 45: "For silence without meditation is death, it is like a man buried alive. But meditation without silence is pure frustration—it is like the struggling of the man buried alive, in his sepulcher. But both silence and meditation together bring great rest to the soul and lead it to perfect contemplation;" from Thomas Merton, *The Silent Life* (New York, Noonday, 1957) 159.

47. Cassian, *Conferences*, 46.

48. Ibid., 514.

49. Cf. Columba Stewart, *Cassian the Monk* (New York, Oxford, 1998) 90–95.

any ecstatic experience of joy and jubilation in prayer. Along with tears of compunction, another important grace was also granted to Romuald—spiritual knowledge or understanding of the hidden meaning of Scripture:

> Then one day, as he [Romuald] was singing the Psalms in his cell, his eyes lit upon the verse: "I will instruct you and teach you the way you should go; I will counsel you with my eye upon you." At that instant tears began to pour from his eyes, and many mysteries of the Bible came clear to him. From that day forth, whenever he so desired, he could shed abundant tears, and the spiritual meaning of Scripture was no longer hidden from him.[50]

According to the hagiographer, on this occasion God raised Romuald to the heights of holiness, from which, by the grace of God's Spirit, he was able to see future events and penetrate with deep insight into many hidden mysteries of Scripture.

This mystical experience was not an isolated instance in Romuald's life but had a lasting effect on him. Tears often accompanied his ecstatic prayer. The descriptions of tears, fire, and jubilation in Romuald's prayer recall the idea of "fiery prayer" (*oratio ignita*) often mentioned by Cassian, who describes a kind of prayer that is fiery, fervent, pure, ineffable, beyond words, expressible only in sighs.[51] He makes *compunctio* a label for all kinds of extraordinary experiences in prayer. Tears, too, are marks of ecstatic prayer.[52]

Likewise, "tears of compunction" is a major theme in John Climacus, even though he emphasizes compunction as repentance and sorrow.[53] In the chapter on prayer, he recommends the use of "monologic prayer" (repetition of a short prayer) as means of guarding against distraction.[54] He advises not to form "sensory images" during prayer and deems the use of words in prayer unnecessary when a person has found the Lord, for the Spirit will intercede with sighs beyond words. Climacus gives great importance to the presence and working of the fire of the Spirit during prayer. One perceives in all these aspects a resonance with Romuald's experience of ecstatic prayer.

It is significant that Romuald obtained the gift of tears, together with spiritual knowledge and ecstatic prayer, when he was singing the Psalms—a way that he recommends in the *Brief Rule*. When one turns to that rule and encounters the words: "If you have just come to the monastery, and in

---

50. Matus, *Mystery*, 222–23.

51. Cassian, *Conferences*, 385.

52. Cf. Stewart, *Cassian*, 114–16. See the entire chapter (114–30) for references to Cassian's texts on ecstatic prayer and for an analysis of the experience of prayer in Cassian.

53. John Climacus, *Ladder*, 122–31, 136–45.

54. Ibid., 276.

spite of your good will you cannot accomplish what you want," one should keep in mind this beautiful chapter 31 in *The Life of Blessed Romuald* and find comfort in the thought that the promised grace will one day be given to those who persist on the way of the Psalms.

The *Brief Rule* continues: "Realize above all that you are in God's presence, and stand there with the attitude of one who stands before the emperor." The exhortation toward the awareness of being in God's presence is found in the *Rule of St. Benedict*. The first degree of humility is based on the awareness of being always and everywhere under the watchful eyes of God (*RB* 7.10-30). This awareness should inspire the monk's behavior especially during the time of common prayer (*RB* 19.1-2). Vigilance and attention are the two correlated aspects of *hesychia*: one strives to be free from the agitation of thoughts in order to be mindful of God's presence. In his chapter on vigilance, Climacus speaks about constantly standing in prayer before God our king.[55] Then in the chapter on *hesychia*, one finds the famous exhortation to unite constant remembrance of Jesus with one's breath: "Let the remembrance of Jesus be present with your every breath. Then indeed you will appreciate the value of *hesychia*."[56]

The *Brief Rule* ends: "Empty yourself completely and sit waiting, content with the grace of God, like the chick who tastes nothing and eats nothing but what his mother gives him." One must empty or strip oneself completely. The whole paragraph recalls Psalm 131: while the image of a chick waiting quietly to be fed by its mother resembles the metaphor of the weaned child on its mother's lap (v. 2), the injunction to "empty yourself completely" reflects verse one of the psalm—"O Lord, my heart is not lifted up, my eyes are not raised too high; I do not occupy myself with things too great and marvelous for me." Both verses are quoted in *The Rule of St. Benedict* as introduction to degrees of humility (*RB* 7.3-4).

C. "Evangelium paganorum—Martyrium" *and Martyrdom of Love*

Two different expressions are given by Bruno of Querfurt for the third good: *evangelium paganorum* and *martyrium*. They are closely related to each other. The Greek word *martys* means one who bears witness. While *evangelium*, or evangelization, means bearing witness to the good news through preaching, martyrdom means bearing witness to the same cause by shedding blood. Therefore, the two are related by the same basic idea of witnessing. From a historical perspective, preaching the gospel to the pagans, or barbarians of the time, often implied a major risk of martyrdom.

55. Ibid., 196.
56. Ibid., 270.

With regard to the terms *evangelium–martyrium*, one may ask which was the primary goal or intention of Bruno and the Brothers when they were planning their expedition to Poland. Jean Leclercq defends the view that their primary concern was with martyrdom, while preaching of the gospel was secondary, which was chosen as a means or occasion for achieving the primary goal.[57] I consider Leclercq's opinion to be well founded. It is quite evident Bruno's heart was set on fire by the recent martyrdom of Adalbert of Prague, for whom he had great admiration, and whose *Life* he wrote. Bruno's primary concern with martyrdom is seen from the original title of *The Life of the Five Brothers*, which, after the Prologue, begins with these words: "*Incipit Passio sanctorum Benedicti et Johannis ac sociorum eorundem.*" Thus the book was intended to be an account of their martyrdom.

Bruno was the first to support the emperor's project of a missionary expedition to Poland. That martyrdom was Bruno's primary goal can be perceived from the way he strove to persuade Benedict to embrace the project. His first argument was related to the idea of dying:

> Why should we stay in this swamp and die for nothing? Wouldn't it be better to go someplace where we could live as hermits and die for the gospel? Here, if we want to seek God in the hermitage, we are not afraid to die. Would we be afraid, then, if preaching the gospel meant that we would have to give our lives for Christ?[58]

To the possible objection that it would be presumptuous for a sinner to seek martyrdom, Bruno replied:

> Don't say that it is pride for a sinner to seek martyrdom. . . . And anyway, we are not looking for martyrdom in order to become saints, but only to have our sins forgiven. For in fact, if Baptism washes away sins, martyrdom totally extinguishes them.[59]

Bruno's primary concern for martyrdom is again evident in the narrative of his farewells with Benedict. The last words Bruno addressed to his parting friend manifest the common ideal that constituted the bond of their friendship. Bruno reminded Benedict to pray constantly for the fulfillment of their desire: to shed their blood "for a worthy cause," i.e., the love of Christ and the gospel.[60]

The intention of preaching the gospel to the Poles was certainly present in their missionary journey. While they were waiting for Bruno to

57. Cf. Jean Leclercq, *Temoins de la spiritualité occidentale* (Paris, du Cerf, 1965) 104–06.

58. Matus, *Mystery*, 99.

59. Ibid.

60. Ibid., 105.

arrive with the papal letter, Benedict and John reminded themselves "they had come here to bear fruit for souls by preaching the gospel."[61] They were also making necessary preparations for their missionary activities. In practical terms, they made an effort to learn the Polish language so as to make it easier for the people to understand the gospel. They adopted their customs by letting their beards grow and shaving their heads. They also started wearing Polish clothing, hoping to be accepted as their fellow countrymen.[62]

But the profound anguish that Benedict experienced during the prolonged wait revealed his deepest concern: "Unable to accept his lot in life, he was at war with himself, afraid that his holy desire might be frustrated and that his hope [for martyrdom] might fail to attain its crown."[63] It is from the same perspective that, just before narrating the scene of their martyrdom, Bruno remarked that God, in his unfathomable wisdom, had fulfilled his promise inasmuch as he had granted the gift of martyrdom to the Brothers, even if they had not had the opportunity to preach the gospel. This affirmation clearly shows that, for Bruno, the primary objective of the missionary expedition of the Brothers was martyrdom, while evangelization had been chosen as an occasion for it.

Nevertheless, the effort of the two Brothers in learning a foreign language and adapting themselves to Polish customs manifested their genuine zeal in spreading the gospel to the pagans. At one point they seemed to place evangelization and martyrdom on the same level: "We did all this so that we could either preach the gospel or suffer martyrdom for Christ's sake. It does not matter which, since the one leads to growth in holiness and the other to eternal salvation."[64] Their expedition probably had a twofold objective—evangelization and martyrdom—the latter being the primary goal for them.

While the first two goods—communion and solitude—clearly correspond to Romuald's personal charism and the nature of his monastic reform, the third good might seem to be the project of Otto/Bruno. However, this project at least obtained Romuald's approval. In reality, the missionary project of Otto/Bruno had a long history in the monastic tradition. From Augustine of Canterbury to Boniface, the monastic missionary tradition reached Bruno Boniface, particularly through Adalbert.[65] Moreover, Romuald fully embraced this project when, after the martyrdom of the Brothers, and especially that of Bruno, he himself "with burn-

---

61. Ibid., 115.

62. Ibid., 129.

63. Ibid., 122. The Latin text is more explicit about martyrdom.

64. Ibid., 132.

65. Cf. Thomas Matus, "Bruno di Querfurt: il Monaco evangelizzatore della Prussia orientale e il Maestro Romualdo," *Monaci e missione*, 129, 133–34; Innocenzo Gargano, "Un monachesimo missionario cristiano: Agostino di Canterbury e Gregorio Magno," Ibid., 49–74.

ing desire to shed his blood for Christ," set forth in an expedition for Hungary, together with twenty-four monks.[66] Periodically, Romuald lived as an itinerant hermit. According to Leclercq, *peregrinatio* as a spiritual path expresses the eschatological sense of detachment and the desire for being exiled from one's own country. It normally includes solitude and asceticism along the journey, offers the opportunity for preaching, and not infrequently martyrdom as well.[67]

Between the two terms *evangelium paganorum* and *martyrium*, as Leclercq points out, the primary object of Romuald's disciples was martyrdom, seen as the highest expression of asceticism. There has always been a close link between martyrdom and monasticism that had its origin or major expansion as intentional substitute for martyrdom in an altered form.[68] Peter Damian considered freely chosen asceticism as "spontaneous martyrdom" which he saw flourishing in Romuald's time: "This was the golden age of Romuald—no one was persecuting Christians anymore, yet spontaneous martyrs abounded."[69] Peter Damian himself defended the ascetical practice of voluntary scourging through the idea of martyrdom.[70] By embracing the ascetical way of life, Bruno Boniface and the other disciples of Romuald looked to martyrdom as the crowning of their asceticism. Since they lived at a time when public persecution by the state or empire no longer existed, the only way to achieve the goal of their desire was to go to a pagan land where they could preach the gospel and receive martyrdom.

Their desire for martyrdom was nothing new. In *The Life of Antony*, the father of all monks already manifested a strong desire for martyrdom. During the persecution under Maximinus, when the holy martyrs were led into Alexandria, Antony also left his cell and followed the martyrs. He yearned to suffer martyrdom with them. But because he did not wish to hand himself over imprudently, he rendered loving and courageous service to the confessors, both in the mines and in the prisons.[71] When the persecution ended, Antony departed and withdrew once again to his solitary place, "and was there daily being martyred by his conscience, and doing

66. Matus, *Mystery*, 235. Cf. Roberto Fornaciari, "Monachesimo—missione—martirio. Bruno Bonifacio di Querfurt dall'eremo del Pereo a Kiev" Unpub. Thesis (Rome, Gregorian University, 1994) 48–49.

67. Jean Leclercq, *Aux sources de la spiritualité occidentale* (Paris, du Cerf, 1964) 44–77.

68. Cf. Gregorio Penco, "La spiritualità del martirio nel Medio Evo" *Medioevo monastico* (Roma, St. Anselmo, 1988) 399–410.

69. Matus, *Mystery*, 259.

70. Petrus Damianus, *Epist.* VI, 27, PL 144, 416. A similar idea of spiritual martyrdom is already found in Gregory the Great, *Dialogues* (New York, Paulist, 1959) 160–61.

71. Athanasius, *The Life of Antony*, 65–66.

battle in the contests of faith. He subjected himself to an even greater and more strenuous asceticism."[72]

Whether it is about secret martyrdom through daily asceticism or public martyrdom by shedding one's blood, the heart of the matter is love, without which all the labor and sacrifice are to no profit (cf. 1 Cor 13:1-3). In this regard, Bruno points to Benedict's ardent love for Jesus as the motivating force of his desire for martyrdom: "Burning with love for Jesus, like wood in the fire, the man of God Benedict was motivated by one desire only: to attain eternal life through a pure and undivided love for divine wisdom."[73] Bruno's vision of Benedict consuming a full chalice of consecrated wine has a symbolic meaning: his martyrdom is a participation in the paschal mystery of Christ.[74] Endowed with eucharistic meaning, the third good means total gift of oneself with unconditional love, just as Christ loved us and gave himself for us (Eph 5:2).

In Romuald's case, after the martyrdom of his disciples, especially that of Bruno, he began a journey for Hungary, burning with strong desire to shed his blood for Christ. Even if he had to return to Italy due to illness and did not achieve martyrdom, the Church rightly honors him as "martyr of love"—*martyr fuit, sed amoris*—for his desire for martyrdom and his ascetical life, compared with "spiritual martyrdom."[75]

3. Conclusion

The 1996 Camaldolese *Consulta* has offered new insight into the meaning of the threefold good. Without denying the reference to external structures of cœnobium or hermitage, the *Consulta* emphasizes the spiritual meaning of the threefold good as a personal journey for each monk. Thus the *Consulta* states:

> Regarding the theme of *triplex bonum*, the priors and formation directors should present it as a journey which each Camaldolese monk or nun is called to live in *koinonia* of fraternal life, in the experience of solitude till the maturity of a total gift of self.[76]

The *Consulta* continues to suggest a comparison of the threefold good with the mysteries of Christ: incarnation, passion, death, and resurrection. It is

---

72. Ibid., 66. The expression "martyrdom of conscience" is taken from 2 Corinthians 1:12.

73. Matus, *Mystery*, 105.

74. Ibid., 104.

75. Cf. Sequence *Plaudant claustra et deserta* of the Mass on the feast of St. Romuald (June 19) in the *Monastic Missal* of the Camaldolese Congregation.

76. Camaldolese Congregation OSB, *Consulta 1996* (Camaldoli, Ediz. Camaldoli, 1996) 7.

possible to reflect on the threefold good—communion, solitude, and preaching—as essential aspects of Jesus' life.[77] The threefold good can be traced back, beyond monastic tradition, to the life of Jesus, the primary source of all Christian and religious life. As the Holy Spirit always led Jesus during his life, the Spirit also marked the threefold good of Jesus. Thus, in the light of Christ's Mystery, the *triplex bonum*—intended as a spiritual journey for each Camaldolese—becomes in concrete the following of Christ (*sequela Christi*), model of the threefold good, under the guidance of the Holy Spirit.

I propose the third good as the maturation of the threefold good and the hallmark of the Romualdian/Camaldolese charism. Understood as a total self-gift with unconditional love, or bearing witness to the point of death, the third good corresponds more to the mysterious character of the Holy Spirit, under the epithets of love, gift, unction, and fire. Like the sparkling fire of the Spirit, the third good animates the other two and manifests itself as self-giving in a variety of ways, beyond any rigid categorization. Since the essence of the third good consists in a total self-gift with unconditional love, the expression "martyrdom of love" can be taken as a catchword for the third good—the flowering of the Romualdian charism.

77. Cf. Joseph Wong, "Il *triplex bonum* nella vita dei primi discepoli di San Romualdo. Dalla prassi monastica al senso teologico-spirituale," Acts of the Conference held at Fonte Avellana, August 23–26, 2000 (to be published).

Koinonia:
The Privilege Of Love

Robert Hale

People tell us that our monastic communities seem particularly warm, friendly, and familial; and they appreciate, they say, our kind hospitality to guests, that breathes of this same spirit. And we do hope it is true; we do try thus daily to live together. Because for us Camaldolese, it all begins with love, and thus with *koinonia*, that is, with Christian community and communion (the wonderful New Testament Greek term *koinonia* indicates all that). And it is this love/communion that sustains us on our journey. And it is this same love/communion that, when fulfilled, will be the heart of the kingdom. So *koinonia* and love are not two values alongside others. Understood in their depth, they converge, and are the "one thing necessary" that enables all the rest for our Camaldolese, Benedictine, Christian, and human existence.[1]

It all begins with love, because God *is* Love (1 John 4:8, 17). And it all begins with *koinonia* because God *is* this communion of Persons: Father, Son and Holy Spirit. One cannot go back further than that. And God the Father so loved the world that he sent the Son to us (John 3:16), to call us, through the Spirit, into communion with God; and in God with all of humanity, all of creation. In this deeper sense, the themes of *koinonia* and love are not just for the beginning stages of the Camaldolese journey, do not characterize just the Camaldolese cœnobium. Rather, they are foundational values for every stage of the Camaldolese—and indeed Christian—

---

1. A favorite maxim of our former Prior General, Benedict Calati, is that before we can be monks we have to be Christians; and before we can be Christians we have to be human beings. This works at the chronological level, but also at a more profound theological level. On all these levels Calati stresses "the primacy of love," "the primacy of communion"— phrases he uses interchangeably.

journey. And they are also, again, about the primordial Beginning before all human journeying, and about the End, about the consummation of all in the loving communion of the Holy Trinity.

1. Camaldolese *Koinonia* Today

To realize this gospel ideal of love/communion in terms of our own monastic charism, a Camaldolese community wants to be a *family* of *brothers* (or *sisters*, for our nuns) in Christ. And our oblates, guests and friends are extended family. Thus the *Constitutions and Declarations* of our Congregation[2] state: "The professed monks of our communities are all brothers without distinction and to the same degree. . . . The brothers' relations among themselves are to be inspired by gospel simplicity and charity."[3]

This bond of gospel simplicity and charity uniting the brotherhood has its ultimate source in the divine communion: "By a life of fraternal dialogue which reflects on earth the communion of the three divine Persons, let the monks 'make every effort to preserve the unity which has the Spirit as its origin and peace as its binding force' until they 'form that perfect person who is Christ come to full stature' (Ephesians 4:3, 13)."[4] Thus the *Constitutions* recommend "shared responsibility and fraternal collaboration."[5] Thus the prior is to seek to deepen this communion: "Let the prior, then, see his brothers in the light of the Spirit and recognize their gifts, needs, and aspirations. Let him support and direct them as they grow in freedom, responsibility, and loving union with God and one another."[6]

If the monks are all bound together as brothers in Christ, friendship is also accepted and encouraged, as a real intensification of Christian communion, as long as it is not closed and exclusive, as long as "in-groups" do not form.[7] The great tradition of monastic friendships encourages us to be open to this great gift in our own communities today.[8]

2. I shall be focusing throughout this chapter on my own congregation; but the substance of what is said is relevant, I believe, also for the various communities of Camaldolese nuns, and for the other men's congregation, the Congregation of Camaldolese Hermits of Monte Corona.

3. Camaldolese, *Constitutions and Declarations*, no. 53.

4. Ibid., no. 31.

5. Ibid., no. 54.

6. Ibid., no. 28.

7. Cf. Robert Hale, "La comunità monastica e 'il gruppo,'" *Vita Monastica* 81 (1965) 45–47. *Vita Monastica* is the official monastic review of our Congregation. I shall be quoting rather immodestly from several of my own articles, simply because they are readily available to me; but a number of our Italian monks have published extensively in these areas.

8. Cf. Robert Hale, *Love on the Mountain: The Chronicle Journal of a Camaldolese Monk* (Big Sur, Hermitage Books, 1999), especially 17f.

A. *The Primacy of Love and Communion*

Whether our bond is simply fraternal, or also fraternal and friendship, the monks seek to "abide in that love" which Christ offers us as brother and friend.[9] Because God is love, and because Christ has summed up the whole of the Law and Prophets in the new commandment of love,[10] our own charismatic Benedict Calati summed up his whole ministry of Prior General for eighteen years with the phrase "the primacy of love." He also used the equivalent phrase "the primacy of communion." In his final conference as General to the General Chapter, entitled simply "The Primacy of Love," he returned again and again to this theme of love/communion. He thanked the whole Congregation for the "active presence of all the brothers, who have worked for this communion and for the human and spiritual growth of the whole Congregation," enabling "this communion" to constitute us as a kind of 'Camaldolese mystical body.'"[11] He then reviewed every aspect of our life, tying it in to his central theme of "the primacy of Love, which is the primacy of the gift of the Holy Spirit . . . within Whom is lived out this pact of love."[12] Thus monastic celibacy "is above all a sign of liberty and of the primacy of the love of Jesus Christ;"[13] so also our liturgical life,[14] etc. In a long section on "communion," Calati notes that our endeavor to live monastic communion is "living image of the Church as communion."[15] He concluded his discourse:

> All that I have I owe to our community, to these fathers and brothers that preceded me and are here. I have loved much and I continue to love. The Bible begins with the song of Adam and Eve, the song of love: Eden. Then there is another garden of the Canticle of Canticles. Finally there is the new garden of the resurrection: the first word of the Risen calls a friend: Mary. The disciple who remains, the one Jesus loves . . . reveals the bond of love of the Spirit in the Church and in history. Only love remains. Only a monasticism shaped through and through with love, singing of love, is credible. I conclude exhorting you all to love one another.[16]

9. Cf. John 15:9.

10. Cf. Matthew 22:37; this is the heart of the great *Shema* or primary commandment of Israel; Cf. Deuteronomy 6:5.

11. Benedetto Calati. *Il Primato dell'Amore: 18 Anni a Servizio dei Fratelli* (Camaldoli: Edizioni Camaldoli, 1989) 5. The whole relation is reprinted in *Sapienza Monastica: Saggi di Storia, Spiritualità, e Problemi Monastici* (Roma, Studia Anselmiana, 1994) 241–79. Regarding the phrase and concept of "Primacy of Communion," see p. 223.

12. Calati, *Il Primato*, 11.

13. Ibid., 12.

14. Ibid., 17f.

15. Ibid., 19.

16. Ibid., 52–53.

B. *Liturgy and Word As* Koinonia *Celebrated*

The culminating moments of our daily life together, whether in the hermitage or the monastery, are constituted by our communal celebration of liturgy. Calati sums it up very succinctly, stating that because of the "primacy of Love . . . our very life is liturgy."[17] Thus our *Constitutions* recall our Benedictine character, and also the teaching of Vatican II, as they affirm:

> St. Benedict wants "nothing to be preferred to the Work of God" (*RB* 43,3). Under the guidance of the Holy Spirit, Benedictine communities have learned to recognize the primacy of the various liturgical forms of celebrating Christ's mystery. . . . Thus "the liturgy" is the summit toward which the activity of the Church is directed; at the same time it is the fountain from which all her power flows.[18]

If we share in the very *koinonia* of Christ with the Father in the Holy Spirit, if we are thus made Christian community, it is primarily through liturgy, and especially in the culminating moment of liturgy which is Eucharist: "The sharing in God's life and the unity of His people are in fact given fitting expression and a mysterious realization in the Eucharist."[19]

The *koinonia* we seek is ultimately nothing less than the very *koinonia* of the divine Persons, which we shall enjoy in fullness in the kingdom; and our daily celebration of Eucharist is privileged foretaste of the *koinonia*. "In the Eucharist, the Church receives an outpouring of the Holy Spirit and enjoys a foretaste of the perfect communion with the Blessed Trinity which will be hers in the age to come."[20] Thus, "the incarnational and also eschatological dimensions of Christian *koinonia* find their privileged expression in the moment of the Eucharist."[21] Consequently, every Camaldolese (as indeed every Christian) should focus their spirituality on Eucharist: "Each monk and the community as a whole are to orient their life in such a way that it is a preparation for, and an extension of the Eucharistic action."[22]

In our spirituality, then, there is not to be an opposition between "liturgy" on the one hand, and "contemplation" on the other, with the former being merely communal and outward, for beginners, and the latter being solitary and truly mystical, for the advanced, or something like that. Rather, in the one Christian *koinonia* our contemplative life is also to be eucharistic and liturgical, and our Eucharist and liturgy are also to be contemplative:

17. Ibid., 17.
18. Camaldolese, *Constitutions*, no. 66.
19. Ibid., no. 67.
20. Ibid.
21. Robert Hale, "La *koinonia* aperta della vita monastica," *Vita Monastica* 126 (1976) 134–35. This whole issue of *VM* is dedicated to the theme of monastic *koinonia*.
22. Camaldolese, *Constitutions*, no. 68.

The Eucharist must be celebrated in faithful adherence to the spirit of the liturgy, so that each individual participant and the community as such may share in it "fully, consciously and actively," according to the nature of the worshiping assembly and the intrinsic demands of the celebration. Thus, by God's gift, the worshipers may attain that total inner openness to God's action which the spiritual masters have called mystical experience or contemplation, and which our monastic fathers have taught by the example of their lives.[23]

Monastic liturgy is not just solemn spectacle, however spiritual, in order to impress and edify admiring guests. Rather, the Eucharist itself calls for an inclusive *koinonia*, and so Camaldolese do everything to facilitate the full *sharing* by their guests in the celebration, as the *Constitutions* direct: "When members of the faithful are present at the Mass of the community, their active and conscious participation in the divine mysteries is to be favored in the most opportune way and with all charity."[24]

If the Eucharist is the splendid jewel of monastic worship, the Divine Office is its magnificent setting—this image used by Cyprian Vagaggini, the famous Camaldolese liturgist and theologian.[25] The *Constitutions*, in explaining the significance of the Divine Office for the Camaldolese, offer a rich theology that is at once ecclesial, christological, and trinitarian; the Divine Office renders present the communion of the Church with Christ, and of Christ with the Father in the fulfillment of Christian love: "In the celebration of the Liturgy of the Hours, the Church offers her sacrifice of praise to the Father, and she thanks Him for the salvation that comes to her in Christ. In the Hours, as in the Eucharist, Christ is acting out His priestly role and bringing to completion the covenant of love that unites the bride to her bridegroom."[26]

Peter-Damian Belisle has thoughtfully explored how the liturgical cycle, that unfolds in the Eucharist and Divine Office celebrations during the year, puts us in profound *communion* with the unfolding of salvation history, and even with the unfolding of the seasonal "natural" cycles; liturgy even puts us into communion with those deep and personal, and also archetypical and preconscious cycles in our own lives. Monastic life is about all these dimensions of *koinonia*:

> We become the music, if we dare to follow the rhythms of divine life . . . .
> We become Love's artifact, the sounding board for that silent Word in the

23. Ibid., with reference to Vatican II.

24. Ibid., no. 69, with reference to the *Rule* and to Vatican II.

25. Cyprian Vagaggini, 1909–99, author of *Theological Dimensions of the Liturgy* and many other books and articles, rector of Sant' Anselmo in Rome, *peritus* of Vatican II, etc. Cf. Robert Hale. "Fr. Cyprian Vagaggini, o.s.b. Cam.," *American Benedictine Review* 50:2 (1999) 214–15.

26. Camaldolese, *Constitutions*, no.71, with reference to Vatican II.

world. By entering the mysteries of Christ, again and again, we experience personal regeneration. Through our wholeness we help to form a Spiritual creation. . . . This is inspirable life, a share in eternity's promise. The liturgical year is a wheel of becoming which invites us to be one with the Word and inspires us to become part of a renewed creation—moving in a convergent circle of love.[27]

Of course it is not at the level of the superficial, false self that we can open up to true communion with these larger realities:

Our patterns of relating to others will hinge on whether we walk on a path of selflessness or pivot around ego's circle. . . . The intimate balance I must know in my relationships with others is one of compassion and sensitivity to others, opening my vulnerable heart to their vulnerable hearts. Intimacy is a precarious journey because openness and vulnerability are its givens. . . . The intimate balance of relating to God is an outward movement of love unto union and communion.[28]

The Word of God in Scripture is a fundamental component of liturgy, of *lectio*, and thus of Camaldolese spirituality;[29] and we understand Scripture as the narration of a salvation history that continues to unfold and to incorporate our own histories, enabling us to share in the one ongoing divine plan.[30] But as the present Prior General Emanuele Bargellini notes, the Camaldolese, in fidelity to the deepest monastic tradition, see "liturgy as the ultimate definitive reading of Scripture" because liturgy renders present salvation history in its culminating moment of paschal mystery.[31] For this reason, Bargellini notes, any spirituality that is not focused on liturgy and the redemptive *koinonia* it establishes is in danger of "groping around in the fog."[32] Thus all Camaldolese spirituality, and indeed all Christian spirituality, is profoundly communal at this deepest level, and "will find necessarily also an opening toward ecclesial community, because it is as a

27. Augustin [Peter-Damian] Belisle, *The Wheel of Becoming* (Petersham, Mass., St. Bede's Publications, 1987) 87.

28. Augustin [Peter-Damian] Belisle, *Into the Heart of God: Spiritual Reflections* (Petersham, Mass., St. Bede's Publications, 1989) 53f.

29. See for instance *Constitutions* no. 75f: "The experience of God in the liturgical celebration has its necessary preparation and its natural unfolding in . . . the reading of His word, 'the food of the soul, the pure and Perennial source of spiritual life.' When a monk hears the word, welcomes it, and treasures it faithfully in his heart, he is brought into the mystery of salvation which the word proclaims and communicates." See also the chapter on the Word in this volume.

30. Cf. Calati, *Il Primato*, 23—the whole section: "Presence in/of the History of Salvation."

31. Emanuele Bargellini, "Esegesi Biblica ed Liturgica. Analisi di un Metodo," *Bibbia e Spiritualità*. A.c. Vagaggini e Penco (Roma, Edizioni Paoline, 1967) 466.

32. Ibid., 470.

member of a people, of the people of God, that the faithful are in relation to God."[33]

C. *Solitude and Contemplation As Intimate* Koinonia

But if our liturgy, as well as our community life of work and hospitality and recreation, is about *koinonia*/love, so also certainly are our solitude, our silence, our personal contemplation. For the monk, it is the Bridegroom, Christ, who invites us into the desert and speaks to our heart (Hos 2:14). Solitary contemplation is that moment of entering into deepest *koinonia* and love with the ineffable God, to seek to fulfill more perfectly that first part of our Lord's commandment of love, to love God with our whole heart, mind, soul, strength. And in that love and *koinonia* we find everything. "For all of us, there is always the primacy of love, founded on the gospel, and beyond that, on the very God who is compassionate Love, loving us with abandon, calling forth our love—filial, friendship, also spousal love."[34] But this intimate and mysterious dimension resists extensive articulation, and the Camaldolese tend to be rather quiet about it.

D. *The Camaldolese Family As* Koinonia *Enfleshed*

The "extended family" of our Camaldolese *koinonia* embraces certainly our other Camaldolese communities, whether rural hermitages or rural cœnobia or urban cœnobia, whether in the U.S.A. or Italy or India or Brazil or Tanzania. Precisely this diversity in unity very much enriches our experience of monastic and Christian community.

The "extended family" includes also our Camaldolese oblates, men and women, lay and clergy, living a whole range of vocations in various parts of the country and world. They are a very rapidly growing community,[35] and the same commitment and experience of *koinonia* obtains here. Thus in the Rite of Admission of Oblates, which is celebrated within the Eucharist, between the homily and the presentation of the gifts, the presider states:

> Friends in Christ: We Propose at this time to receive _____ as a Camaldolese Benedictine Oblate. He/she has requested to be a member of the larger Camaldolese Benedictine family, and to live by the Rule of the Camaldolese

33. Ibid.
34. Hale, *Love*, 188.
35. See the chapter in this volume by Jeffry Spencer and Michael Fish on Oblates. See also Randy Sweringen, *The Camaldolese Benedictine Threefold Good: Seeds of Growth for the Christian People*. Thesis (Berkeley, GTU, 1999), especially ch. 4: "Seeds of Growth for American Camaldolese Oblates," 106f.

Benedictine Oblates. We desire to honor this request and commitment. By the power of the Holy Spirit, this *koinonia* shall be a mutual bond of strength and consolation as we endeavor to live together the life of our one Lord, Jesus Christ.[36]

E. The Benedictine Family As Extended Koinonia

As Camaldolese we are Benedictine, and so our *koinonia* extends to the entire Benedictine family. St. Romuald never thought of himself as founding a distinct congregation, and down through the centuries Camaldolese and other Benedictines "considered themselves of one family, and lived in the spirit of a great monastic unity and intimacy."[37] It was thus inevitable that the Camaldolese would join the "fraternal communion" of the Benedictine Confederation, in which each Benedictine congregation "is equal."[38] The Benedictine family thus represents a larger extension of the *koinonia* that the Camaldolese experience and rejoice in.

F. Camaldolese Ecumenism As Ministry to Koinonia

The reverencing of *koinonia*, also in its widest extension, explains the Camaldolese commitment to ecumenism and interreligious dialogue. So our *Constitutions* affirm: "The whole world is aware of a new ecumenical climate which is creating, or enhancing the condition for dialogue among believers of the great living faiths. Catholics, Christians of other confessions, Jews, Muslims, Hindus, Buddhists, and all persons of good will are seeking new ways of growing in the truth and in communion."[39] These "new ways of growing in the truth and in communion" are explored through study and writing, ecumenical dialogue, covenant relations, and in a special way through ecumenical hospitality, through a welcoming into our *koinonia* of our brothers and sisters who journey from elsewhere. Thus the *Constitutions* continue: "The monastic community, adhering to the tradition of our fathers of ages past and to their spiritual freedom, is ready

36. "The Rite of Admission of a Camaldolese Benedictine Oblate," *Oblate Rule of the Camaldolese Benedictine Monks* (Big Sur, Hermitage Publications, 1997) 14.

37. Giovanni G. Donati, "San Romualdo e il suo Istituo in rapporto alla Confederazione benedettina," *Vita Monastica* (1963) 36. Regarding how emphatically St. Peter Damian felt himself and the Fonte Avellana tradition to be Benedictine, cf. Mansueto Della Santa, *Ricerche sull'idea monastica di San Pier Damiano* (Camaldoli, Edizioni Camaldoli, 1961) 197f: "Peter Damian and the Rule of St. Benedict," for example p. 199: "It would be inconceivable to St. Peter Damian that the hermit movement of Fonte Avellana not be Benedictine."

38. Donati, *San Romualdo*, 37.

39. Camaldolese, *Constitutions*, no. 125.

to welcome all with sincere affection and to recognize the 'seeds of the Word' mysteriously present in all who seek the face of God . . . let the monks remember that ecumenism is today an especially monastic way of responding to the Lord's call to preach the gospel."[40] One of the great pioneers of the East-West dialogue was Bede Griffiths who not only wrote extensively about this encounter, but also lived it in his community and in his heart in the Camaldolese ashram of Shantivanam in India.

In the spirit of Vatican II, the Camaldolese seek to be in communion also with the joys and hopes, the griefs and anxieties of the entire human family of our time,[41] indeed with the whole of creation in its yearnings to be free.[42] Thus Camaldolese communion is an "open *koinonia*" that embraces ultimately all of creation in the one *koinonia* of the Holy Trinity.[43]

G. The Prophetic Dimension As Call to Fuller Koinonia

This stress on *koinonia* and love, which runs throughout Camaldolese spirituality, is today definitely countercultural and prophetic.[44] Our American society especially, but more and more Western society as such, is characterized by a deep-seated individualism, which threatens to isolate each person from real community and the possibility of authentic, permanent love.[45] What is deeply needed by our society and time is precisely the lived experience of *koinonia*, loving community of memory and commitment.[46] Specifically Christian communities can foster members who, nourished by Eucharist, are committed to "being Eucharist for other . . . it's about life; it's about giving life to others."[47] Camaldolese *koinonia* wants to be about all this.

40. Ibid. See the chapter of this volume, dedicated to this theme (p. 157).

41. Cf. Vatican Council II, *The Constitution of the Church in the Modern World*, 1. See also Robert Hale, "Comunità monastica, comunità cristiana e famiglia umana" *Vita Monastica* 115 (1973) 227–31. See also Robert Hale, "Il monaco e il mondo," *Vita Monastica* 106 (1971) 182–92.

42. Cf. Romans 8:22. See also Hale, ibid.

43. Cf. Robert Hale, "La *koinonia* aperta della vita monastica," *Vita Monastica* 126 (1976) 128–62.

44. Regarding the prophetic dimension of Camaldolese and other forms of monasticism, see for instance Robert Hale, "Dimensione profetica della vita monastica," *Vita Monastica* 120 (1975) 40–74. The whole issue of the review is dedicated to that theme.

45. Cf. Robert Bellah, and others, *Habits of the Heart: Individualism and Commitment in American Life* (Berkeley, University of California Press, 1985).

46. Ibid., 152f.

47. The phrase is quoted with appreciation by Robert Bellah in his "Religion and the Shape of National Culture," *America* 181 (1999) 14.

2. The Camaldolese Heritage and *Koinonia*

A. St. Romuald and His Disciples

An intense fraternal and friendship love bound together the first disciples of Romuald. We read, for instance, in the earliest document of the tradition, *The Life of the Five Brothers*:

> Every time John spoke about Master Romuald (who was then in the prime of his life and famous throughout the land for his virtues), Benedict's heart burned within him. He wondered how it could be that a man like Father John, who was qualified to be a teacher in his own right, always presented himself as somebody else's disciple. . . . Romuald missed John and was eager to see him again. . . . He admired John's many virtues, especially his refusal to speak ill of people behind their back or to listen to those who do so. When news arrived that Romuald was coming, Benedict, like someone who has just inherited a great fortune, jumped on his horse and galloped off to meet him. From the moment they met, they were inseparable . . . [when Romuald became sick] Benedict strove to outdo everyone in nursing Romuald and serving his every need.[48]

Monks have rejoiced in Christ's proclamation, "I no longer call you servants but friends" (John 15:15). Thus Christian friendship has been highly valued in the monastic tradition[49] and certainly in our Camaldolese tradition, and from the earliest period. St. Bruno Boniface, for instance, disciple of St. Romuald and author of *The Life of the Five Brothers*, rejoiced in the bond of deep friendship with this same Benedict who nursed Romuald. Bruno Boniface writes of "the long hours Benedict and I spent together—it was my privilege to enjoy his friendship and to hear him call me 'my brother.' . . . Benedict was like the other half of my soul."[50] It should be noted that St. Bruno Boniface and his close friend St. Benedict, both martyrs, represent the Camaldolese "third good," but the values of love and communion that we are here discussing under the heading of the "first good" were nevertheless at the heart of their heroic lives. The deepest values of one stage of the threefold good are not abandoned at the next, but

---

48. Matus, *Mystery*, 87f.

49. Cf. Brian Patrick McGuire, *Friendship and Community: the Monastic Experience 350–1250* (Kalamazoo, Cistercian Publications, 1988). The classic monastic treatise is Aelred of Rievaulx' *Spiritual Friendship* (Kalamazoo, Cistercian Publications, 1977). One of the most authoritative scholars on Aelred was our own Aelred Squire; see his *Aelred of Rievaulx: A Study* (Kalamazoo, Cistercian Publications, 1981).

50. Ibid., 98, 100. This phrase recalls similar descriptions of monastic friendship throughout the centuries. See also for instance how John Cassian characterizes his bond with Germanus, his constant companion for at least twenty-five years: "everyone used to say we were one mind and soul inhabiting two bodies" (*Conferences* I, 1).

if anything lived more deeply; and this is particularly the case with love and communion.

Monastic *koinonia* is able to open out and embrace others because it is first of all a communion with the Triune God. At the heart of Romuald's experience was his deep, loving, Spirit-inspired communion with the Father and with Christ. So his biographer, Peter Damian, writes: "Often he was so taken up in divine contemplation that he felt he was melting away in tears, and the fire of God's love burning within him made him cry out, 'Jesus, dear Jesus, sweetness beyond compare, desire of my heart, joy of the saints, delight of the angels . . . !' As the Spirit descended upon him, his prayer went beyond words into a jubilation the human mind cannot comprehend."[51]

Out of this love, Romuald journeyed throughout Italy and as far as Spain, "gathering disciples in the power of the Holy Spirit. . . . The Holy Spirit fell like rain on the brothers' hearts."[52] Lino Vigilucci, an historian of the Congregation, characterizes the warmhearted Romuald thus, "The rigor with which he disciplined himself did not in any way hinder him from opening up to others. We see him as available and human, familiar, gentle, and good with all, so that 'he always appeared cheerful, even serene.'"[53] He also regularly had "recourse to a vein of good humor"[54] and also healed, once with a kiss.[55]

There was an apostolic dimension to Romuald's life, which also flowed out from his intense love, and so bore fruit in the lives of those he ministered to: "For them, Saint Romuald was beyond compare, like one of the Seraphim, all aflame with the love of God. Wherever he went, his words would set others on fire as well."[56]

St. Romuald preached against simony and corruption to diocesan priests, and urged also for them the great Christian resources of community: "he had them live in community as canons . . . they were to submit to a superior and live together as brothers."[57]

His love extended to those who did not always act lovingly towards him; for instance, he showed compassion and mercy to a thief the monks had discovered robbing a monastic cell:

> The monks grabbed him and dragged him off to Romuald, who was waiting for them with a big smile on his face. They asked him, "What do you want

51. Matus, *Mystery*, 223.
52. Ibid., 91.
53. Lino Vigilucci, *Camaldoli: A Journey into Its History and Spirituality*. Trans. Peter-Damian Belisle (Big Sur, Hermitage Books, 1995) 33.
54. Ibid.
55. Ibid.
56. Matus, *Mystery*, 229.
57. Ibid., 230.

us to do with this guy? He is guilty of sacrilege." Romuald answered, "I really don't know. Should we poke out his eyes? But then he won't be able to see. Or cut off his hand? But then he won't be able to work and may even die of hunger. And if we hack off his foot he won't be able to walk. Anyway, take him inside and give him something to eat. Then we can decide what to do with him." When the burglar had eaten, Saint Romuald, rejoicing in the Lord, gently corrected and admonished him with a few kind words and sent him on his way in peace.[58]

The former Camaldolese Prior General and expert on Camaldolese sources, Anselm Giabbani, thus summed up Romuald's life and ministry: "Saint Romuald was a man of unity. What he wanted at Camaldoli was harmony between contemplation and action, between solitude and communion, between prayer and service. He wanted the monks to learn how to love undividedly, and to let their love flow freely toward God, toward one another, toward the poor."[59] Thomas Matus writes that "Master Romuald, the liturgy says, 'was a martyr, yes, but a martyr of love' . . . the love in the hearts of Romuald and his disciples for the Christ who rose from the dead, the love of friendship that bound them so strongly with one another, the love of the two disciples who joined Poland's first martyrs in overcoming by the power of love alone, their own bodily death and the death in the hearts of their slayers. It is a story for all times."[60]

B. St. Peter Damian

Another primary source for the Camaldolese heritage is St. Peter Damian. A great promoter of solitude, he himself sacrificed his solitude to labor mightily for the *koinonia* of the Church of that time, serving as cardinal and working tirelessly for Church reform. But his heart was always in the Hermitage. And he understood its solitude not as a distancing from the larger ecclesial communion, but rather as an entering into a more profound *koinonia* with all the faithful, indeed with the saints of all times. So he affirmed in his most important tract, "*The Lord Be With You*":

> The Church of Christ is united in all her parts by such a bond of love that her several members form a single body and in each one the whole Church is mystically present; so that the whole Church universal may rightly be called the one bride of Christ, and on the other hand every single soul can, because of the mystical effect of the sacrament, be regarded as the whole Church . . . although the hermit is separated in space from the congregation of the faithful yet he is bound together with them all by love in the unity of faith; al-

58. Ibid., 231.
59. Quoted in Matus, *The Mystery*, 70.
60. Ibid.

though they are absent in the flesh, they are near at hand in the mystical unity of the Church.[61]

Because of the limits of space, we shall limit ourselves to some quotes from one other writing of St. Peter Damian, *"On the Perfection of Monks,"* which also eloquently expresses his teaching regarding love and communion as the heart of the monastic life:

> We are embracing the whole body of this holy monastery in the outstretched arms of brotherly love. . . . So now, dearly-beloved brethren, I speak to every one of you; I entreat you by the name of Christ, in which every knee shall bow. Remain steadfast in brotherly love; unite together in the zeal of your mutual affection against the wiles of our ancient enemy. Let the whole structure of your holy way of life be raised on the foundations of charity; let the whole edifice which you are building from the living stones of virtue be cemented by the mortar of a genuine love.[62]

C. The Later Camaldolese Heritage and Koinonia

This *koinonia* ecclesiology also explains the participation and creative contribution of notable Camaldolese in the significant humanistic movements and achievements of their own time. The Camaldolese were not cut off from these ferments, according to a certain "separatist" understanding of monasticism, but rather were in collaborative communion with the best of the renaissance achievements. Thus the creative work of Guido of Arezzo (d. 1050), "the father of modern music" whose innovative principles set the foundation for modern notation. So similarly the work of Gratian (d. ca. 1197), "the father of canon law" and the contribution of Lorenzo Monaco (d. ca. 1424), "perhaps the most important Florentine artist of the first half of the 15th century."[63]

And so, too, Ambrose Traversari (d. 1439), General of the Order, described by Pope Eugene IV as "the light of the Church," a pioneering ecumenist whose tireless efforts strengthened the bond between Catholicism and the Eastern Churches."[64] It is still moving to read Ambrose Traversari's "Invitation to Concord" addressed to his Camaldolese monastery of Florence and also to the Camaldolese monks of Camaldoli itself. As General, he exhorts the brethren to communion, utilizing simply a string of quotes from the new Testament to encourage them on:

61. Patricia McNulty, *St. Peter Damian; Selected Writings on the Spiritual Life* (London, Faber, 1959) 57, 74.

62. Ibid., 121, 134.

63. Hale, *Camaldolese Spirituality*, 109.

64. Ibid.

I pray you, beloved, to be "united among you in speaking, and that there not be among you divisions" (1 Corinthians 1:10). "Be of one spirit and with one voice praise the glory of God our Father in our one Lord Jesus Christ" (Romans 15:6). "Seek to conserve the unity of spirit through the bond of peace" (Ephesians 4:3). "Love one another" (Romans 12:10). "Carry the burdens of one another" (Galatians 6:2). "Let no one seek his own interest but that of Jesus Christ"(Philippians 2:21). And persevering in the practice of holy humility "be subject one to another in the fear of Christ" (Ephesians 5:21).[65]

3. The Roots of the Camaldolese Heritage

Space limits permit only the briefest reference here to the deeper roots of the Camaldolese heritage regarding *koinonia*. The *Constitutions* begin, for instance, by noting our communion with the earliest pre-Christian forms of monasticism in India.[66] Thus there exists the inevitable commitment of the Camaldolese to the East-West dialogue.

In the West, much of ancient Greek culture considered friendship to be the highest human value, and defined friendship as simply the living out of *koinonia*: thus Aristotle observed, "It is quite true that 'among friends everything is shared,' for friendship consists in sharing (*koinonia*)."[67] And this esteem for *koinonia* extended into the religious realm; thus Flavius Josephus praised the quasi-monastic Essenes for the "marvel" of their *koinonia*.[68]

Given this historic context, it is not surprising that in the New Testament the apostolic community is noted for its living out of holy *koinonia* (Acts 2:42; 4:32), concrete manifestation of friendship love, so that "the ancient Greek ideal of friendship achieved upon unexpected new foundations its own concrete realization."[69] The theme of *koinonia*, like that of *agape*, is woven throughout the New Testament, and thus also throughout the early monastic literature; and often, as in Acts, the terms are used synonymously.[70]

65. Ambrose Traversari, *Ep.* XIV, 30, 672. Cf. C. Somigli and T. Bargellini, *Ambrogio Traversari, Monaco Camaldolese* (Bologna, Dehoniane, 1986) 254.
66. Camaldolese, *Constitutions*, Introduction.
67. Aristotle, *Nicomachean Ethics*, VIII: 11; 1159 B, 31. Cf. also Euripedes, *Andromache*.
68. Flavius Josephus, *The Jewish War*, II: 122.
69. Jacques Dupont, *The Salvation of the Gentiles: Studies in The Acts of the Apostles* (New York, Paulist, 1979) 102.
70. The Camaldolese biblical scholar, David Holly, in his *Complete Categorized Greek-English New Testament Vocabulary* (London, Bagster, 1978) notes that *agape* occurs 116 times in the New Testament; its verbal form, to love, occurs 142 times; the adjectival form, beloved, 61 times, and *koinonia* with its cognates occur 66 times. Obviously we are dealing with major New Testament themes. See for instance the survey by Ceslaus Spicq, *Agape in the New Testament*, 3 vols. (St. Louis, Herder, 1963). Regarding the use of *koinonia* as synonymous with *agape*, cf. Dupont, *Salvation*, 102.

In Egypt the early monasticism of the Pachomian communities presented itself as simply the living out of "holy *Koinonia*" as found in the apostolic community[71] so that "the term *koinonia* is undoubtedly the key concept of Pachomian monasticism."[72] So also the apostolic *koinonia* remained foundational for St. Basil's monasticism, "erected on the ideal of the apostolic church as presented in the first chapters of Acts."[73] In the West the same ideal of loving communion is central to the monastic vision of Augustine.[74] Tapping from all these sources, the *Rule of St. Benedict* is fully within this tradition in its intention simply "to concretize *koinonia* for celibate Christians. . . . Thus Benedict legislates simply and only to establish and sustain *koinonia*."[75]

Benedict Calati, medievalist and Camaldolese General, delighted in stressing that the same foundational value of loving communion is present throughout Pope Gregory's *Life of Benedict*.[76] And Calati noted that the theme of *koinonia* as loving communion continues to weave through medieval and later monastic writers of the larger Benedictine and specifically Camaldolese family.

4. Conclusion

All these sources, and so many others, have impacted significantly upon Camaldolese spirituality and our experience of *koinonia/agape*.[77]

71. Adalbert de Vogüé, *Pachomian Koinonia* (Kalamazoo, Cistercian Studies, 1980) I, 431, and "Forward," xv.

72. Timothy Fry, "Introduction," *RB 1980: The Rule of St. Benedict in Latin and English with Notes* (Collegeville, The Liturgical Press, 1981) 25. Cf. also Armand Veilleux, *La Liturgie dans le cénobitisme pachômien au quatrième siècle* (Rome, Studia Anselmiana, 1968), especially II, 1: "Pachomian monasticism, an ecclesial Koinonia" 161f; II, 1, v: "The liturgical character of Pachomian Koinonia" 195f; and II, 3: "The Eucharist of the Pachomian Koinonia" 226f.

73. Pier Scazzoso, *Reminiscenze della polis platonica nel cenobio di S. Basilio* (Milano, Istituto Editoriale Italiano, 1970) 6.

74. Cf. T. Van Bavel, "The Evangelical Inspiration of the Rule of St. Augustine," *The Downside Review* 311 (1975) 83f.

75. Sister Augusta Marie, "*Koinonia*: Its Biblical Meaning and Use in Monastic Life," *American Benedictine Review* 18 (1967) 200f.

76. Cf. Benedetto Calati, "Comunità e Scrittura nel pensiero di Gregorio Magno," *Vita Monastica* 80 (1965) 3–24. Cf. also Luigi Lezza, "Il monaco nella Chiesa secondo I Dialoghi di S. Gregorio Magno," *Vita Monastica* 97 (1969) 96f. Cf. also Calati, *Sapienza*, 315–64.

77. Regarding the many sources of Camaldolese spirituality, as revealed in Camaldoli's ancient library, see the carefully researched study by M. Elena Magheri Cataluccio and A. Ugo Fossa, *Biblioteca e Cultura a Camaldoli: Dal Medioevo all'umanesimo* (Roma, Editrice Anselmiana, 1979). Regarding the sources of St. Peter Damian and an early catalogue of Fonte Avellana's library, see McNulty, *Selected*, 47f. See also Della Santa, *Ricerche*, 190–204.

Because of the limits of space, we have been able only to trace a brief overview of the key themes of *koinonia* and love in the Camaldolese heritage and its roots. But hopefully this sketch has made clear that *koinonia*/love constitute the very substance of our heritage, whether in the hermitage or the monastery, and daily nourish our spirits, expand our horizons. They also reveal to us the way to the kingdom itself, where all of us, whatever be our vocation here on earth, shall be ushered into the fullness of this *koinonia* and love, reunited with loved ones, established in communion with all the redeemed and the whole heavenly host, sharing in the very life of our loving "Three-Personed" God.

These studies demonstrate the major influence on Camaldoli and Fonte Avellana of the sources we have considered here, that is, Pachomius (through St. Benedict's *Rule*), Cassian, Basil, Augustine, Gregory, and of course, Benedict.

Psychological Investigations and Implications for Living Together Alone

Bede Healey

1. Introduction

The phrase "living together alone" evokes a paradox. Yet this is exactly what the monastic call is about and how the monastic way is lived. So much so, that this was the title of a book on monastic forms written in the 1970s.[1] The Camaldolese Benedictines have this paradox at the center of their lives that witness to the profound meaning of these three words.

The Camaldolese way of life has always included both the eremitical and cenobitical traditions of monastic life. The history of this combination and its ramifications has been well covered elsewhere in this book. It is important to note that this way of life is not a life of "either or"—either eremitical or cenobitical—but "both and"—both eremitical and cenobitical. The introduction to the Camaldolese *Constitutions and Declarations* states, "The hermitage retains elements of cenobitic living."[2] The Camaldolese way of eremitical life is more that of the ancient laura of the Egyptian desert monastics who lived separately, but came together for prayer. Indeed, the Camaldolese see an aspect of their inspiration coming from this desert tradition.

Camaldolese life, then, blends solitude and communion. It is not always an easy blending. A monk in the early period of his formation was talking recently about the seemingly contradictory demands of a life that calls for radical solitude and deep communion. He said it was impossible. Left to ourselves, we would have to agree. For it is only with God's call and grace that we can attempt to live out this mysterious life.

How does this grace and call become manifest? In the human arena, certainly, and this is the arena that will be the focus of my thoughts.

1. Charles A. Fracchia, *Living Together Alone* (San Francisco, Harper and Row, 1979).
2. Camaldolese, *Constitutions*, no. 2.

Specifically, I will be looking at the role psychological insights provide in helping us understand ourselves and the demands of this unique way of life. The aim is not simply self-understanding, although that is a part of the process, but to help those living this life to embrace it more fully, seeking God in solitude and communion. Innumerable articles and books have been written on solitude and community, on approaches to the healthy living of these expressions of life, and of the dangers associated with them. I will be focusing on three human issues that I believe are at the core of an expanded spiritual life and required for work on growth in the Camaldolese Benedictine monastic path: the capacity to be alone, the true self, and transitional phenomena. And work it is! The process of transformation requires all of our efforts that are, paradoxically, really our response to God's call of increasing surrender to the mystery that ultimately consumes us.

2. Psychological Theory

I will be weaving together a number of strands of psychological theory in this next section. Specifically, I will be outlining a dynamic psychological process that has at its center the belief in the essential need for relatedness in the human person. This theory, known broadly as object relations theory, is a development within the psychoanalytic movement begun by Freud, a movement that is continually growing and advancing. Within this framework I will explore the psychological dynamics involved in living in solitude and in community, and the work needed to make these experiences vital parts of our path to interiority. For it is not so much a process of aligning with a cenobitical or eremitical way of life, but in making use of these expressions as needed to promote the development of interiority. I would say at the outset that one could only grapple with the three human issues I will discuss by intentionally living out a life that embraces, in its own time and at the right seasons, elements of both solitude and communion.

In the psychoanalytic literature, object relations is a technical term that refers to human relations, specifically to the inner, largely unconscious web of relationships developed early in life with significant caregivers that then tend to color and shape current "real" external relationships. From this perspective, human beings are not organized around sexual and aggressive drive discharge, as Freud would have it, but are (human) object seeking from birth. This relational drive, if you will, is the hallmark of this radical break with Freudian psychoanalytic approaches.[3] John McDargh describes the object relations approach eloquently. It is

---

3. A recent book that provides a useful and approachable introduction to this area: Lavinia Gomez, *An Introduction to Object Relations* (New York, New York University Press, 1997).

the continuous inner theater that is human life, the way in which each of us from childhood carries on an intense private dialogue with the real and imagined, and in all cases, constructed characters of our past and present. . . . The human person is born with a primary and irreducible need for confirmation and affirmation of relationship.[4]

The basic question is not simply "who am I?" but rather "who am I there for?" and "who is there for me?" This highlights the core relational element that forms the deepest part of our being.

The traditional psychoanalytical approach to understanding people would focus on the sexual and aggressive drives and their derivatives, on the developing structure of the ego and the manifold defenses erected to assist the person in the assimilation of the disparate aspects of self with the demands of the culture and society. The object relations approach focuses on the relational world, both real and imagined, and the vicissitudes of these relationships in the individual's life. It is important to note that we perceive our relationships with others in the "real world" colored by these earlier experiences, now uniquely rarified in our inner world. It is also important to note that for us, the so-called "real world" is not the real world at all. Insofar as our experience and evaluation of it are filtered through the inner world, that inner world is more real. Therefore, it is essential that we attend to this world.

This approach has special utility to understanding humans in relation with themselves, with others, and with God. To quote McDargh again, "Psychoanalytic object relations theory . . . has developed from the effort of analysts to understand and heal the acute suffering of persons whose primary presenting complaint is that they do not have a self, or that they feel empty inside, isolated, cut-off from others and from any personal center of vitality and meaning."[5] It is axiomatic that the issues seen in patients seeking therapy are not unique to that class of individuals. Rather, the issues are differences in degree, not in kind. All of us have much to learn about our relational selves, especially those seeking God "with the help of many brothers (and sisters)," as the old monastic saying goes. In the Camaldolese way, with its opportunity for both solitude and community life, it is essential to understand our relational selves so that we can use the experiences of solitude and communion as resources on the journey to the heart of God and not alternately using one as an escape from the demands of the other, as so often happens.

4. John McDargh, "God, Mother & Me: An Object Relational Perspective on Religious Material, " *Pastoral Psychology* 34:4 (1986) 251–63.
5. John McDargh, "The Life of the Self in Christian Spirituality and Contemporary Psychoanalysis," *Horizons* 11:2 (1984) 351.

Operating from the object relations perspective gives us a rich perspective from which to see how we engage and also avoid the demands of this life of living together alone. In addition, it can give us some insights as to why we do or do not make the changes that will help us on the path to God, and even more importantly, what we might do to make those needed changes. In essence, everything revolves around relationship: with ourselves, with others, and ultimately with God.

Once again, I will treat three concepts about which D. W. Winnicott,[6] a British pediatrician and psychoanalyst, has written that are immediately helpful: the capacity to be alone; the true and false self, and the development of representations of others, especially the God representation; transitional phenomena and space and its related topic—the capacity to play.

3. The Capacity to Be Alone

Winnicott notes that more has been written on the fear of being alone and the desire to be alone than on the *capacity* to be alone. Indeed, Winnicott sees this capacity as one of the hallmarks of psychological maturity. It is a developmental process, beginning early in life. First, according to Winnicott, the infant must learn to be alone and, to begin this process, to be alone in the presence of the mother. Paradoxical, isn't it, being alone in the presence of another? This is the process of being in relationship with the mother without physical touch, without basic needs like feeding being immediately met. It implies a psychological relationship whereby the infant brings inside, if you will, the physical presence of the mother. She is experienced as reliably present, although not in physical contact, and later, present without being physically so. The infant (and later the child) undergoes a series of stages to develop this capacity. At first, continual physical contact is required, or the infant feels abandoned. Then follows the gradual movement away, but requiring the reconnection by actual physical touch. A further capacity grows to experience this reliable "other" throughout longer periods without physical contact, then through only auditory contact. Many mothers will tell you of their children calling out to them from another room, the mother responding from that room "what do you want?" and the child replying "nothing." Exasperating, yes, but necessary—the child is continuing to develop the capacity to be alone.

Ultimately, the individual develops the capacity to be alone. The continuing reliable presence of the mother during the early years has become

6. Cf. D. W. Winnicott, *Collected Papers* (New York, Basic Books, 1958) and *The Maturational Processes and the Facilitating Environment* (New York, International University Press, 1965).

internalized such that the individual is alone, but never alone. Her sustaining presence is a part of the individual without the individual's conscious awareness. Psychologically, this internalized "mother" functions, in part, as a basis for the development of the God representation. Thus the individual arrives at the capacity to be alone because the internal world is peopled with positive, good objects or representations that provide a deep, sustaining, unconscious presence. We can be alone because we are not abandoned. These are two distinct psychological experiences. The capacity to be alone reflects a developed human and spiritual maturity, while the experience of abandonment reflects a psychological trauma, often with related issues in the spiritual realm that will likely need reparative work.

This capacity to be alone is also the capacity to be at home—at home, comfortable with ourselves, but not in a static way. We are comfortable with ourselves as changing, growing persons-in-relationship. There is a dynamic tension in us all, struggling with the wish to stay as we are and the pull to grow and change. The reliable other, who is at the root of our capacity to be alone, supports us in this tension and allows us to be at home in the struggle.

Now this capacity is not usually fully developed in the early years, and for most adults, it is not complete, i.e., there are situations, circumstances and events which threaten the return of the primitive fears of infancy and childhood that lead us to feel not at home. Camaldolese monastics need to attend to these fluctuations and to the current state of their own capacity to be alone, and to know the situations, circumstances, and events that trigger fears and their subsequent responses. This is related to their need to move into a deeper surrender and lessen their grip on their lives. Whether in the monastery or hermitage, monastic life requires a highly developed capacity to be alone—to be at home with oneself—whether for solitude or community life. If we have a diminished capacity to be alone, then we *need* community.

In her book *Being and Loving*,[7] Althea Horner makes an important distinction between loving and needing. She discusses the difference between needing people and loving people. When we need people, we need them to be and act in certain ways to meet our own needs, and to sustain our sense of ourselves. Without them behaving in certain, needed ways, we lose our sense of ourselves. Thus, we work to keep people in certain roles to meet our needs. This diminishes their humanity because we are relating to them out of a fear-based need, not authentic love. Similarly, when we need community, we need others to be and act in certain ways. We may try to orchestrate others to bring about an environment where we can keep

7. Althea Horner, *Being and Loving*, rev. ed. (Northvale, N. J., Jason Aronson, 1999).

our particular fears at bay. There is a world of difference between primarily need-based living and engaging in the transformative energy of communal life, just as between being isolated and separate—living in fear that we are or will be abandoned—and embracing the life-altering power of solitude intentionally engaged. The transfiguring energy of community and the power of intentional solitude facilitate our growth in holiness, our openness to surrender to God.

What are some of the signs of problems in this area? I will look at three: loneliness, depression, and sexual preoccupation. Although there are other issues, these occur with significant frequency and raise issues central to our continuing human and monastic development. There has been research done on loneliness. People have been surveyed about whether they have ever been lonely. As one wag puts it, "95 percent said yes and the other 5 percent were lying!" Obviously we all experience loneliness at various times in our lives. It is part of the human condition. At a deeper level of desire, we are always seeking the God within. This is our driving force that animates us and gives us direction. Neale[8] suggests that loneliness has two aspects in the human dimension: the sense of separation and the seeking to overcome the separation. This notion of seeking is important. If the separation is seen in a positive light, then there will be no seeking and thus, no loneliness. If there is no hope of restoring the relationship with the one from whom we are separated, we become hopeless, not lonely.

In times of solitude it is common and expectable to experience the separation inherent in solitude positively, while at other times to experience a sense of loneliness. To be lonely in solitude is not a sign of failure in solitude, although monastics new to solitude might think so. Our task, after all, is to seek God, and the experience of loneliness can be a lively and driving force to bring us closer to God by reshaping our humanness, perhaps by making us more aware of how much we *need* and how little we *love*, to borrow again from Horner's use of these words.

We can, and do, have some of our most poignant experiences of loneliness when we are not alone, but physically present with others. To be physically present with others and yet experience disconnectedness, can painfully highlight our distance from others—our deeper, human separation that goes beyond physical proximity. This experience of loneliness calls us to a closer, deeper relationship with our fellow monastics, to Christ manifest in them. Often this communal loneliness is mistaken for a sign of deeper need for solitude. This is not the case. It is a sign of the need for deeper relational work: "What keeps me from experiencing a sense of con-

8. Robert E. Neale, *Loneliness, Solitude, and Companionship* (Philadelphia, Westminster, 1984).

nection with others?" "Why am I afraid to reveal myself to others?" "Where does the pain I experience originate?" "What does this experience say about my relationship with myself, with others, and with God?" These and many more questions may need to be explored in order to work through the experience and understand the ultimate personal meaning of loneliness for each of us.

Depressive experiences can often be part of what we experience in loneliness, but it would be a mistake to misdiagnose, as it were, loneliness for depression. Medication will not treat loneliness. We need to acknowledge the separation and actively seek to overcome that separation. It appears that loneliness and depressive experiences are likely occurrences in a life oriented to a monastic/contemplative existence, like the Camaldolese way of life. We must seek out the deeper meaning beneath depressive experiences and loneliness. Our inner work will naturally bring us to a deeper, and often painful, awareness of our deep separation from ourselves, others, and God. The work is hard, and we can experience listlessness, sadness, and *acedia* (or the "noonday devil" of the ancient monastics).

This can shock those who have previously considered themselves spiritually advanced people, well on the path to God. These experiences of loneliness and depression can seem detours and sidetracks, or signs of failure, but are in reality the necessary road to further growth. We must embrace them—painful as they are—as we do our inner work. In the course of a lifetime of such work, we have many opportunities to review our lives and reflect on the sins of omission and commission. Mistakes, errors, missed opportunities, losses, ever-increasing awareness of our weaknesses: all can bring about depressive experiences. Again, the deeper meaning of these experiences must be explored and the issues worked through. This means going through these experiences, not trying to get around them. The life of increasing interiority has as its hallmark what I call contemplative *knowing*. This *knowing* comes about only by sitting with, and working through, the various experiences in our lives. Both the sitting with and working through are essential to the process, allowing for the development of resilient, open vulnerability, so necessary for our way of life.

Sexual preoccupation is another natural, expectable human occurrence that we will experience from time to time. Sexual fantasies and craving for genital sexual experiences occur. We must engage our contemplative *knowing* here as well. Although it may be our first consideration to rid ourselves of these thoughts, we need to sit with them, to understand them. Sexual fantasies and craving for genital sexual behavior can be indicative of many things, including a whole range of unacknowledged emotions, loss, boredom, disconnection, hunger of various kinds, deep fear, painful aspects of our life that are surfacing and part of us wants to avoid. These fantasies and cravings may be a way of our wanting to escape from the hard work at hand.

Rather than consider these thoughts and cravings as something larger than life and having an exaggerated sense of their importance (for example, automatically assuming that this means a person does not have a call to celibate chastity), it may be more useful to see them as just one of many expressions of the complicated reactions we have to the work of developing interiority. Careful, respectful attention to our sexuality and its ebb and flow, seen in the context of our larger experiences, will be a more productive and growth-enhancing process than simply repressing these fantasies and cravings. It seems prudent to point out here the wisdom of the centuries of monastic experience in calling for a spiritual guide to assist us in the inner work. Try as we might, we are self-deluding by nature, and the help of a wise guide is essential to our work of surrender to God.

4. The True Self

In his article on solitude and loneliness, Davies[9] reminds us that psychological theorists such as Karen Horney, Eric Fromm, and Rollo May all believed that, unless we know and accept our deepest self, we will experience a deep loneliness at our very center. This deepest self is very similar to Winnicott's concept of the true self, and is also connected to our relational capacities.

Writing about the growth of the human person, Winnicott highlights the inevitability of imperfect human development and stresses that perfect development is unnecessary. In his discussion of the concept of the "good enough mother,"[10] Winnicott states that some basic needs must be met to provide a facilitating environment for the total growth of the infant and child. But as a matter of course, we encounter limits, failures, wrongs, sins of omission and commission in our parents, family, world and ourselves. This leads to the development of what he calls a "false" self. The term "false self," although commonly used, is really a misnomer. As we meet the shortcomings of this world and those who inhabit it over the course of our development, we develop many false aspects of ourselves, efforts we use to protect our truest essence. We develop layer upon layer of false aspects of many facets of ourselves.

According to Winnicott and other object relations theorists, these false aspects of ourselves develop to protect us, to enhance our capacity to

---

9. Mark G. Davies, "Solitude and Loneliness: An Integrative Model" *Journal of Psychology and Theology* 24:1 (1996) 3–12.

10. Cf. D. W. Winnicott, *Collected* and *The Maturational*.

live safely with others in this world. This is an effort of adaptation and self-preservation—to adjust to the demands placed upon us. Early in our lives we do not have a wide repertoire of approaches to respond to demands, so we change ourselves instead. Although these changes are often the best we can muster under the circumstances, we unfortunately do not automatically reevaluate these changes based on new capacities. The perception of threat or demand, and our response to it, often happens outside our conscious awareness. Thus the change is not necessarily very noticeable and we do not sense a need to reevaluate the changed behavior. Unconsciously, there is no perceived need for change, because the problem has been solved. If anything, such a change would likely be a further expansion of the false self, since our basic need to be safe and to protect what is truest in us is so strong.

Dynamically, it takes a significant experience to influence the inner world that houses, metaphorically speaking, the representations of the highly charged relationships developed in response to the perceived threat or demand. A crisis, a significant unbalancing which foils our usual adaptive approaches, suffering, guided inner work: these and other events can be significant enough to effect change in our inner world of guiding perceptions and appraisals. Such events can either reinforce the continuing development of the false aspects of ourselves or break through, to varying degrees, to bring us closer to our true self.

In reality, both will happen. We see the subtle and not so subtle energies at work, thwarting our awareness of our true self. We want to be open, but fear disclosure. We want to share with others, but fear rejection. The fear of the loss or corruption of our deepest good unconsciously mobilizes us to retrench in myriads of ways, while simultaneously, our deepest, truest self desires to be free. Since much of this happens beyond our awareness—resulting in an accumulation of disowned and unacknowledged aspects of ourselves that, in their own way, contribute to the development of the false self—a true guide is essential.

This concept of the true self is very important in psychoanalytically informed clinical practice, but is also useful in explaining many other aspects of the human condition. Thomas Merton[11] wrote extensively about the true self and false self, moving us beyond a purely psychological experience to

11. In his introduction to Merton's *Contemplative Prayer,* Douglas Steere uses the simile of the raising of stage curtains to describe Merton's thought in this area. As each curtain rises, it seems to be the real scene, but is not. More and more curtains are raised until the final curtain that reveals the real stage setting, the true self. Merton also discusses this issue in his prologue to *No Man Is an Island,* in *Seeds of Contemplation,* and in *New Seeds of Contemplation.*

one of our transcendent, ontological, spiritual self. Basil Pennington has recently written a book[12] on this topic. There is something quite compelling for us in this concept, perhaps because complicated shifts are taking place in today's understanding of the self—philosophically, culturally, and at many other levels. The deconstruction of the self, a particularly lively topic these days, can call us to a more critical and fresh understanding of the self.

What does this have to do with our life of solitude and communion? The inner work we must accomplish involves, and ultimately requires, our facing and shedding the many layers of falseness within ourselves. Both solitude and communion, properly embraced, will bring us face to face with our falseness. Indeed, the interplay of solitude and communion is the recipe for the deepening of interiority on our path. Knowing loneliness, deep connection, acceptance and love in solitude and communion—as well as being open to interplay of these experiences throughout our lives—is our monastic contemplative path to being at home with our truest self and our sure path to God.

Related to the development of self is the development of our representations of others. These processes go hand in hand. In our earliest development we "take in" images, representations of our most basic relationships, both positive and negative. These then become the dramatic characters in the theater of the mind (to use John McDargh's image). For most of us, these representations are a mixture of positive and negative characteristics, so when we experience individuals in the external world through the lens associated with this internal world, we see people as having both positive and negative characteristics. Those with pronounced relational deficits have a different inner organization, one where representations are either exclusively positive or negative, good or bad. This latter organization is a necessary part of early development and becomes problematic only when one becomes stuck there.

In any event, our task is to work at seeing people in the external world as they really are, not as receptacles for our own projected inner representations. A rich and varied inner world can allow us to see others more and more as they truly are, while a constricted and arrested inner world makes that task much more difficult. Some have theorized that the completion of our psychological relational world would result in the eradication of our inner representations, because we internalize only those relationships about which we are in some form of conflict. The end result of our inner work would then be an empty stage, not the emptiness of an aching void, but the inviting openness to allow others—as they are—to be a part of our lives, to come and go, but always be remembered.

12. Basil Pennington, *True Self False Self: Unmasking the Spirit Within* (New York, Crossroad, 2000).

A particular representation that has broad ramifications for Camaldolese life is the development of God representation. Psychoanalyst Ana-Maria Rizzuto has written extensively on this topic, here briefly summarized.[13] The young child creates a highly personal mental representation of God drawn from inner representations of parents, self, and significant others. The development and maintenance of this representation, aspects of which may change, involves both conscious and unconscious processes. The representation contains visceral, emotional, and conceptual components; it is not simply an intellectual concept. It can be used in its original form as developed in childhood, repressed, or transformed. Often it is a combination of all three: aspects may change, while others are repressed and still others, transformed. If this object representation does not change along with other developmental changes in our object world, God either becomes irrelevant or threatening. The repressed aspects will likely surface, especially during times of stress or life transition.

It is important to note that this is a psychological representation of God, not God as God truly is. We need to ask ourselves, "Has our image of God changed as we have grown and matured?" A particular Achilles' heel for contemplative monastics is to move too quickly to an apophatic approach to God. This is often seen as a "higher" form of relating to God, and thus something to strive for. However, much can be said for the richness of cataphatic experience, while acknowledging that apophatic experience is not something we can control, but only humbly receive when it is offered. To move too quickly into this form of prayer can shortchange us. We need to attend throughout our lives to our relationship with God and to the nature of our God representation that speaks volumes about us and our relationships with God, ourselves, and others. How we see God, experience God, attribute reactions to God, dismiss God, avoid God, distance ourselves from God, desire God: all these are rich sources not to be overlooked, but often are in our hurried pace to "spiritual maturity." This moment occurs only in God's time and usually not at the pace we set. Here is where the great monastic virtue of patience comes into play.

5. Transitional Phenomena

The notions of transitional phenomena and potential space are perhaps Winnicott's finest contributions to the field of psychology and religion and have been adopted by many writers. Potential space is an

13. Cf. the summary of Rizzuto's ideas in Marilyn and William Saurs' "Images of God, a Study of Psychoanalyzed Adults" *Object Relations Theory and Religion: Clinical Applications*, eds. Mark Finn and John Gartner (Westport, Conn., Praeger, 1992) 129–40, esp. 131.

"intermediate area of experience," as he calls it, a "resting place for the individual engaged in the perpetual task of keeping inner and outer reality separate yet interrelated."[14] Winnicott hypothesized that an area of mutual creativity develops between the infant and the mother, and is dependent on "good enough" maternal care. The consistent, facilitating presence of the mother leads to the development of creativity.

Briefly, transitional phenomena develop early in life as maternal substitutes, and are especially important during the phase when the infant is separating from the mother and developing a separate identity and the capacity to be alone. The development of this capacity assists us in maintaining self-sufficiency and protects us from being overwhelmed by feelings of abandonment. Although articulated separately by Winnicott, there is much interconnection between potential space and transitional phenomena. They both address the need for experiences that are simultaneously *me* and *not-me*, something *more than* me, some thing or place *between* others and me. For Winnicott, this is the area of *play*. Creativity, culture, and religion are all transitional phenomena, belonging to that intermediate area of experience also called transitional space.

Play, for Winnicott, is a medium for the expression and elaboration of the true self—it is progressive, creative and developmental. Play can be the "work" of psychotherapy. I believe it is also applicable to the "work" of growing in interiority that is the task for contemplative monastics. We are at play with God when we are about the work of transformation. When we meditate or pray, for example, we are entering an area of potential space, transitional space. In this generative space created between God and us, we encounter God and God encounters us. We are no longer completely inside or outside ourselves, but in this space co-created by God and ourselves, a place to play, where we can be our truest self and pray.

This potential space is not concrete, so it would be a misapplication to apply it to the cell, for example. We may indeed be able to co-create this space in our cell, and it may be a place of profound prayer. But this ground of encounter with God cannot be limited to a concrete place. It is, in fact, something that is part of our heart, here defined from a biblical and early Christian perspective. We take our heart with us wherever we go. In many ways the process of growing in interiority can be considered "heartwork" that takes place is solitude and in community. The potentiality of potential space means it can be co-created anywhere. I believe we can see the co-creation of this potential space in our relations with our fellow monastics. Our openness to their needs, our responsiveness, and our willingness to

14. D. W. Winnicott, *Playing and Reality* (New York, Basic Books, 1971) 2.

engage with them at a deep level in matters of the heart: all these can be just as rich as our finest moments of solitude.

6. Human Issues and Growth in Interiority

The richness of these three concepts lies in their broader applications, beyond a merely clinical understanding of the human person. There is something mysterious in each of these concepts, a way in which each points to something beyond what we can understand from a purely human or psychological perspective. The capacity to be alone, the true self, and transitional phenomena/potential space can all be useful tools for the work of seeking God in the Camaldolese Benedictine way of life. That life points to the other, the beyond, the transcendent, while remaining incarnationally grounded in the here and now. Our use of these psychological insights is not purely for psychological growth—certainly not in the service of simply building ourselves up in a self-centered way—but also to free us from ourselves and the tyranny of our inherent falseness.

Part of the tension in Camaldolese monastic life can arise from the mistaken belief that eremitical life is inherently better than cenobitical life, and that we must move to this higher good, leaving behind the cenobitical experience. I would argue that the richness of our life is precisely the formal opportunity for both. Our growth in each of the three concepts discussed—and ultimately growth in interiority—is best accomplished by a life that includes both eremitical and cenobitical elements. The wisdom of our founder, St. Romuald, shines through here. He left us as our only rule the *Rule of St. Benedict*, yet simultaneously encouraged growth in solitude. For him, they were not mutually exclusive. Growth in interiority occurs in both aspects of life. We must work with our spiritual guide to find the vital balance for ourselves, and be ready for the inevitable shifts in that balance. We will truly continue to grow fully only through guided experience in both the eremitical and cenobitical elements of our lives. Both community and solitude must be embraced for what they truly *are* and not be used as escapes, one from the other. Each has its moments of pain and suffering; each has its moments of tranquil peace and deep connection, joyful experiences of God in God's many manifestations.

7. Conclusion—Ultimate Issues

Why be concerned about all of this? Why is this important? Where will it lead us? John Cassian has told us that the ultimate goal for those who follow the monastic path is the kingdom of God. That is our ultimate end.

To achieve this end, we are to strive for purity of heart, that deep love that undergirds all things. It can be useful to think of purity of heart as a symbol, a mysterious concept that attempts to reveal to us a deeper, greater experience than words can convey. Perhaps purity of heart is akin, in some way, to: a life wherein we have progressed and continue to progress in our capacity to be alone, so as to be fully open to God and others; our searching for and continuing to find the richness that is our truest self, and joyfully embracing it as the vital center of God within us; our ability to attend to our inner and outer worlds, and more importantly, to enter that transitional space that is both everywhere and nowhere, where we can playfully engage with God in the re-creation of who we are and ultimately, who we will become.

The Camaldolese *triple good*—here named solitude, communion, and mission—can also be considered an expression of purity of heart. Camaldolese Benedictines strive to engage as fully as possible in the interplay and interpenetration of this *triplex bonum*: laboring in solitude, toiling in communion and, with the overflowing hearts that come from this toil and labor, spilling ourselves for God's people. Through a life devoted to an ever deeper understanding of our charism of combined solitude and communion, we embrace others, find ourselves and encounter God. We are transformed.

Golden Solitude

Peter-Damian Belisle

It seems almost tautological to mention "Camaldoli" and "solitude" within the same sentence, since solitude has been such a hallmark of the Camaldolese tradition from the moment of its inception. Fulfilling a distinct need within the monastic world, Camaldolese solitude became the historical springboard for the growth of its congregation and has formed a mainstay of Camaldolese spirituality throughout its first millennium of existence. The purpose of this chapter is to glean the theory of solitude from the early Camaldolese sources and discuss its praxis in Camaldolese spirituality.

1. Romuald of Ravenna

What we substantively know of Romuald's life and ministry can be found in Peter Damian's *Life of Blessed Romuald* and Bruno-Boniface of Querfurt's *Life of the Five Brothers.* In the latter work we find reference to Otto III's threefold advantage suggested to Romuald and his followers, the second advantage being "golden solitude, for those who are mature and who thirst for the living God."[1] Romuald, who devoted most of his life to living monastic solitude, organizing hermits to live in community, founding hermitages and monasteries, as well as reforming already extant monastic houses, was at least tacitly compliant with Otto's monastic schema vis-à-vis the mission in Poland, but continued to live his own vocation to "golden solitude" in an exemplary fashion, for at least protracted periods of several years, alternating

---

1. Bruno of Querfurt, *The Life of the Five Brothers* in *The Mystery of Romuald and the Five Brothers; Stories from the Benedictines and Camaldolese* by Thomas Matus (Big Sur, Hermitage Books, 1994) 95.

with various itinerant journeys concerned with founding and reforming monastic groups. As can be seen in Peter Damian's biography, Romuald had a bit of the *wanderlust* about him, always eager to make new foundations. Bruno-Boniface corroborates this view: "Abbot Romuald—always a wanderer, now here, now there, gathering disciples in the power of the Holy Spirit."[2]

In his life of Romuald, Peter Damian tells us the saint already experienced solitude's call as a young man:

> For example, when he was out hunting and happened upon a pleasant glade, he immediately felt drawn into solitude and said to himself, "How fine it would be to live like hermits, deep in these woods, how easy to stay quiet and free from the world's turmoil!" Heaven put these thoughts into his mind, like a prophecy, and he began to fall in love with what was to be his life's work.[3]

He became a monk at the newly Cluniacized abbey of St. Apollinare in Classe at Ravenna, but left after a few years of frustration with his fellow monks' lack of fervor and, with the permission of his abbot at Classe, began to live a master/disciple relationship with a hermit named Marino in the countryside near Ravenna. "A rough and ready type he [Marino] was, without any formation for the solitary life,"[4] Peter Damian quotes Romuald in later years.

After they had moved to the Abbey of St. Michael of Cuxa (a successfully Cluniacized house), this same duo built a hermitage[5] close to the abbey but the roles of the master and disciple were now reversed. Soon other disciples joined them and the little group studied the monastic sources and performed their ascesis. It is instructive to read Romuald's teaching from these idyllic years near Cuxa, sensing in his wisdom why he quickly became known as a spiritual master for solitaries.

> Be constant in your practice, and one day He who gave you the desire for the prayer of the heart will give you that prayer itself. When your heart's intention is fixed on God, it will keep lit the incense of your prayer, and the wind of distraction will not put it out. Do not worry about stray thoughts; they may come and go, but they will not take your attention away from God.[6]

Romuald was single-minded and went about his life's work of engendering monastic solitude and bringing solitaries together into community wholeheartedly.

2. Matus, *Mystery*, 91.

3. Peter Damian, *The Life of Blessed Romuald* in *The Mystery of Romuald and the Five Brothers; Stories from the Benedictines & Camaldolese* by Thomas Matus (Big Sur, Hermitage Books, 1994) 173.

4. Ibid., 179.

5. Ibid., 182.

6. Ibid., 188.

Romuald's unique vocation seemed to vacillate between periods of relative seclusion or reclusion and those times when he felt impelled to journey forth in founding and reforming activities. Two lengthy periods of seclusion occurred at Parenzo and Sitria. "Romuald dwelt in the territory of Porec (Parenzo) for three years, one of which he dedicated to the building of a monastery and the other two to seclusion."[7] "At Sitria, Romuald lived as a recluse for seven years, never breaking his silence. Although his tongue was silent, his life was a sermon, and he continued to work as never before, drawing men and women to monastic life and sinners to repentance."[8] In his seminal work on Peter Damian, Jean Leclercq[9] views these years of reclusion as the underpinning of all Romuald's activities:

> His need of solitude is clearly the ground of all his activity: what he did was only the consequence of the radiance emanating from within himself; but what he wanted was to be alone with Jesus Christ and die on the cross. These years at Pereo and Sitria are the summits of his life.

Clearly, solitude was central to Romuald's spirituality. Unfortunately, we suffer the paucity of documentation regarding his spiritual teachings. As with many great mystics and saints throughout the centuries, we must rely on what few accounts of Romuald's life and testament form the tradition of Romuald's teaching on solitude. Peter Damian indicates that mindfulness in solitary prayer was central to Romualdian spirituality:

> "Better to sing one psalm with feeling," he said, "than to recite a hundred with a wandering mind." But if you haven't yet received the grace of singing from your heart, do not give up hope. Be constant in your practice, and one day He who gave you the desire for the prayer of the heart will give you that prayer itself. When your heart's intention is fixed on God, it will keep lit the incense of your prayer, and the wind of distraction will not put it out. Do not worry about stray thoughts; they may come and go, but they will not take your attention away from God.[10]

We also know that Romuald viewed the solitary vocation within the context of obedience. He reprimands the monk Veneric to be a hermit under authority: "Thus the house of your holy life, which your good will is building, will rest on the foundations of humility and will have the strong support of obedience."[11] One of the monastic houses he tried to reform was at Biforco.

---

7. Ibid., 222.

8. Ibid., 248.

9. Jean Leclercq, *Saint Pierre Damien, Ermite et Homme D'Église* (Roma, Edizioni di Storia e Letteratura, 1960) 30.

10. Ibid., 188.

11. Ibid., 207.

Romuald spent a rather long time at Biforco. In addition to instructing the hermits in spiritual practice, he also tried to convince them that they should elect an abbot and live a full community life. But each of the hermits had his own benefactor to provide for him, and they were all accustomed to privacy and the freedom to do as they wished; so they gave little heed to Romuald's advice.[12]

Bruno-Boniface makes Romuald's stand on obedience clear when he calls him "Romuald the father of hermits who live according to right reason and follow the monastic Rule . . ."[13]

The main gem of teaching we have, again from Bruno-Boniface, has been called the *Brief Rule* of Romuald:

Sit in your cell as in paradise. Put the whole world behind you and forget it. Watch your thoughts like a good fisherman watching for fish. The path you must follow is in the Psalms—never leave it. If you have just come to the monastery, and in spite of your good will you cannot accomplish what you want, then take every opportunity you can to sing the Psalms in your heart and to understand them with your mind. And if your mind wanders as you read, do not give up; hurry back and apply your mind to the words once more. Realize above all that you are in God's presence, and stand there with the attitude of one who stands before the emperor. Empty yourself completely and sit waiting, content with the grace of God, like the chick who tastes nothing and eats nothing but what his mother brings him.[14]

For Romuald, solitude accords the possibility to commune with God, to speak with God as with a real living person.[15] And the grace derived from this living relationship enabled Romuald to journey forth from solitude quite literally, to bring to fruition his own spiritual freedom and immense love of God. This freedom expressed itself in many ways, so that his works of monastic foundation and reformation were not restricted to one model or type of being monastic. He was a "free spirit" of the first caliber and perhaps, precisely this quality of being liberated from restrictions or constraints was his most attractive characteristic.

2. Peter Damian

Romuald's biographer not only champions the memory of a holy hermit given to wandering, reforming, and itinerant preaching; he also embraces

12. Ibid., 228.
13. Ibid., 88.
14. Ibid., 158.
15. Giovanni Tabacco, "*Privilegium amoris*: aspetti della spiritualità Romualdina" in *Spiritualità e Cultura Nel Medioevo* (Napoli, Liguori, 1993) 177.

the founder's great passion for solitude and propagating sanctuaries for living that solitude. "Romuald represents the creative and visibly dynamic moment of an experience which Peter Damian wants to prolong,"[16] writes Tabacco. Like his predecessor, Peter Damian also became quite the monastic founder and reformer in his own right. And like Romuald, Peter Damian also founded cenobitical and eremitical houses without undue prejudice toward a set form that those houses might take. But again, the biographer's own preference is for solitude and the eremitical life. "Faithful to the traditions inherited from St. Romuald, Peter Damian respects a certain variety of form in the monastic groupings. His ideal, like St. Romuald's, always remains eremitical."[17]

Among his monastic writings are the so-called "Avellanita Constitutions" (Opus XV) written for a monk named Stephen who had joined the Congregation of Fonte Avellana—describing the eremitical life in general and depicting some of the life and customs at Fonte Avellana itself in particular. True to Western monastic culture, Peter Damian immediately centers on purity of heart in his praise of eremitism. "In the solitary life it is one's duty to be so engaged in bravely performing great deeds, that one always takes pains to display the beauty of a heart that is pure."[18] To keep that heart pure, the hermit must be able to enjoy certain conditions of life that will be constant and familiar companions: an atmosphere of quiet, the maintenance of silence, and the asceticism of fasting. All three of these external conditions must be tempered by the traditional monastic virtues of moderation and discretion. Sounding like an excerpt from John Cassian's *Institutes of the Cœnobia*, he writes, "Like a prudent and busy farmer you should constantly till your soil, furrow the field of your heart and of your body with the plow of holy discipline, harrow the hard earth and strive to pull up the weeds of sin, and thus you will be prepared each day, with eyes intent on heaven, to await the downpour of rain from above."[19] But the hermit must take care not to underestimate the need for obedience in eremitical life, sometimes referred to as the "Cross" of obedience for one who might want to tamper with a "go it alone" spirituality. "One must be especially careful not to depreciate the obligation of obedience under the guide of leading a hermit's life."[20] The hermit is meant to be an obedient apostle of love. In both of his works already cited in this chapter, Tabacco

16. Giovanni Tabacco, "Romualdo Di Ravenna e gli Inizi Dell'Eremitismo Camaldolese" in *L'Eremitismo in Occidente Nei Secoli XI e XII* (Milano, Società Editrice Vita e Pensiero, 1965) 83.

17. Leclercq, *Saint Pierre Damien*, 62.

18. Peter Damian, "Letter 50" in *Letters 31–60*, trans. Owen J. Blum (Washington, The Catholic University Press, 1990) 291.

19. Ibid., 325.

20. Ibid., 313.

has emphasized how the mainstay of the Romualdian movement at Cuxa, Venice, and Ravenna was the bonds of love formed among the members of this small group of solitaries gathered *pro privilegio amoris,* for the privilege of love. Peter Damian, too, speaks for love and freedom among hermits: "When love takes the place of fear, and freedom slavery, then necessity is turned into desire, and by the unspeakable fire of charity, whatever until then seemed harsh and unfeeling will become sweet and agreeable."[21]

Probably the most popularly known work by Peter Damian is his Opus XI, the so-called *The Lord Be With You* ruminations about solitude, the eremitical life and the relationship between hermit and Church. The point of departure is the query about the propriety of a hermit-priest who celebrates Eucharist alone responding to the words: "The Lord be with you." This immediately brings into question the hermit's relationship to the greater Church. For Peter Damian, the solitary represents the Church; the Church subsists in the person of the hermit.

> Since the whole Church is symbolized in the person of one individual, and since, moreover, the Church is said to be a virgin, holy Church is both one in all and complete in each of them; that is to say, simple in many by reason of the unity of faith, and multiple in each through the bond of love and the various charismatic gifts, since all are from one, and all are one.[22]

His ecclesiology is sound, even if the air in Peter Damian's cell seems a bit lofty, and rarified. The Church is present in each individual member of the Mystical Body; and each member is substantially the Church which is one in all. "If they are one who believe in Christ, then wherever an individual member is physically present, there too the whole body is present by reason of the sacramental mystery."[23] And so, dedicated solitude within the Church is also a collective act. "By the power of the Holy Spirit who dwells in each and at the same time fills all, our solitude is at once plural and our community is singular."[24] It is a matter of presence through the bonds of love. By love, the entire Church is present in the hermit. "By the mystery of intimate unity, to be sure, the entire Church is there spiritually present when one person is present, participating in the same faith and fraternal love. For where there is unity of faith, it allows neither for solitude in one, nor for a schism of diversity in many."[25] André Louf[26] refers to this sacra-

21. Ibid., 322.

22. Peter Damian, "Letter 28" in *Letters 1–30*, trans. Owen J. Blum (Washington, The Catholic University Press, 1989) 262.

23. Ibid., 263.

24. Ibid., 265.

25. Ibid., 268.

26. André Louf, "Solitudo Pluralis" in *Solitude and Communion; Papers on the Hermit Life given at St. David's, Wales in the Autumn of 1975* (Oxford, SLG Press, 1977).

mental unity stressed by Peter Damian as "shared solitude . . . corporate solitude"[27] because the hermit is united to all in the Holy Spirit.

> By the adhesive of love, *caritatis glutinum*, the solitary is united with all his brothers [and sisters] and that in an almost sacramental way by the mystery of the sacrament, by inviolable sacramental unity—*per mysterium sacramenti, per unitatis inviolabile sacramentum*. In him are thus realized two basic qualities which the Church receives from the Holy Spirit: that which unites and that which diversifies.[28]

The final third of *The Lord Be With You* treatise is a rather elaborate paean to the hermit's cell and eremitical solitude. True to St. Romuald, his mentor, Peter Damian calls the cell "paradise" and enlists a number of metaphors to describe its paradisiacal qualities. It is a school where the arts of heaven are taught and in which dwell the virtues:

> God is there, where one learns where life is heading, and one attains there to the knowledge of the highest truth. The hermitage is truly a paradise of delights, where like various savory spices or the perfume of red-glowing flowers the fragrant scents of virtue give forth their odor. There the roses of charity blaze in crimson glory; there the lilies of chastity glisten in snow-white beauty, and with them the violets of humility, since they are content with lowly spots, are never disturbed by the wind; there the myrrh of perfect penance gives forth its fragrance and the incense of incessant praying fills the air.[29]

The cell is a mirror of souls where self-knowledge leads to spiritual growth, and a bridal chamber that leads to intimate contemplative union: it is a fountain of life. As a haven and refuge, solitude nurses the soul to health, watches and protects what has been accomplished, and encourages one to embrace simplicity.

But the cell is not only paradise, because it forms a crossroads between heaven and earth. Since it is a meeting place—a halfway post—solitude is also a purgatory: a furnace or kiln or workshop wherein the work of perfection is fashioned and molded and brought into being. It is a bath which cleanses, purifies, and shines. The solitary's way is a road of return to God, on whose path one travels through the desert wastelands of the heart. The cell is also a great storehouse where bartering between heaven and earth leads to eternal life.

However, the cell's activities can often move from purgatorial struggles into the full combat of an inferno in the spiritual arena. So, solitude is also

27. Ibid., 22.
28. Ibid., 17.
29. Peter Damian, *Letter* 28: 281.

a real battlefield, sometimes a bloody one. The cell must become a fortress
to fight off the onslaughts of demons whose attacks can become deadly serious. And at times the solitary cell will become a tomb in which reality is
brought to light and life in the breath and power of the Holy Spirit. Paradise,
purgatory, inferno: solitude's cell is all this and more for Peter Damian. The
desert solitude of eremitical monasticism seems to many to have more than
a tinge of individualism about it, but for Romuald and Peter Damian, the
community bonds of obedience and communion are intended to protect the
solitary from such individualistic pursuits. Still, when reading Peter Damian,
one can sense the individual coming to the fore between the lines of the text.
Calati, in fact, sees Peter Damian as a precursor to the *devotio moderna* of the
thirteenth century. Speaking of the monastic desert, Calati writes: "And so,
one finds this 'monastic desert' at present in the cell. We can already see from
some excerpts of Opus 11 Peter Damian's insistence already has the flavor of
the subsequent *devotio moderna*."[30] And again,

> The crisis of the communitarian idea of cluniac monasticism fostered a re-
> action at the level of individualistic asceticism. The latter attained the height
> of its expression in the 13th-century *devotio moderna* movement, but is al-
> ready contained "in a nutshell" within the spiritual writing of St. Peter
> Damian and later, in that of St. Bernard.[31]

But even if he has a strong individualistic strain running through his spiritual writings, Peter Damian is deeply concerned that the hermit is intentionally part of the Church and intimately concerned with the life of the Church.
Solitude is meant to foster love for and within the Church communion.

3. Rudolf of Camaldoli

Rudolf, the fourth prior of Camaldoli, wrote his *Constitutions* in
1080, producing a shorter version in 1085. As with the previously mentioned *Avellanita Constitutions* by Peter Damian, we must keep in mind
that these "constitutions" really form more of a "customary" wherein Rudolf
describes life as it was lived at eleventh-century Camaldoli. They are not a
list of rules and restrictions, but of customs and descriptions.

Naturally, the early founders of Camaldoli developed a spirituality of
the cell consonant with Romuald's teaching in the *Brief Rule*. The monastic
cell is the *locus* of solitude, the place of grace. "Let the solitary cultivate a
continual and perpetual fidelity to the cell, so that through the grace of God

30. Benedetto Calati, *Sapienza Monastica; Saggi e Storia, Spiritualità e Problemi Monastici* (Roma, Studia Anselmiana, 1994) 383.
31. Ibid., 536.

and his assiduous stability, living in the cell will become sweet to him."[32] But from their humble beginnings as hermits in the Romualdian mold and then down through the Camaldolese centuries, the monks did not let the cell of solitude detract from the communal aspects of their monastic life.

> At the sound of the signal let all the brothers except the recluses and any who are sick hasten to the Divine Office whether for the Hours of day or night, and perform the work of God with great reverence, according to the practice of the monasteries of this Congregation.[33]

If the solitary's life might have seemed busy to an outsider, it was meant to be so. Human nature ensures that "it is possible to wander about all day within the cell itself . . ."[34] True to the monastic desert tradition, "Everyone ought to be so diligent either in prayer, reading, or performing disciplines, prostrations and flagellations, that the whole space of day and night seems brief and insufficient to him."[35]

Like Peter Damian's view of solitude, Rudolph's solitary cell is the spiritual arena for the development of the various virtues. Camaldoli does not lack the Benedictine stress on humility; in fact, Rudolph views it as even more important for hermits! "While this virtue [humility] is for everyone . . . it is nevertheless especially necessary for hermits, so that where the life is stricter, the mind may be humbler."[36] Romuald consistently encouraged hermits to place themselves under obedience in order to live the monastic virtue of *discretio*, discretion. Rudolph insists that obedience "is very necessary to solitaries, and since they lead a harder life they should observe a fuller obedience."[37] And of course, moderation, that "mother of the virtues," should not be lacking at Camaldoli: "Sobriety . . . ought to be applied to all our actions so that eating, fasting, keeping vigil, sleeping, standing, walking, speaking, keeping silence and all our other actions be performed soberly and moderately."[38]

But perhaps the virtue that speaks most significantly in Rudolph's document is piety—which he equates with kindness and gentleness. "Piety is also very necessary to solitaries, so that they may be humane, kind, merciful and meek. Piety is a kind inclination of the heart, bending with merciful

32. Rudulphus Camaldulensis, *Constitutiones* in *Annales Camaldulenses Ordinis Sancti Benedicti* . . . 9 vols. Comp. By Johanne-Benedicto Mittarelli (Venetiae, 1755–1773) III, App., col. 529.

33. Ibid., col. 521.

34. Ibid., col. 527.

35. Ibid.

36. Ibid., col. 531.

37. Ibid., col. 532.

38. Ibid., col. 533.

humanity to another's infirmity."[39] We may be tempted to think that eleventh-century hermits might have been a bit gruff, introverted, and fiercely focused, as they lived the hard rigors of Camaldoli. Rudolph's comments on piety speak more to the bonds of love that characterized the Romualdian world where the "privilege of love" was of the utmost importance. André Louf also happily notices that Rudolph's eremitism culminates in tender love and gentleness.

> The consummation of solitude, its ripe fruit, is the sweetness of love, that with which God has filled the solitary, and which now, through him, is available to all. . . . The true solitary finally appears as gentle among the gentle. He radiates *pietas*, the tenderness which Blessed Rudolph of Camaldoli recommends as an indispensable eremitical virtue, that "loving-kindness which comes out to meet disease and weakness with mercy and humanity."[40]

Here is the monastic key that opens the heart and gentles the spirit of the hermit's life at Camaldoli. Love is the point behind the call and the clearest expression that the call has been heard and answered.

4. Solitude in Camaldolese Benedictine Spirituality

Extolled by Romuald and preserved by Peter Damian of Fonte Avellana and the early hermits of Camaldoli, solitude's place was assured in the history and spirituality of what became known as the Camaldolese Congregation. To greater and lesser degrees, hermits and cenobites have espoused solitude as a necessary part of their monastic journey throughout this first millennium of Camaldolese history. To be "alone with the Alone" has long been the deep yearning of solitaries. Far from mere loneliness, this aloneness is a Spirited way of being present to God attentively, expectantly. "The Spirit alone can join itself to the spirit without violating identity or intimacy, in a union so respectful and profound that it transforms the solitude of ego's self-centeredness into a solitude of address: 'Abba, Father.'"[41]

Presence, not absence, is the point of monastic solitude. To be alone in order to be away from realities, without being present to spiritual reality, is an experience of isolation. I have written previously of the "hermit" archetype in monasticism: "The monastic response in solitude to the call voiced by the 'hermit within' is not a call to romanticized loneliness nor an existential *angst* experienced in bitter isolation. Here is a call to honest

39. Ibid.
40. Louf, *Solitudo Pluralis*, 28.
41. Marguerite Lena, "Solitude" in *Dictionnaire de Spiritualité* 14b (Paris, Beauchesne, 1989) cl. 1015.

aloneness where one is really not alone at all, but awake to God's presence. For solitude entices us into Presence."[42] Thomas Merton has also described this enticement, or invitation, metaphorically: "The door to solitude opens only from the inside. . . . The one who has entered freely, falls into the desert the way a ripe fruit falls out of a tree."[43]

Camaldolese spirituality embraces this ripeness, to use Merton's metaphor, which promotes growth in the awareness of God's pervasive presence. "Persons comfortable with solitude can grow in an awareness of God. They experience their own personal emptiness and yearning for wholeness. They wait expectantly for God's Word to sound forth from their hearts."[44] The ensuing dialogue can best be heard in an atmosphere of cultivated silence, so the Camaldolese *Constitutions* promote both silence and solitude as monastic ideal "givens": "Monastic solitude and silence entail a relative material separation from others; these practices are at the service of the monk's inner work as he meditates on the Word of God. Thus with the exercise of self-denial and prayer, the monk remains in loving dialogue with God (cf. *RB* 6)."[45] Generally, though not exclusively so, Camaldolese foundations have been located in rural settings to promote and protect these essential elements of monastic spirituality. "Our houses are to be established in appropriately secluded locations, so as to provide the community with the necessary climate of solitude and silence."[46] Here Camaldolese live in an Advent expectation of watching and waiting for God's epiphanies of presence. Here we listen to God's Word and speak to God within the sanctum of the stilled heart. For in solitude and silence our hearts find rest.

But it is not only rest we discover in the bosom of solitude! As we already know from Peter Damian's eloquent "song of solitude" as well as monastic tradition dating back to the fourth-century Egyptian, Syrian, and Palestinian deserts, solitude is also a battlefield. In his book on eremitical Camaldolese spirituality, Anselm Giabbani describes this climate of struggle: "Loving God and seeking God's will force the monk in the hermitage cell to battle unceasingly against the spirit of evil and to strive toward absolute

42. Peter-Damian Belisle, "The *Hermit* Archetype within the Monastic Spiritual Journey" in *Word & Spirit; a Monastic Review* 15 (1993) 41.

43. Thomas Merton, "Notes for a Philosophy of Solitude" in *Disputed Questions* (New York, Harcourt Brace Jovanovich, 1960) 196–97.

44. Augustin [Peter-Damian] Belisle, *Into the Heart of God, Spiritual Reflections.* (Petersham, St. Bede's Publications, 1989) 18.

45. Camaldolese Congregation of the Order of Saint Benedict, *Constitutions and Declarations of the Camaldolese Congregation of the Order of Saint Benedict*, trans. Thomas Matus (Camaldoli, 1985) no. 90.

46. Camaldolese, *Constitutions and Declarations*, no. 96.

fidelity to the Father's call and invitation."[47] As with much medieval hagiography, *The Life of Blessed Romuald* is populated with demonic forces. This is also true of Peter Damian's monastic writings. "The hermitage is a place of ineffable contrasts, the experience of good and evil as imminent powers, seeking and confronting each other in a heroic tension within the soul."[48] Like the *abbas* of the Egyptian desert wastes, Romuald and his early followers battle the demons in the great adventure of solitude. "For the privilege of love, a test is asked of the hermits which is so difficult that they find themselves at the very roots of evil itself—the immediate battle with diabolical powers."[49] To translate these demons into modern psychological struggles, spiritual conflicts, and physical suffering does not denigrate either the immediacy or intensity of the battle.

Because the psychological and spiritual stakes are high in solitude's arena, Camaldolese encourage a formative process that will best prepare the monk to respond to God's call with a mature dialogue of the "whole" person. "In order that the monks may live their life in the most authentic way, it is necessary, even for those who spend their time habitually or always in solitude, that they have an adequate cultural and spiritual preparation, as is required for the complete maturity of the person."[50] For seeking God's will demands the attention and response of the mature, developed person. To strip oneself of all vestiges of personhood in a misguided kenotic fervor is clearly not the answer when there is no person remaining to respond to God's will. But to denude oneself of self-will and egoism while preserving the integrity of personhood in discerning God's will is the authentic battle of Camaldolese solitude. To find oneself in God's will without annihilating the person in the process is the wisdom needed for combat.

> The solitary is placed in the situation where the temptations of self-pleasing and self-preoccupation are at their most acute, and it is there that he has to struggle with the demonic assaults on the spirit as well as on the flesh. Therefore the combat merges into the final *agonia* and experience of dereliction as the privilege of the mountain is succeeded by the demands of Gethsemane to keep awake and pray with Christ, to endure that fierce stripping of the will until it has nothing left but the Will of God.[51]

47. Anselmo Giabbani, *L'Eremo. Vita e Spiritualità Eremitica nel Monachismo Camaldolese Primitivo* (Brescia, Morcelliana, 1945) 82.

48. Tabacco, *Privilegium amoris*, 188.

49. Ibid., 184.

50. Camaldolese, *Constitutions and Declarations*, no. 93.

51. Roland Walls, "The Biblical Background to the Solitary Life" in *Solitude and Communion: Papers on the Hermit Life Given at St. David's, Wales in the Autumn of 1975* (Oxford, SLG Press, 1977) 51.

Seeking God's will and finding oneself therein is ultimately the reality of humility—that "mother" of virtues which has held a central place within the tradition of monasticism. It is a humbling experience to discover repeatedly that one is not the center of existence and must leave behind the seemingly insatiable demands and obsessive limitations of the self in order to reach out authentically to another and to the Other. That is the work of humility and is the fruit of genuine solitude. Merton writes: "The whole purpose of the solitary life is to bring the soul into the 'center of her humility' and to keep it there. The hermit does not pretend to have acquired any esoteric secret or any exalted technique by which he penetrates into the mystery of God. His only secret is the humility and poverty of Christ and the knowledge that God lifts up those who have fallen."[52] It is paradoxical that we find our "true" self in selflessness, but solitude, like monasticism, is a place of paradox in the stream of life. "The waters which rise from the monastic core pull us into a world of paradox: encounters within solitude; celebration of Word in silence; stability within a mobile world; marginality at life's core; creativity within aridity."[53]

Solitude is not only a place for aloneness and an arena for battle, but it is also a *locus* for communion. In solitude we not only wait in God's presence and prepare ourselves to know God's will, but we also move into union with God. For solitude is a meeting-place and a crossroads for covenant. "Vocational solitude is not the desert of abandonment, but the meeting-place, the Ark of the Covenant: it is an interior Sinai."[54] We strive to enter the burning bush, to become the flame. Perhaps that is what Abba Joseph of Panephysis meant by his startling action in the Egyptian desert:

> Abba Lot went to see Abba Joseph and said to him, "Abba, as far as I can I say my little office, I fast a little, I pray and meditate, I live in peace and as far as I can, I purify my thoughts. What else can I do?" Then the old man stood up and stretched his hands towards heaven. His fingers became like ten lamps of fire and he said to him, "If you will, you can become all flame."[55]

At its most efficacious moment, solitude is a spousal reality that ushers the heart into loving communion with God. The rest and work of solitude prepares just for this moment. "Only the heart which is solitary enough to recognize the presence of the Wholly Other within itself truly becomes a place of communion . . . it can welcome beings and things, the

52. Thomas Merton, "A Renaissance Hermit" in *Disputed Questions* (New York, Harcourt Brace Jovanovich, 1960) 173.

53. Belisle, "The *Hermit* Archetype," 41.

54. Lena, *Solitude*, cl. 1015.

55. *The Sayings of the Desert Fathers, The Alphabetical Collection*, trans. Benedicta Ward (London, Mowbrays, 1975) 88.

world and history."[56] To use a favorite term of the medieval English mystics, solitude's true aim will be a "one-ing" with the Word. "The entire flow of aloneness (as opposed to loneliness) is one of integration, wholeness. We wait for God to give us meaning and unity. Expectant of heart, we grow in the silence of the Word and find fulfillment in the communion of solitude."[57] Really, one is never alone at all when one is living an authentic solitude whose focus is presence and whose aim is communion. "One who is 'at ease' with being alone will be 'at home' with the world and 'at one' with the Word."[58] If solitude is peopled with "demons," then it is also peopled with angels and indeed, the Church! Echoing Peter Damian, André Louf writes: "From whatever side one looks at it, Christian solitude passes into fullness of communion; it is always corporate—*solitudo pluralis*. The cell, in the words of St. Peter Damian, is '*conclave sanctae Ecclesiae*'—the meeting-place of Holy Church."[59]

This Church-connectedness about which Peter Damian wrote in his monastic writings, particularly *The Lord Be With You*, has naturally been a concern for Camaldolese monastics throughout the second Christian millennium. An unhealthy or distracted approach to solitude can find a monastic feeling, for all practical purposes, "outside" the Church! Of course, any authentic ecclesiology would not allow this to happen. And the Camaldolese *Constitutions* remind the members that they are very much a part of that Church. "The monks should realize that monastic solitude does not separate them from the Church community, to which they are united by the bonds of charity and their journey toward the Kingdom of God."[60] Even from the beginnings of Romualdian eremitism, the monastic movement which later became codified and constituted as "Camaldolese" was intimately connected to the *Rule of Saint Benedict* and the Benedictine monastic tradition, and as such, was profoundly concerned with "community." Calati writes:

> This whole experience of life that found its outlet in Romualdian eremitism could not be the decisive moment of the monastic project, intuited by St. Romuald, St. Peter Damian and the first founding fathers of Camaldoli. The riverbed of the *Rule of St. Benedict* and its pluralistic tradition always remained a concrete solution capable of guaranteeing that the great prophetical intuitions of evangelical radicalism of these Fathers would not be lost. This explains why the same eremiticism of the Camaldolese tradition had

56. Lena, *Solitude*, cl. 1016.
57. Belisle, *Into the Heart of God*, 18.
58. Ibid.
59. Louf, *Solitudo Pluralis*, 27.
60. Camaldolese, *Constitutions and Declarations*, no. 91.

always nurtured the most profound connection to the *Rule of St. Benedict*, despite the arduous experiences of charismatic life.[61]

The Camaldolese way was never a movement away from community and from the Church. A distinct part of Romuald's own ministry was to bring isolated hermits and disparate eremitical groups *into* community, under a religious superior. To view Camaldolese solitude as an escape from community or a flight from Church would render a great disservice to Romuald and his followers. Camaldolese are not deadened to the realities of the Church or the world. If the cell is seen as a tomb, it is the tomb of Christ that is indeed the womb of the Church. The entire life of the Church is resurrection life.

> Buried with Christ in the solitude and silence of his cell—which the Desert Fathers called a tomb—he [the solitary] demonstrates in an extreme form the truth behind the existence of the Church. Any life that emerges from this buried life can only be Resurrection life, a sheer gift of God which faith alone can receive.[62]

If solitude is a place of refuge and healing, of purification and death, it is only so in the grace of resurrection.

There is yet another dimension to solitude which is arguably its most important gift to the Church—its prophetic character. Throughout salvation history revelation and prophecy have strong links to solitude. From Moses on the mountain, to Elijah listening to the tiny whispering sound, to Jesus on his postbaptismal desert experience: a revelatory moment arrives in solitude. Monastic solitude does not cultivate private revelations, but does stand witness to a Church still-in-waiting for the ongoing work of revelation. "This revelatory aspect of the hermit's vocation removes him from that ever-present danger of reducing his role to the requirements of personal devotion, either of his own or of others. He is where he is for a radical purpose, related to the contemporary reception of the revelation by the faith of the present-day Church."[63] Solitude fashions the person not so much to see revelation as to *be* revelation for the Church. To be transformed, indeed, to be transfigured in Christ is the prophetic dimension of solitude. It is no accident that the Camaldolese foundations at the Holy Hermitage of Camaldoli, the hermitage of Monte Giove in Italy, Mogi daz Cruzes in Brazil, and Transfiguration Monastery in New York were all founded under the patronage of the Transfigured Christ. We find that Christ in the forests, on the mountains, in the ocean, in all of nature and

61. Calati, *Sapienza Monastica*, 536.
62. Walls, *The Biblical Background*, 51.
63. Ibid., 50.

the cosmos, as well as in the Church and hermitage cell. Expansiveness of heart and mind flow from the solitary cell because the calls to union and communion are boundless.

A Wild Bird, with God in the Center: The Hermit in Community

Donald Corcoran

1. Introduction

Clement Roggi, one of the founders of the Camaldolese Benedictine hermitage in Big Sur, California, once described the Camaldolese charism as "an eremitical cœnobium and cenobitical hermitage."[1] Whether in a solitary hermitage or a cœnobium, the Camaldolese life and spirit has always had a sense of the solitary dimension marking each person—and marking *both* poles of its expression—the cœnobium and the hermitage. Though at times in history there were great tensions between the two poles, the Camaldolese leadership of the twentieth century has led the whole congregation to a deep appreciation of both poles and their fruitful interrelationship. The "return to the sources" recommended by Vatican II has been an evident factor in recovering the primary and revitalizing energy of the charism among the Camaldolese. All dimensions of the charism—hermitage, cœnobium, reclusion, evangelization, ecumenical leadership, study and writing have had remarkable expressions.

America's most well-known monk, Thomas Merton, a Trappist of Gethsemani, was for a time considering a transfer to the Camaldolese, until the Vatican intervened and discouraged it on the grounds that Merton was such an important witness to monastic life in America that it would be a great loss if he were to move to Europe.[2] One of Merton's poems puts very aptly the essence of the solitary vocation, lived apart in a hermitage or in the very heart of a community:

1. Related by Thomas Matus, in a personal conversation in June 2000.
2. Related by Emanuele Bargellini, in a personal conversation.

> Under the blunt pine
> Elias becomes his own geography
> (Supposing geography to be necessary at all),
> Elias becomes his own wild bird, with God in the center,
> His own wild field which nobody owns,
> His own pattern, surrounding the Spirit
> By which he is himself surrounded:
> For the free man's road has neither beginning nor end.[3]

In this poem, with great economy of words, Merton points to the essence of the solitary vocation—its center is God. The hermitage is not about the luxury of living alone, a comfortable distance for introverts, a place to concentrate on one's work, a zone free from the moment-to-moment challenges of interpersonal relatedness. There are reasons why Benedict would strongly suggest that all monks receive a foundation in the cœnobium or community. Basil the Great is noted for a famous comment on hermits, "Whose feet do they wash?"[4] Yet the hermit, the solitary, the anchoress, stand there for all times as a signal-bearer, a lighthouse, an eschatological sign: someone who says "God is enough" because all things are in God and can be found in God. And that is quite an extraordinary statement to make with one's whole life.

Merton had a longtime romance with "the hermitage." Whether or not he had a true solitary vocation may be debatable, yet in a sense he grew into it. For years he struggled for permission to "be a hermit"—perhaps a bit idealistically. Yet the notion was, for him, perhaps also the projection of his best and deepest spiritual yearning. A year or so after finally receiving permission to withdraw to his hermitage on the property of the Abbey of Gethsemani, he realized that he had somehow inadvertently spoiled the opportunity by inviting too many of his friends. He had filled the physical and the interior space with too much business, no matter how worthy or honorable. With frank honesty that makes him all the more charming and deserving of our respect, Merton realized that, after one year or so in his hermitage, he had somewhat wasted his opportunity and too many friends were visiting. He wrote, with a kind of lighthearted humility, that he "blew it." Merton grew into a deeper and deeper realization of the simple demands of real solitude. He could not continue to live with a label "hermit" and whittle away the time and space of his hermitage. Prayer and reflection recalled him to a greater commitment to his solitary vocation.

---

3. Thomas Merton, *The Collected Poems of Thomas Merton* (New York, New Directions, 1977) 245.

4. Augustine Holmes, *A Life Pleasing to God: The Spirituality of the Rules of St. Basil* (Kalamazoo, Cistercian, 1999). See chapter 11, "Whose Feet Will You Wash? Solitude or Community"—Longer Rule 7, 139–67.

A hermit with a large cœnobium in the background—or in the surround—has many benefits, everything from soap powder to the protection of time and space. Antony of Egypt withdrew in the fourth century for a number of years of prolonged solitude to the so-called "Inner Mountain"—with two monks guarding the entrance. In a sense, Antony was a solitary supported by a small cœnobium. One has to admit there is a certain luxury to that spiritual system.

2. The Camaldolese in History

There is no discernible, uniform "Camaldolese pattern," either presently or historically. What Leo XIII said of the Benedictine Order at large, because of its plurality of forms, expressions and lack of centralization—"the Benedictine Order is a great disorder"—might also be said of the historical Camaldolese family. While the current model expressed at Camaldoli itself expresses the tradition of the two poles (cenobitical and eremitical) strongly and visibly, it is hardly the only expression, or standard pattern, or even the ideal pattern. The merits of the Camaldolese charism are its diversity, its manifold expressions, and its flexibility. The Camaldolese often use the term "hermitage" (derived from the Greek word for *desert*) when referring to the individual hermitage cell, as well as to the "cluster" of cells—for example, the "Holy Hermitage" of Camaldoli.

Hermits were not unusual in the medieval monastic world. Even the Cluniac monasteries—the very image of strong centralized cœnobia—generated small *cellae* of one or two monks connected to the home monastery. Though far-flung *cellae* and granges may not have been expressly founded for purposes of solitude and simplicity, they certainly provided it for those who lived in them. The eleventh century saw the flourishing of a widespread eremitical, ascetical movement, as well as several movements of monastic reform. St. Nilus, a Calabrian, had founded Grottaferrata[5] near Rome in the late tenth century, following the *Rule of St. Basil*. Through this monastery and the presence of other Greek monks in Italy, the notion of the eremitical or desert ideal touched many. In 1080 St. Bruno of Cologne gathered a few others to found the Carthusians near Grenoble. St. Norbert, a secular canon, founded a group of "regulars" (i.e., following a Rule) in the early twelfth century.

Thus Romuald of Ravenna, founder of the Camaldolese Benedictines, lived in an era hungry for reform and the desert ideal. Romuald's traveling put him in contact with many independent recluses who were taken with

5. Christian Leisy, "Grottaferrata: Greek Monks at the Gates of Rome," *Cistercian Studies Quarterly* XXI (1986) 171–75.

his example and asked to join him. He brought regularity, accountability, and mutual support to their lives, while preserving the integrity of the eremitical ideal. Romuald brought to the monastic world a combination of cœnobium and hermitage. He was a Cluniac Benedictine monk at the monastery of St. Apollinare in Classe, near Ravenna. Seeking greater monastic seriousness—and with perhaps an inchoate call in his heart to be alone—he "hit the road," so to speak. It is likely that he came into contact with Greek monks in Italy, such as the monks of the previously mentioned Grottaferrata near Rome, who were more historically given to the solitary ideal. There was even a monastery of Benedictines on Mount Athos at the time known as "Amalfatines," since they were from Amalfi. The Christian monastic East had always preserved, for example, the possibility of the *skete*, a small cluster of semi eremitical monks gathered around a spiritual elder—a monastic expression clearly linked to the early Desert Fathers and Mothers.

At any rate, Romuald was not a "founder" in the modern sense; he had no self-conscious plan like Dominic or Ignatius, for example. Romuald was a kind of monastic "Johnny Appleseed." The impact of his strongly spiritual character as he moved on from place to place, planted seeds of small eremitical brotherhoods that eventually became stabilized foundations. Thus contemporary scholars tend to distinguish between Romualdian spirituality and Camaldolese spirituality, the latter a more clearly self-conscious and articulated formula expressed in the early Camaldolese *Constitutions* set down from 1080 to 1085 by Blessed Rudolph of Camaldoli. The first generations of Camaldolese also lived in the century before the more formal articulation of canon law in the twelfth century. Ironically, a Camaldolese monk, Gratian, eventually became the great codifier of canon law. Interestingly, Gratian was virtually a recluse of his cell and the monastery's scriptorium. He did for Roman Church law what Abelard did for Church teaching, i.e., compiled inconsistencies (pros and cons in the tradition regarding specific legal questions) that made evident the need for rational elaboration. A carved statue now graces the entrance to the Notre Dame University Law School—a testament to the importance of his contribution to Roman Church law.

3. Monastic Vocation: Solitary and Cenobitical

It is evident in the *Rule of St. Benedict* that Benedict had a personal bias in favor of the cenobitical path. It stemmed partly from his personal experience—he knew that a life of solitude had its pitfalls—and partly from his wish to provide a monastic way of greater accountability (witness his comments on sarabaites and gyrovagues). Yet it is clear that he saw the hermitage as a little "window of possibility," a calling for some who, having been formed in the monastery and by community living, listen to a particular call of the search for God in solitude. The cultural disintegration of Western Europe at the time of Benedict and during the first centuries following his death would call for tightly centralized, almost fortress-like monasteries. This reached a heightened institutionalization in the reforms of Charlemagne when the *Rule of St. Benedict* was imposed in 810 upon all monasteries of his realm. The reforms of Benedict of Aniane were geared to standardization and shoring up strong cenobitical monasteries. Thus the eremitical character of monastic life—such as survived in the Christian East—was eclipsed. It survived on the margins of western Europe, particularly the Celts who had been influenced by the more eremitical or semi-eremitical varieties of monastic life in the ancient Christian Near East.

Both the solitary hermitage and the cœnobium can be a trap. Solitude (eremitism) is not about spiritual elitism or preciousness. It is not the luxury of living alone, with great gaps of time to do one's work or enjoy one's hobbies, or even to rest comfortably in one's introversion. It is not about woolgathering. Solitude can promote fierce and deep inner work—painful and sweaty toil, as the Desert Fathers and Mothers put it. They also called the monk's cell the "furnace of Babylon." Ascetical struggle, painful inner work towards true self-knowledge can, and should be a refining fire.[6] Though such inner asceticism may be particularly occasioned by solitude, it can also happen in cenobitical life. Certainly a healthy cœnobium ought to be able to provide time (and space) for deep reflection, long prayerful *lectio*, and a place for peace of heart.

St. Benedict calls his monastery a "school of the Lord's service." The way of life, instruction, and the example of fellow members, especially elders are formative. The cœnobium is a school, a testing ground, and vehicle of formation by osmosis. The immediate living of solitude can be dangerous, though not necessarily so. It presumes a certain maturity and readiness to deal with deep inner work, and a freedom to follow one's own rhythm—a great boon. The cœnobium *can* be a trap of "group think"—a climate and environment in which there is a loss of individuality, a subtle and insidious conformism. Succumbing to the "cultural trance" of even a very small group can swallow one up, slowly and subtly. One is in danger of never achieving individuality, or what C. G. Jung more properly calls "individuation." Speaking of her discipline as a kind of sacred enclosure (as is a true hermitage), an American Zen teacher (on her way to becoming a fully authenticated Zen *roshi*) speaks of being carried to a point in where "being ONE means being ALL ONE. That is very hard to admit. But

6. Mary Caroline Richards, "The Vessel and the Fire," *The Evolution of Consciousness*, ed. Sugerman (Middletown, Conn., Wesleyan University Press, 1976).

AL-ONE also means EVERYTHING. It means fullness and aliveness and life itself. Ultimately it means freedom."[7]

The hermitage can provide greater distance from "noise"—the disturbance of guests and the business of the inevitable hubbub of community concerns. But it can also heighten inner noise, one's own "stuff,"—a door to greater self-transformation and not to be avoided. Whether in one's own hermitage or in a cœnobium, one might say that the goal of monastic life is *always* to be a hermit, to develop the hermitage of the heart—a sacred "space" at the center of one's self—where one is always more or less conscious of God, or at least deeply attentive and attuned to the Spirit. It is an empty space, a *point vierge* as Merton, borrowing from the Sufis, described it: a place of deep abiding rest and peace.[8] But it is also a place where one is empowered, as one flows from the Center of all centers that is within. *Caritas Christi urgit nos*: the love of Christ urges us, impels us. At the Center we are empowered, inspired to bring light, love, peace, healing, joy—and perhaps, prophetic confrontation—to the circumference, to the whole, and to all of life. That urging comes not from an "apostolic" agenda, a self-conscious program or ministry that also overflows from the Spirit's work in one's deepest self. That is why, at the summit of his ladder of humility, Benedict says there will be "ease in virtue" and the Spirit will manifest in the "workman" (the monk).[9]

Prayerfulness of heart has much to do with finding the Center and then living out of that Center in everyday centeredness. Space and time for God are necessary for that centeredness that becomes *habitus*—the very baseline of one's personal melody in the Spirit. I once ventured to ask a markedly prayerful married woman how she prayed. She gave a surprising answer: "I just putter." She worked and accomplished tasks, but with a free interior heart—free for God, free for holy musings, and free for praying for others. Puttering is rather right-brained; it is not highly focused, not agenda-oriented, and not a charge up a mountain. Artists, poets, writers—creative and spiritual people—need non-agenda time in which to putter and live in "interior space" where inspiration can happen. They need to cultivate the vessel of the heart: open, empty, and ready for inspiration—gift of the Spirit.

7. Janet Abels, "How Zen Found Me," *Cross Currents* (Spring/Summer 2000) 15.

8. Sister Abdelnour, "*Le Point Vierge* in Thomas Merton," *Cistercian Studies Quarterly* VI (1971) 153–71.

9. Terrence Kardong, *Benedict's Rule: A Translation and Commentary* (Collegeville, The Liturgical Press, 1996) 159–60.

4. Silence, Stillness: The Matrix of Solitude

Isaac the Syrian, a great seventh-century mystic, wrote his ascetical homilies for "the dwellers in stillness."[10] Hermitage, cell, and anchorhold: all have to do with "sacred space" more than with "sacred time." It is feminine—the womb, the enclosure, the containment. And speaking in such archetypal terms, one must be aware that the womb is both positive (nourishing, birthing) and negative (devouring . . .). It can be both hell and paradise, pressure-cooker and place of repose.

The hermit (and any monk who lives the solitary core of his or her vocation) is a special voyager of inwardness and interiority. The monk, and especially the hermit, knows that the privileged place of access to God—beyond Sacrament and Word, of course—is the deep self, the heart. Thus Isaac the Syrian bids the dweller in solitude,

> Enter eagerly into the treasure house that is within you, and so you will see the things that are in heaven, for there is but one single entry to them both. The ladder that leads to the Kingdom is hidden within your soul. Flee from sin, dive into yourself, and in your soul you will discover the stairs by which to ascend.[11]

The solitary could, even *should* have an edge of perception and clarity. There is abundant evidence that simplification, centering down, and sensory deprivation can lead to heightened insight. And so the solitary hermit *can* live with greater distance from both social fiction and distortion, but at the same time have deeper solidarity with human struggle, pain and the best riches of the human heart. This is the meaning of Evagrius Ponticus' famous dictum, "The monk is separate from all and united with all."[12] Searching the depth of one's heart—working through the maze of one's life story—can be both difficult and universalizing. Theophane Boyd makes this point very well in his fictional "The Monk Whose Face Was Red," relating the story of a monk who dies but is sent back for further work, further transformation. The "cave" is an image of the heart; in fact, in Sanskrit the word *guha* means both care and heart. It is symbolic of deep, mysterious, inaccessible regions that are fathomless, but where we also find the hard-to-find treasure:

> Standing beside a cave was a monk whose face was red. He smiled at me and said, "I guess you're wondering why my face is so red."

10. Cf. Isaac the Syrian, *The Ascetical Homilies of Saint Isaac the Syrian*, trans. Holy Transfiguration Monastery (Boston, Holy Transfiguration Monastery, 1984).

11. Ibid., 11.

12. Evagrius Ponticus, *Praktikos and Chapters on Prayer*, trans. Bamberger (Kalamazoo, Cistercian, 1981). Cf. prayer no. 124.

I sure was. "Well, it was this way. When I was fifty I died. When I went to judgment, they asked me, 'What have you accomplished?' That's when my face turned red. I pleaded with them to give me more time. 'All right,' they said, 'we'll give you seven more years.'"

So I came back to my cave. I went in and kept going. I went deeper than I'd ever gone before, in and down. I must have walked for several days, although it was so dark I couldn't see day from night. I just wanted to think, to think about how I would spend those seven years, but it was scary. I didn't know what I'd meet down there, and I wasn't sure I'd be able to find my way but I kept going. Finally I began to hear a rumbling sound, like mighty water! I heard the bitter tears of EVERYONE'S fear, hurt, despair, disappointment, rage. Everyone's. And I heard the sweet tears too—you know, when you're loved, when you're safe at last, a loved one restored, those tears of joy. Yes, I heard the death of Christ and His Resurrection. I must have been at the heart of the earth, because while I couldn't hear any words, I heard ALL the tears—therefore I experienced total communion. I was separated from my separateness.

I don't know how long I stayed there in that state of communion—days, weeks, but I finally decided how I would spend my seven years. I would go back to the mouth of the cave and conduct people back and forth to the depths.[13]

Arnold Toynbee commented on the number of world spiritual leaders who began their careers in chosen marginality, in separation, in desert or wilderness, and often quite literally in the earth—in caves, a kind of womb of spiritual gestation. The hermitage is not a privatized cocoon, a comfortable "aside" from life and the human fray. It is a way to the Center that connects to all. One contemporary hermit writes,

True solidarity requires a profound sense of inner integration into the pain and horror—and awe and beauty—of being human. I have read so many books about the holiness of aloneness, and the psychological neediness of loneliness. For me, both run together in a river. I am alone—and lonely—in the same indrawn breath I feel the awe and the sharp wounding pain of my loneliness. The two become so one that it is impossible for me to say, like coffee and creamy sugar, what part is bitter, and what the sweet milk?

The first step toward true solidarity is accepting our human poverty. It is hard to keep one's heart open to the enormity of one's pain, and not rush back to human consolation. And why? Why not run to our brothers and sisters? We are meant to be human, to be in communion. What strange disorder possesses the solitary to seek a solidarity that cannot be seen, touched, or affirmed?[14]

13. Theophane Boyd, "The Monk Whose Face Was Red," *Tales of a Magic Monastery* (New York, Continuum, 1982) 27.

14. Barbara Erakko Taylor, *Silent Dwellers: Embracing the Solitary Life* (New York, Continuum, 1999) 65.

5. The Great Tribe of Hermits and Hermit-Types

Who are models of the solitary way? St. Seraphim of Sarov,[15] perhaps the greatest saint of modern Russia and hermit monk who lived in the woods near the Sarovka River, became a person resplendent with the radiance of the Holy Spirit. St. Seraphim and his pet bear! He initiated his hermitage in the woods by praying continually while kneeling on a stone for a thousand days and nights. People gradually recognized him as a healer, wonder-worker, and great counselor of souls. After robbers had attacked him, his abbot asked Seraphim to return to the monastery. Soon recognizing Seraphim's extraordinary gifts, the abbot told him that he must "never close the door of his cell" because his gifts of prayer and discernment were meant for others. Seraphim tried to help all who came to him. Certainly there must have been some asceticism in that. Was Seraphim less a hermit with such ministry, or was his heart so given to God in continual prayer that, alone or in community, he was still "alone with God?"

Solanus Casey, a Capuchin friar who died in 1957, was a hermit of sorts. He was not a monk, but a Franciscan of the Capuchin tradition—a sort of monkish friar. A farm kid from Wisconsin, Solanus barely made it to the priesthood. He found languages very difficult; German and Latin almost did him in. So he was ordained a priest *simplex*, allowed to celebrate Mass but not to preach. A humble servant in his order, he was assigned for years to be the porter (gatekeeper, welcomer). His service was hospitality and extraordinary prayer. His "radiance" was like Seraphim's, a century earlier. Solanus found his desert within his community and daily task—a true wild bird with God in the Center.

Staretz Siloan the Athonite, spiritual father of Fr. Sophrony who founded a monastery in England, was once the director of two thousand employees on Mount Athos, and did so with a hermit's heart. "When the tribes go up to Jerusalem," reads Psalm 121. When the tribes of hermits go up, one can imagine an odd, ragtag, joyous band: Aelred of Rievaulx' sister, a recluse who, when she prayed, "held the whole world in her arms"; Julian of Norwich and her cat; Solanus and Seraphim; Robert Lax and St. Sabas of Palestine; Thoreau and St. Romuald; Gratian the legalist, arm in arm with a holy fool who lived saintly anarchy. One thinks of Hugh of Lincoln, a Carthusian who loved his cell at La Grand Chartreuse, but consecrated bishop of Lincoln and

---

15. There are several biographies of St. Seraphim by Irina Gorainov, Lazarus Moore, and Valentine Zander. See, for example, Valentine Zander, *St. Seraphim of Sarov* (Crestwood, N.Y., St. Vladimir's Seminary Press, 1975). Also, more recently, Harry M. Boosalis, *The Joy of the Holy Spirit: Saint Seraphim of Sarov and Orthodox Spiritual Life* (St. Tikhon, Pa., St Tikhon's Seminary Press, 1993).

whose funeral cortege spread for miles because he was so well loved. One could go on with the imaginative procession.

The ecological crisis has created concern about the disappearance of entire species. For years I taught students at the Institute of Religious Formation at St. Louis University, a program that trained formation directors from around the world. Each year one met a panoply of charisms and traditions, members of ancient venerable orders and newly founded institutes, canons, friars, Daughters of Charity, social activists and hospitallers, monks and anti-monks (an interesting tension). It was a kind of spiritual zoo, a plethora of spiritual life forms, and a precious treasure trove of experience in the Church. May they all not only survive, but also flourish! Certainly the Camaldolese, a small family within the Benedictine Order, is a thousand-year-old "wisdom gene," about the eremitical experience, as it were. Merton remains a great model for our times—a unique monk, perhaps, sometimes summarily dismissed and frowned upon by "official" institutional types. Yet he worked his way through his personal maze and emerged with a sense of his own "eremitical nonsense," an ego-trap, into a true solitude of honesty and spiritual poverty. The following poem, written in a time of arrival at excruciating inner honesty, expresses Merton's greater readiness for true solitude:

> When in the soul of the serene disciple
> With no more Fathers to imitate
> Poverty is a success,
> It is a small thing to say the roof is gone:
> He has not even a house.
>
> Stars, as well as friends,
> Are angry with the noble ruin.
> Saints depart in several directions.
>
> Be still:
> There is no longer any need of comment.
>
> It was a lucky wind
> That blew away his halo with his cares,
> A lucky sea that drowned his reputation.
>
> Here you will find
> Neither a proverb nor a memorandum.
>
> There are no ways,
> No methods to admire
> Where poverty is no achievement.
> His god lives in his emptiness like an affliction.
>
> What choice remains?
> Well, to be ordinary is not a choice:

It is the usual freedom
Of men without visions.[16]

In his journal of April 14, 1996, Merton put it very well: "One thing has suddenly hit me—that nothing counts except love and that a solitude that is not simply the wide-openness of love and freedom is nothing. Love and solitude are the ground of true maturity and freedom . . . true solitude embraces everything, for it is the fullness of love that rejects nothing and no one, is open to All."[17] This is a place beyond eremitical or cenobitical—contemplation or action—because the truth and humility of the empty Center embraces all.

Hermit is an "easy" label to use; finding true solitude before God is an immensely hard work. The monastic vocation is always at its very deepest level "solitary" because it means living for God alone. The classic emphasis in the tradition is to honor the cell as a special place of encounter with God in prayer. The word "monk" or "monastic" derives from the Greek *monos*, meaning one, alone, solitary, but it also (even St. Bernard saw the significance of etymology) means one, complete, integrated, a person who is "one." That reality can be found in the midst of the fray, so to speak. Come to think of it—if I may finish with a bit of whimsical irony—one of the best hermits I know is a traffic cop in the heart of New York City at the intersection of Fifth Avenue and 42nd Street.

16. Merton, *Collected Poems*, 279–80.
17. Thomas Merton, *Learning to Love: Exploring Solitude and Freedom (Journals of Thomas Merton)* (San Francisco, Harper, 1998) 168.

The Camaldolese in Dialogue: Ecumenical and Interfaith Themes in the History of the Camaldolese Benedictines

Thomas Matus and Robert Hale[1]

If one can speak of an "undivided Church"—as in, "the Church of the first four [or seven] ecumenical councils"—such a Church is the home of the Camaldolese monks and nuns, who look back beyond divided Christendom to their origins in the *Rule of Saint Benedict* (fifth to sixth centuries) and in the charismatic example of Saint Romuald (tenth to eleventh centuries). On the other hand, if we recognize that the history of Christianity is also a history of its divisions, beginning with the disciples at Corinth,[2] and continuing with the separation of the body of Christians from the Jewish people,[3] then we Camaldolese are challenged today as never before, in virtue of our historical origins, to become a unifying presence within the Church and among the various faiths that mingle in all the nations where we now live.

A contemplative life tends by its very nature to unity, and in this life the task of unification is both an ascetical practice and a spiritual goal. Prayer may begin with and include the chanting of many psalms and the reading of many sacred texts, but the inner thrust of monastic prayer is from the many to the one. St. Romuald found one, key word in Scripture (for him, it was Psalm 32/31:8, "I will instruct you and teach you the way you should go; I will counsel you with my eye upon you"), and from that moment "many mysteries of the Bible came clear to him . . . and the spiritual meaning of Scripture was no longer hidden from him[;] . . . his prayer went beyond words into a jubilation the human mind cannot

---

1. Thomas Matus is the principal author of this chapter; Robert Hale is the secondary author, whose contribution lies mainly in the footnotes.

2. Cf. 1 Corinthians 1:11-17.

3. Cf. Revelation 2:9.

comprehend."[4] Since among Christians (and often within other faiths as well) divisions have arisen largely over questions of names ("Apollos," "Cephas," etc.) and words (*homoousios, homoiousios,* etc.), the experience of God beyond names, words, and essences has conveyed on those who have had such experience a strong sense of unity and of their own responsibility for establishing unity.

Hence the "ecumenical" viewpoint expressed in the introductory paragraphs of our *Constitutions and Declarations* did not arise only, or primarily, from the Second Vatican Council; much less was it the fruit of a "modern" mentality; it was a natural outgrowth of our monastic life. As contemplatives, we see that "long before the coming of Christ, humanity's quest for the Absolute gave rise in various religious traditions to expressions of monastic life. The many different forms of monastic and ascetical life bear witness to the divine destiny of the human person and to the presence of the Spirit in the hearts of all who seek to know what is true and ultimately real."[5] We find ourselves in communion not only with fellow members of our Church but also with men and women who have practiced the ascetical-contemplative life in other spiritual traditions. And while "the whole world is aware of a new ecumenical climate which is creating or enhancing the conditions for dialogue among believers of the great living faiths," we Camaldolese look to our origins to find the ultimate motivations for our own ecumenical commitment: "the monastic community, adhering to the tradition of our [ancestors] of ages past and to their spiritual freedom, is ready to welcome all with sincere affection and to recognize the 'seeds of the Word' mysteriously present in all who seek the face of God."[6]

In the hospitable and ecumenical practice of monastic presence, we make no distinction of persons. "Christ himself is received" in every guest, of whatever church or faith or of no particular faith.[7] At the same time, we understand the need to differentiate the specifically ecumenical dialogue among Christians of various denominations from the wider dialogue with the Jewish people and other religious bodies and traditions. With all of

---

4. St. Peter Damian, *The Life of Blessed Romuald,* in Thomas Matus, *The Mystery of Romuald and the Five Brothers: Stories from the Benedictines and Camaldolese* (Big Sur, Hermitage Books, 1994) 222–23. Some have called St. Romuald "the last saint of the undivided Church," although the absence from the Catholic calendars of St. Symeon the New Theologian, who died five years (1022) before Romuald did, would seem to indicate a de facto division, at least between their respective followers (Niketas Stethatos and Peter Damian).

5. The Camaldolese Congregation of the Order of Saint Benedict, *Constitutions and Declarations to the Rule of Saint Benedict,* Introduction.

6. Camaldolese, *Constitutions,* no. 125.

7. Cf. *Rule of St. Benedict* 53.1.

them we share a certain basis for unity; with other Christians we share the same Lord, the same gospel, and the same baptism. Individual Camaldolese monks and nuns since Vatican Council II have dedicated themselves to studies that have made them specialists in one or the other form of dialogue, but all agree that dialogue in whatever direction enlarges the horizon of our relations with other faiths in general.

Our first ecumenical "specialist," in this sense, was certainly Blessed Ambrose [Ambrogio] Traversari (1386–1439), a central figure in the failed attempt, at the Council of Florence (1438–39), to reestablish eucharistic communion between the churches of Rome and Constantinople. To justify his interest in the Christian East, Ambrose could invoke the memory of St. Romuald's earliest disciples, chief among them St. Bruno-Boniface of Querfurt. St. Peter Damian identified Bruno-Boniface's pagan interlocutor as "king of the Russians," and although this identification was historically erroneous, the reference to "Russia" was enough to suggest that Romuald's spiritual progeny ought to look to the East. Toward the end of the nineteenth century, with the rediscovery of Bruno's authentic writings, the Camaldolese learned that he was a friend and a guest of Saint Vladimir, king of the Rus' of Kiev, and a preacher of the gospel to the pagan Prussians, enemies of Vladimir and the Kievan Christians.[8] The disciples of Romuald, missionaries in Poland, "Russia," and Hungary, were in full communion with missionaries sent from Constantinople, and in no way did they work in competition with them. This sense of a shared faith and a common vocation survived among the Romualdian monks and hermits even after Rome and Constantinople excommunicated each other, a half-century later.

Another connection with the Christian East can be seen in the physical structure of the Holy Hermitage of Camaldoli. It escapes no one today that the model of the *eremo*—small cottages clustered around a church and a common building for meetings and meals—is that of early Palestinian hermit colonies, and this connection was equally apparent in St. Romuald's time. Although Romuald almost certainly did not visit the *lavras* on Athos, in Palestine, or in southern Italy, he may well have met (or heard of) monks from there, who circulated freely in Italy and elsewhere in the West, including Romuald's family properties on the Istrian peninsula (now part of Croatia). But well before the founding of the *Sacro Eremo*, monastics who read and practiced the *Rule of St. Benedict* learned to refer to St. Basil of Caesarea as "our holy father Basil" and to study the "*Conferences, Institutes* and *Lives of the fathers*," that is, the writings of John Cassian (who traveled widely among the Christian monks of Palestine and Egypt) and

8. Cf. Quotations from Bruno-Boniface's correspondence in Matus, *Mystery*, 60.

the lives and sayings of the "fathers and mothers" of the Egyptian desert.[9] St. Romuald saw nothing better for his own disciples than to recommend these same readings.[10]

Returning to Ambrose Traversari, we find that the first Camaldolese ecumenical "specialist" was also a typical monastic "generalist." His activity as translator of Greek patristic texts into Latin shows nothing of the academic "publish-or-perish" syndrome; these texts were part of his initiation into monastic life, and he translated the Greek texts as he encountered them in his reading.[11] Only one secular work received his attention: *The Lives of the Philosophers* by Diogenes Laertius. At the insistence of friends he did it into Latin, using spare moments of time between the reading of one patristic work and the translating of another. While he considered it only a duty of friendship, his reluctant contribution to the study of the ancient philosophers anticipated the founding of the Platonic Academy. It should be remembered that the Academy's first publication, issued at the behest of Cosimo de' Medici, was Christopher Landino's translation of the *Corpus Hermeticum*, a collection of philosophical speculations dating from the first centuries of the common era but then believed to be of ancient Egyptian origin. Hence it could be said that Blessed Ambrose opened the way to interreligious studies as well.[12]

9. Cf. *RB* 73.5.

10. Cf. St. Bruno-Boniface of Querfurt, *Life of the Five Brothers*, ch. 2, in Matus, *Mystery*, 87. On the reading of the monastic literature of Eastern Churches at Camaldoli, Fonte Avellana, and other communities under St. Romuald's patronage, see M. Elena Magheri Cataluccio and A. Ugo Fossa, *Biblioteca e cultura a Camaldoli* (Rome, Editrice Anselmiana, 1979). In recent years, Byzantine-style icons have come to occupy a significant place in the churches of Camaldoli, San Gregorio, and New Camaldoli, and also in the Camaldolese nuns' convents in Rome and in Windsor, N.Y. Another important component of Eastern spirituality, the Jesus Prayer, has become a key practice of many Camaldolese monks and nuns. The American Camaldolese have been guided in this practice by Bishop Kallistos Ware, who has given several conferences on the Jesus Prayer to the monks at New Camaldoli.

11. Cf. Costanzo Somigli and Tommaso Bargellini, *Ambrogio Traversari monaco camaldolese: La figura e la dottrina monastica* (Bologna, Edizioni Dehoniane Bologna, Edizioni Camaldoli, 1986) 211–58. See also Costanzo Somigli, *Un Amico dei Greci: Ambrogio Traversari* (Camaldoli, Edizioni Camaldoli, 1964), and Charles Stinger, *Humanism and the Church Fathers: Ambrogio Traversari* (Albany, SUNY Press, 1977), especially chapter V: "Patristics and Union of the Greek and Latin Churches." Stinger notes that in the dialogue with the Eastern Churches leading up to the Council of Florence, Traversari's thorough "knowledge of Greek and his long years of study of the Fathers and the early Ecumenical Councils proved invaluable both for the theological discussions and in establishing personal rapport with members of the Greek contingent. From the mid-1420s Traversari had been an advocate of union between the Latin and Greek Churches. The resuscitation of patristic antiquity implied for him the re-establishment of the ecumenical unity which animated the first centuries of Christianity," 205–06.

12. Cf. Somigli and Bargellini, *Ambrogio*, 33–34.

A younger contemporary of Traversari also merits mention: Fra Mauro the mapmaker (for whom a moon crater was named) of our monastery of St. Michael in the lagoon of Venice.[13] He designed several large world maps (that did not include the Americas, as Columbus had yet to "discover" the lands beyond the Atlantic Ocean), one of which shows a world that is anything but "Eurocentric." Africa is at the top of the map; northern Europe is at the bottom. The Italian "boot" points upward, and the Mediterranean itself is but a small lake on the edge of the great landmass, dominated by Asia. These are the true proportions of the world, as Fra Mauro saw it, and his vision suggests a cultural openness that would one day lead to attitudes of dialogue toward the great Asian civilizations and their spiritual traditions.

As Renaissance evolved toward Reform in the sixteenth century, the Camaldolese Benedictines continued to be involved in the cultural and ecclesiastical ferment of the times. A Christian humanist of Venice, Thomas Giustiniani (1476–1528), entered the Holy Hermitage of Camaldoli, taking the name Paul. In spite of his fellow hermits' begging him to remain, Paul Giustiniani left the Tuscan *eremo* and initiated a new eremitical movement that he called "The Company of St. Romuald, *Societas eremitarum sancti Romualdi*," which after his death became the Congregation of the Camaldolese Hermits of Monte Corona.[14] Blessed Paul's reform reflected, on the Roman Catholic side, the spirit of austere simplicity that inspired the church reform of his contemporary, Ulrich Zwingli of Zurich (1484–1531), especially in the reduction of church ornamentation and ceremonies and the suppression of liturgical music. Doctrinally, Paul Giustiniani never deviated from the official teachings of the Roman See; yet he was one of the strongest Catholic proponents of precisely those reforms of Church practice that came to characterize Protestant Christianity. Writing to Pope Leo X, Blessed Paul advocated the translation of the Bible into the vernacular and the education of the laity in biblical and patristic spirituality, the celebration of liturgical rites in the language of the people, radical reform of the Roman Curia, the clergy, and the religious orders, etc.[15]

Paul Giustiniani also dreamed of sailing to the "Indies," which after the journeys of Columbus and Verrazano were understood to be the newly discovered lands across the Atlantic.[16] The dream of Camaldolese monks

13. Cf. A. Peters and S. Frigerio, *Dalle carte di Fra Mauro alla carta di Peters: La riscoperta del "nuovo mondo"* (Camaldoli, Edizioni Camaldoli, 1993).

14. Cf. Alberigo Pagnani, *Storia dei Benedettini Camaldolesi: Cenobiti, Eremiti, Monache ed Oblati* (Sassoferrato, Tipografia Garofo, 1949) 129–30; 185–90.

15. Paolo Giustiniani, *Lettera al Papa: Libellus ad Leonem X*, trans. Bianchini (Modena, Artioli Editore, 1995); see especially "Parte Quinta: Riforma della Chiesa."

16. Cf. Jean Leclercq, *Un humaniste ermite, le bienheureux Paul Giustiniani* (Rome, Istituto grafico Tiburino, 1951) 112.

and hermits settling in exotic (Far Eastern or Far Western) lands was never to be fulfilled before the twentieth century, but it was cultivated under the surface and emerged symbolically from time to time, as in the seventeenth-century frescoes in a corridor of the Camaldolese monastery of San Gregorio in Rome, representing peacocks, monkeys, palm trees, and other tropical flora and fauna. On the one hand, this imagery may signify no more than a vague attraction to the "missions" easily aroused in any Christian soul, but on the other hand, the gradual broadening of our Congregation's horizons indicates a basic availability to the idea of "inculturation" and consequently of dialogue with Far Eastern and Far Western cultures and spiritualities.

Another significant, although anonymous, source for Camaldolese openness to other church traditions and to the universal wisdom of humanity can be found in the "Metaphysical Meditations" or "Reflections on the Attributes of God," penned by an unnamed Camaldolese monk or nun of the eighteenth century.[17] What is most interesting is the author's abundant use of the *Corpus areopagiticum*, especially *De divinis nominibus* ("On the Divine Names") and frequent references to other Eastern Church writers (Gregory of Nazianzen, John Chrysostom, Theophylact, and others). His or her blending of apophatic mysticism with affective prayer—Indian thought would say: *jnana* with *bhakti*—make the work an interesting basis for comparison, not only with similar works of Byzantine and Russian mystics, but also with the writings of Sufi, Hindu, or Mahayana Buddhist contemplatives.

The nineteenth century saw a pope of our order: Gregory XVI, who reigned from 1831 to 1846.[18] This paradoxical papacy, to which a humble but extremely conservative Camaldolese monk had been unexpectedly called, furthered the expansion of the Catholic Church into new mission territories, especially in the Americas and Asia. Gregory founded the first diocese in California, Monterey, where today the monks of New Camaldoli Hermitage form one of the most ecumenically committed communities among American Benedictines. He also erected the vicariate apostolic in southern India that would eventually become the diocese of Tiruchirappalli, hosting the Christian ashram of Shantivanam, founded by Jules Monchanin, Henri Le Saux, and Bede Griffiths; the ashram is now affiliated with our Congregation. In the history of dialogue, Gregory XVI can

---

17. Anonimo Camaldolese, *Riflessioni sugli attributi di Dio* (Camaldoli, Edizioni Camaldoli, 1965). Precisely the purposeful anonymity of the writer justifies our overcoming prejudicial ascription to a person of male gender and suggesting, at least as a remote hypothesis, that the author was a learned nun, perhaps the abbess of one of our monasteries in Pisa.

18. Cf. Pagnani, *Storia*, 288–94.

perhaps be mentioned for his desire to promote "indigenous clergy" in the missions, a policy that would eventually favor openness to the incorporation of local culture and custom, hence of local religious traditions, into the life of the Church.

In the twentieth century, the two outstanding Camaldolese monks in ecumenical interfaith dialogue were Bede Griffiths (1906–93) and Cyprian Vagaggini (1909–99). Both had made their monastic profession in other Congregations of the Order of St. Benedict and joined the community of Camaldoli after years of dedicated service to dialogue, Griffiths chiefly with Hinduism and Vagaggini with the Orthodox Churches. Shortly after his ordination and the completion of two doctoral dissertations, Vagaggini's monastery (St. Andrew's of Brugge in Belgium) assigned him to Rome as rector of the Pontifical Greek College, which from its establishment by Pope Leo XIII offered hospitality and theological training not only to Eastern rite Catholics but also to Orthodox students (including the present Patriarch of Constantinople). Vagaggini's academic career continued at the Benedictine Athenaeum of Sant' Anselmo in Rome and at the Catholic University in Milan, but his most important service to the Church was as a *peritus* at the four sessions of the Second Vatican Council, where he made decisive contributions to the documents on liturgy (*Sacrosanctum Concilium*) and ecumenism (*Unitatis Redintegratio*). His major work, *Theological Dimensions of the Liturgy*,[19] itself contributed to the ecumenical dialogue, both because he cited the liturgical research of the Anglican scholar Gregory Dix, monk of Nashdom Abbey, and because the work has been an important source for the liturgical renewal in other Christian communions, especially among the Anglicans and the Reformed (see the monastery of Taizé, for example). Vagaggini ended his long life on the first day of the Octave of Prayer for Christian Unity, January 18, 1999.[20]

In 1980 Bede Griffiths brought to the Camaldolese Benedictines not only his quarter-century experience of Hindu-Christian dialogue in India, but also the nascent community of Saccidananda Ashram, Shantivanam, in Tamil Nadu, whose direction he had assumed from Henri Le Saux (known in India as Swami Abhishiktananda), cofounder of the ashram with Jules Monchanin. Shantivanam was and is a witness to dialogue and to the incorporation of all the riches of India's spiritual wisdom into a monastic life lived according to the gospel and the principles of the Benedictine

19. Cyprian Vagaggini, *Theological Dimensions of the Liturgy* (Collegeville, The Liturgical Press, 1976).

20. On Vagaggini, see the collective volume *Lex orandi lex credendi: Miscellanea in onore di p. Cipriano Vagaggini*, eds. Gerardo Békés and Giustino Farnedi (Roma, Editrice Anselmiana, 1980).

Rule. While not a theologian, Griffiths developed a coherent and convincing vision of the "universal wisdom" common to all religions, the basis for a unity that transcends their divisions.[21] His gentle character and wise understanding of the spiritual problems of contemporary humanity drew a great many persons of different denominations and faiths to Shantivanam, where the "Benedictine ashram" offered them a common ground for opening their minds both to Asia's great religious traditions and to the teachings and sacraments of Catholic Christianity.

Both Vagaggini and Griffiths (who knew and admired each other's work before they joined the Camaldolese) found in the Congregation a congenial home, in part because of the presence at Camaldoli of the monastic and patristic scholar Benedict Calati, who served as Prior General from 1969 to 1987. Although his extensive bibliography does not contain much that would be considered a direct contribution to ecumenical and interfaith dialogue,[22] the general thrust of his thought, solidly based in Holy Scripture, the writings of St. Gregory the Great, and those of other Church doctors of East and West, pointed in the direction indicated by the Second Vatican Council. Above all, he encouraged the younger monks of his own and other communities to prepare themselves theologically for the dialogue with the churches, the Jewish people, and the other world faiths.

As an instrument for furthering dialogue, the quarterly review of the Camaldolese Benedictines in Italy, *Vita Monastica*, has produced a rich bibliography of articles by Camaldolese monastics and other authors.[23] Among the latter we can name Johannes Cardinal Willebrands, A. M. Allchin, Thomas Provatachis, Traian Valdman, Valdo Vinay, Renzo Bertalot, Luigi Sartori, Thomas Berry, Jean Leclercq, Spencer Bonnel, O.H.C., and Bede Thomas Mudge, O.H.C. A frequent Camaldolese contributor to the review, who was also its editor-in-chief for a number of years, is Innocenzo Gargano, professor of patristic exegesis at the Pontifical Oriental Institute and consulter to the Vatican's Congregation for the Oriental Churches.[24]

---

21. Cf. Bede Griffiths, *Universal Wisdom: A Journey through the Sacred Wisdom of the World* (San Francisco, Harper, 1994). Another important work of his maturity was the only full Christian commentary on India's most popular sacred text, the *Bhagavad Gita:* Bede Griffiths, *River of Compassion* (Warwick, New York, Amity House, 1987).

22. See the anthology of his various essays and articles: Benedetto Calati, *Sapienza monastica: Saggi di storia, spiritualità e problemi monastici*, eds. Alessandra Cislaghi and Giordano Remondi, with an Introduction by Innocenzo Gargano (Roma, Studia Anselmiana, 1994).

23. Cf. *Vita Monastica* 52:209 (July–December 1998).

24. By Innocenzo Gargano, see: "Towards a Monastic Ecumenism," *Vita Monastica* 23 (1969) 98, 178–92. In 1971–72, after an extended visit to Greece and Mount Athos, where he made important contacts with Orthodox monks and Orthodox Church leaders and faithful, Gargano published in *Vita Monastica* "Letters from Greece," *VM* 25 (1971) 106,

In 1973 the Italian Secretariat for Ecumenical Activities established a Mixed Theological Group, with Catholic, Orthodox, and Protestant participation; Gargano was a key participant from the beginning. From 1972 *Vita Monastica* published a special annual issue dedicated entirely to the work of this theological group.

Robert Hale, former prior of New Camaldoli Hermitage in California, was instrumental in establishing bonds between the Camaldolese and the Anglican Communion, especially the covenant between the Camaldolese Benedictines and the Order of the Holy Cross, a Benedictine community in the Episcopal Church, the oldest and largest men's order among American Anglicans.[25] In 1977 the Camaldolese and Holy Cross launched the Fellowship of St. Gregory and St. Augustine, dedicated to the reunion in diversity of the Roman Catholic Church and the Anglican Communion. The Fellowship has sponsored numerous ecumenical activities, published a newsletter, "The Cross & Dove," and cosponsored several ecumenical pilgrimages to the Camaldolese houses in Italy, to Canterbury, and to Anglican monasteries in England. Other activities include "Benedictine Experience," a yearly ecumenical retreat that explores Benedictine spirituality not only through conferences, but also through the lived rhythm of liturgy, *lectio divina*, and work, characteristic of Benedictine life. The participants are mainly Anglican and Roman Catholic, and the leaders are frequently Camaldolese and Holy Cross monks.[26]

153; 26 (1972) 42ff; "On the spiritual/theological characteristics of Orthodoxy," *VM* 27 (1973) 5–37; "The Ministry of Spiritual Paternity in the Eastern Orthodox Tradition," *VM* 33 (1979) 59–87; "The Orthodox Church in the Ecumenical Movement," *VM* 35 (1981) 13–29; "Icons and the Word: Proposals for an Iconographic Theology," *VM* 43 (1989) 36–68. Gargano has also authored a number of books on monastic spirituality in Eastern and Western Churches, and on *lectio divina*.

25. According to Vatican II and the Agreed Statements of the Anglican/Roman Catholic theological commission, spiritual ecumenism is central to our dialogue, in which Roman Catholic and Anglican religious orders are called to play a special part. In obedience to this call, the Camaldolese and Holy Cross decided to draw up a formal Covenant of Friendship. This was ratified at Camaldoli during the Octave of Unity in 1977. The Covenant, which committed the two communities to mutual prayer, exchanges, study, and ecumenical ministry, continues in force to this day. See *New Life* (May 1977) 17: "Holy Cross and Camaldolese Join in a Covenant."

26. By Robert Hale, see: "Monks in Ecumenism," *VM* 32 (1978) 106–16; *Vita Monastica* also dedicated an entire issue to the Anglican//Roman Catholic dialogue at the level of spiritual, monastic ecumenism, edited by Hale, "La Comunione Anglicana: Chiesa ponte, Chiesa sorella," *VM* 134 (1978). Also by Hale: *Canterbury and Rome: Sister Churches*, with a Foreword by the Roman Catholic Bishop Alan Clark, of the International Anglican/Roman Catholic Commission, and with an Afterword by A. M. Allchin, then Canon of Canterbury Cathedral. The book was published simultaneously in the U.S.A. (Paulist Press) and in England (Darton, Longman & Todd) at the same time as the pope's visit to England in 1982.

In addition to Gargano, Hale and other Camaldolese Benedictines who have devoted years of study and practice to furthering ecumenical and interfaith relations, individual communities of our order have made a special commitment to one or the other form of dialogue. The motherhouse of the Camaldolese Congregation, Camaldoli in Tuscany, became aware of its calling to dialogue through the experience of certain epochal and tragic events of the twentieth century. One such event was World War II and the Holocaust of the Jews. Like some other religious during the war, the Camaldolese in Rome sheltered a number of Jewish men; the monks clothed them in their white habits to shield them from detection. Reflecting on this experience at the time of the Second Vatican Council, the monks of Camaldoli decided to host a yearly *Colloquio ebraico-cristiano*, which has become the most important annual event in Italy's Jewish-Christian dialogue. The *Foresteria di Camaldoli* has frequently hosted individuals and groups belonging to other faith traditions, and many of the retreats and seminars offered in the summer *Settimane di Camaldoli* program have an ecumenical and interfaith dimension.

With the opening of the Anglican Centre in Rome, a few blocks from the Camaldolese Monastery of San Gregorio, fruitful contacts were facilitated between Camaldolese monks and Anglican representatives.[27] It was from San Gregorio, established by Pope Gregory the Great in the sixth century (it became Camaldolese in the sixteenth century), that St. Gregory sent his prior Augustine and two groups of monks to England to renew Christian life there. Not only St. Augustine, the first archbishop of Canterbury, but also the four subsequent archbishops of Canterbury, the first archbishop of York, the first bishop of London, and the first bishop of Rochester were monks of San Gregorio. The Venerable Bede revered Gregory as "the apostle of the English"; for

---

27. The second director of the Anglican Centre, Dr. Harry Smythe, was invited to Camaldoli, where he gave conferences to the community regarding Anglicanism and the Anglican/Roman Catholic dialogue. He pointed out that the Anglican Communion has a particularly monastic spirit, because of the "Benedictine centuries" that so shaped Christianity in England, and because of the insistence upon continuity of the Anglican reformers. As the Anglican theologian John Macquarrie has noted, "Anglicanism has never considered itself to be a sect or denomination originating in the sixteenth century. It continues without a break the *Ecclesia Anglicana* founded by St. Augustine thirteen centuries or so ago": "What Still Separates Us from the Catholic Church? An Anglican Reply," in *Concilium* 6 (1970) 45. In the words of the Anglican bishop Stephen Neill, "The English Churchman regards himself as standing in the fullest fellowship and continuity with Augustine and Ninian and Patrick and Aiden and Cuthbert and perhaps most of all, that most typically Anglican of all ancient saints, the Venerable Bede": Stephen Neill, *Anglicanism* (Middlesex, Penguin, 1960) 419. It should be noted that all the saints named by Bishop Neill were monks. On the other hand, it is often the Anglican laity, including women, who most appreciate the monastic shape of their spirituality; see the writings of Esther de Waal, Norvene Vest, and others.

this reason the Monastery of San Gregorio is a place of pilgrimage for Anglicans as well as Roman Catholics. In recent years Pope John Paul II and the archbishops of Canterbury have visited San Gregorio to pray and to issue joint statements regarding the Anglican/Roman Catholic dialogue.

Shantivanam in India has been a dialogue center from its very beginning a half-century ago (1950); the intuition of its founders and its place in India have made it a community radically committed to spiritual exchange with Hinduism and India's other spiritual traditions.

The Camaldolese in the United States have benefited from the ecumenical contacts and friendships of their former prior and have conducted in-depth dialogues with the Anglican Communion and with other Christian churches and denominations. The guest and retreat facilities of New Camaldoli have always welcomed persons of other faiths, and many members of the community have had occasion to practice ecumenical and interfaith dialogue at the simplest and often most spiritual level.

The Camaldolese presence in Berkeley, California began in 1979 with the project of a "joint community" of Camaldolese Benedictines and Holy Cross (Anglican) monks at Incarnation Priory.[28] The Camaldolese participants in this ecumenical experiment later needed more space for their own ministry, and so they purchased a separate dwelling, now called Incarnation Monastery, but the two communities continue in close friendship and regularly exchange visits. A quite different, and very delicate, ecumenical ministry has been carried on in recent years by Joseph Wong of New Camaldoli, a native of Hong Kong, in his several trips to mainland China. There, through his teaching in seminaries and dialogue with Church leaders and faithful, he has contributed to the journey towards reconciliation of the Chinese "Patriotic Church" and the "underground Church" in communion with the Holy See. Together with his brothers in Big Sur and Italy, Wong organized and chaired an interreligious symposium at New Camaldoli (June 2000) involving representatives of Christian churches, Buddhist and Hindu monastic bodies, and the Taoist and Confucianist traditions of China.

In the United States, many of the Camaldolese oblates are Anglican. Indeed, the Camaldolese *Oblate Rule* was significantly influenced by the Holy Cross *Rule* for its Associates. But several other denominations, including Lutheran, Presbyterian, Baptist, etc., are represented in the American Camaldolese oblate family. As of this date (September 2000), more

---

28. Through its friendship with the Camaldolese, the Order of the Holy Cross decided to make explicit its own Benedictine character and nature on the occasion of its chapter in April 1980; see Adam McCoy, O.H.C., *Holy Cross: A Century of Anglican Monasticism* (Morehouse-Barlow, 1987) 231. See Robert Hale, "The Benedictine Spirit in Anglicanism" in *American Benedictine Review* 30 (1979) 226–48.

than 40 percent of the some 350 members of the American Camaldolese oblate family are non-Catholics.

Down through the centuries, the Camaldolese Benedictines have grown in their commitment to Christian ecumenism and interfaith dialogue. Since our whole charism can be summed up in terms of the New Testament theology of *koinonia*, it is not surprising that the advancing and deepening of Christian *koinonia* and interfaith fellowship has become a central ministry of the Camaldolese today.

The Camaldolese Oblate Program: History, Tradition, Charism

Jeffry Spencer and Michael Fish

From its earliest beginnings, monasticism has extended its influence beyond the confines of the cloister, not only through the ministry of hospitality—an especially vital aspect of the Benedictine tradition—but also more indirectly through the recognition, tacit if informal, of the "*monastic* dimension in every human life."[1] As contemporary culture increasingly distances us from the inner life, it becomes more difficult to perceive and acknowledge this vital aspect of our spiritual selfhood. In his *Blessed Simplicity*, Raimundo Panikkar asserts, "the monk is the expression of an archetype which is a constitutive dimension of human life. This archetype is a unique quality of each person."[2] In support of Panikkar, Randy Sweringen suggests, "the monastic impulse is widespread and not solely located in the professional religious. It may, in fact, reside in all people to a greater or lesser extent."[3]

Once those drawn to the contemplative life could respond to the "monastic impulse" in only one way. "In the past, if you wanted to be a mystic, you went into a monastery and you lived a very austere life and you separated yourself from the world. Today we believe that the mystical experience is open to everybody. We all have this capacity for God, deep in ourselves. It's buried in most people."[4] Today increasing numbers of men

1. *Oblate Rule of the Camaldolese Benedictine Monks* (Big Sur, New Camaldoli Publications and Tapes, n.d.) 1.
2. Quoted in Randy Sweringen, *The Camaldolese Benedictine Threefold Good: Seeds of Growth for the Christian People*. Unpublished M.A. Thesis (Berkeley, G.T.U., 1999) 94.
3. Sweringen, *Camaldolese*, 95, n. 7.
4. Bede Griffiths, quoted in Beatrice Bruteau, ed., *The Other Half of My Soul* (Wheaton, Illinois, Quest Books, 1996) 327.

and women whose vocation has not led them into monasteries or convents are encouraging the growth of "the monk within" by formally associating themselves with a community of monastics. A well-known example is the writer Kathleen Norris, who has described her experiences as a Benedictine oblate in a recent best-selling book.[5] And she is only one of the many individuals throughout the United States who have made similar commitments to monastic foundations.

The Camaldolese Benedictine oblate program in the United States is of comparatively recent origin; however, there is ample evidence of a vigorous and thriving lay movement associated with Camaldolese foundations in Italy from the time of the late Middle Ages.[6] Though throughout the centuries lay participation may have waxed and waned as the Congregation's development and mission changed, lay associates have remained historically a vital part of Camaldolese life. For a comparatively brief period in the mid-twentieth century, however, the oblate program was allowed to lapse at Camaldoli when Augustine Modotti, then oblate chaplain, left Camaldoli in order to attempt the establishment of an American Camaldolese foundation in the United States. After his departure, the monks reviewing the oblate program perceived it as having become too "devotional" and too "third order." So they gradually phased out the program, only to revive it some decades later. At present Camaldoli has a thriving oblate program.[7]

The American oblate program began at Incarnation Priory, an experimental Anglican/Roman Catholic monastery in Berkeley. Robert Hale, at that time co-prior at Incarnation, provided the impetus for the program and based much of its design on a flourishing program for "associates" of the Episcopal monks of the Order of the Holy Cross. He was careful to give the program a specifically monastic character, emphasizing liturgy, personal prayer and service. It was inaugurated in January 1984, at the beginning of Unity Week—underscoring its ecumenical emphasis from the start. The first oblates, received at Incarnation in August and October 1984, were members of the Fellowship of Saint Gregory and Saint Augustine, an Anglican/Roman Catholic ecumenical society. At first, New Camaldoli declined to participate in the program, fearing it could lead to a diminishment

5. Kathleen Norris, *The Cloister Walk* (New York, Riverhead, 1996).

6. Cf. Cecile Caby, *L'Érémitisme Rural au Monachisme Urbain. Les Camaldules en Italie à la fin du Moyen Âge* (Rome, École Française de Rome, 1999). Caby describes several diverse groups of individuals (*conversi, commissi, oblati*) who were linked to the monastery. These included benefactors, relatives, and "spiritual friends" who participated to varying degrees in the life of the monastery.

7. This information and the following concerning the origins of the oblate program at Incarnation Priory and New Camaldoli Hermitage derives from notes provided by Robert Hale, prior of New Camaldoli, 1988–2000.

of that foundation's eremitical emphasis. Several years later, when Robert Hale had been elected prior of the Hermitage, the monks at Big Sur revised their policy, and an oblate program was established there as well, with the chaplain chosen from among the monks in residence at New Camaldoli.

There are now over three hundred and fifty Camaldolese Benedictine oblates affiliated with the Hermitage at Big Sur and with the house in Berkeley (now called Incarnation Monastery), "roughly ten times the number of monks."[8] This number increases by about ten or twelve each year, and the present oblate chaplain at Big Sur receives, on average, at least two or three inquiries weekly.

Many of those inquiring cite the books of Thomas Merton as influential in their own spiritual development and identify with Merton's struggle to incorporate an eremitical dimension into his monastic vocation. Others, especially those who are from non-Catholic or non-Christian backgrounds, mention Bede Griffiths' radical ecumenism as a compelling model for their own spiritual growth. Still others are drawn to explore Camaldolese spirituality through their own experience as retreatants at New Camaldoli or Incarnation, or they hear by word of mouth about the oblate program.

Helping prospective oblates discern whether or not the Camaldolese Benedictine monastic tradition fits their personal spiritual needs, the oblate chaplain interviews them and points out the unique qualities that characterize Camaldolese Benedictine spirituality. He first outlines those elements that are broadly Benedictine: life in community and a commitment to continuing conversion within the context of traditional monastic vows, including that of stability. He emphasizes the commitment to hospitality, welcoming all who come to the monastery as though each were Christ himself. Of key importance in Benedictine spirituality is an approach to work that views any type of meaningful work as a form of prayer. After summarizing these elements, the chaplain imposes a metaphorical "grid" on this Benedictine foundation, emphasizing those aspects of Camaldolese spirituality that are its unique heritage from the tradition's founder, St. Romuald.

Living five hundred years after Benedict and influenced by eastern Byzantine traditions in his native Ravenna, Romuald sought a more flexible pattern of monastic life, one that was "idiorhythmic," adaptable to the differing needs of individual monks, and rejecting the more rigidly structured lifestyle of other Western monastic communities.[9] Joined to this

---

8. Sweringen, *Camaldolese*, 106.

9. Thomas Matus has observed that the combination of Benedict's *Rule* and Romuald's reforms led to the "flexibility and pluralism characteristic" of Camaldolese communities. This "heritage of monastic pluralism" is advantageous to the Congregation's ability to respond creatively and flexibly to today's culture. See Thomas Matus, *The Monastic Life of the Camaldolese Benedictines* (Big Sur, Hermitage Books, 1994) 12, 15.

flexibility was a concern for solitude that went beyond that defined by imposing periods of silence within the community to a solitude created through geography and residence, explicitly through individual hermitages grouped around a central church, thus combining the cenobitical and eremitical monastic modes. Moreover, these new foundations were usually small and quite simple—very different from the large, wealthy monasteries that flourished in Romuald's day.[10] Thomas Merton celebrates this return to St. Benedict's ideal: "It is probably not exaggerated that the Father of western monks would feel himself more at home in a simple mountain hermitage than in many a greater and more splendid monastery amid the cities of the plain."[11] Finally, Camaldolese Benedictines have, over the years, established a tradition of openness to other faiths and have accepted the encouragement of the Vatican to become involved in intercultural and interreligious dialogue.

In summarizing these aspects of Camaldolese Benedictine life, the oblate chaplain stresses that those who do not seek a highly structured rule, who appreciate that solitude is at the heart of what it means to be a Camaldolese Benedictine, who willingly embrace a lifestyle characterized by simplicity and hospitality, and who value ecumenism and work for tolerance and understanding among faiths probably will fit in well as oblates and benefit from sharing in the "supple and flexible"[12] spirit of Camaldolese life. Camaldolese Benedictine oblates are individuals who feel called to a deeper life of prayer and "experience a bond of friendship"[13] with the monastic community, sharing in its ancient spiritual tradition. Described in the *Rule* as "extended members of the Camaldolese Benedictine family," oblates benefit from the Congregation's idiorhythmic approach, which allows them to shape a balanced spirituality suited to their individual needs but informed by the *Rule of St. Benedict*, the Camaldolese *Constitutions*, and the *Oblate Rule*. All of these spiritual resources provide a context for the shaping of their daily lives within a harmonious rhythm of prayer, work, and service to others in their local church or the larger community. Oblates all promise to live by the *Oblate Rule*, adapted from the Camaldolese *Constitutions*, in a way that balances the obligations of the *Rule* with whatever secular commitments—professional or familial—inform their lives.

10. Peter-Damian Belisle points out "the fact that all these houses were rather small says something about the movement's spirituality" as this impetus was counter to the prevailing preference for "large, prosperous monasteries." See Belisle, *Primitive*, 418.

11. Thomas Merton, *The Silent Life* (New York, Farrar, 1957) 158.

12. Merton, *Silent*, 165.

13. *Oblate Rule*, 3.

Formal admission as an oblate occurs after a period of one year of study and prayer under the direction of the oblate chaplain. Those beginning their probationary period are provided with a list of books and tapes—most prepared by previous oblate chaplains Peter-Damian Belisle and John Powell—that are designed to help in their formation and familiarize them with Camaldolese history and spirituality. The *Oblate Rule* also provides detailed guidelines for various approaches to prayer. These include preeminently the frequent celebration of the Eucharist, so that the oblate's life becomes "a preparation for, and an extension of, the eucharistic action."[14] Oblates are recommended as well to incorporate the Liturgy of the Hours, at least Lauds and Vespers, into their daily prayers for the purpose of "the sanctification of the entire day."[15] Reflecting the Camaldolese emphasis on Scripture, *lectio divina* as "a method of approaching scripture in order to listen to the depths . . . hidden in the words of the text" is also urged as a "principal practice"[16] of the Congregation's spirituality. Finally, the practice of interior prayer morning and evening in an atmosphere of silence is recommended so that "prayer gradually becomes expansive," enhancing the awareness of "God's continual abiding presence."[17]

Within this general framework, however, allowance is made for the diversity of the oblates' lifestyles and background. While most oblates are lay Roman Catholics, some are priests or vowed religious; others, both clerical and lay, may come from Protestant, Jewish, or Buddhist traditions. Since affiliates come from throughout the United States as well as from Canada, Australia, New Zealand, South Africa, Saudi Arabia, and even China; not all are able to journey to California for a retreat, though a surprising number manage at least an annual visit. Whatever their lifestyle or religion, all strive to incorporate into their daily lives the Benedictine balance of work and prayer, and to encounter "God in silence and solitude," a "distinctive" part of the Camaldolese tradition.[18]

That tradition also guides the oblates by grounding them in the rich history of the Congregation. Besides studying that key document in monastic literature, the *Rule of St. Benedict*, oblates are encouraged to become familiar with the uniquely Camaldolese charisms through such sources as Peter-Damian Belisle's comprehensive overview tracing the historical development of Camaldolese Benedictine spirituality.[19] Relevant as well is

14. *Oblate Rule*, 6.
15. *Oblate Rule*, 7.
16. Ibid.
17. *Oblate Rule*, 9.
18. *Oblate Rule*, 10–11.
19. Peter-Damian Belisle, *Romualdian/Camaldolese Benedictine Spirituality*. Four audiotapes (Big Sur, Hermitage Books and Tapes, 1995).

Thomas Matus' translation of the eleventh-century sources for the life and work of St. Romuald, the Congregation's founder.[20] Within this small book is found St. Romuald's *Brief Rule* which encapsulates the goals of the monastic life:

> Sit in your cell as in paradise; put the whole world behind you and forget it; like a skilled angler on the lookout for a catch, keep a careful eye on your thoughts. The path you must follow is in the psalms—don't leave it. If you've come with a novice's enthusiasm and can't accomplish everything you want, take every chance you can find to sing the psalms in your heart and to understand them with your head; if your mind wanders as you read, don't give up but hurry back and try again. Above all realize that you are in God's presence; hold your heart there in wonder as if before your sovereign. Empty yourself completely; sit waiting, content with God's gift, like a little chick tasting and eating nothing but what its mother brings.[21]

The Camaldolese *Constitutions* have been praised for their "spirit of remarkable discretion and breadth of view" as well as for their "balance and sanity and supernatural good sense."[22] In the revised Article 4 of the Camaldolese *Constitutions* (1993) appears the following restatement of a foundational philosophy: "The characteristic element of the Camaldolese tradition is the unity of the monastic family in the threefold good of cœnobium, solitude and *evangelium paganorum* . . . " These terms, derived from St. Bruno-Boniface's *Life of the Five Brothers* (translated by Thomas Matus),[23] provide additional guidelines for monk and oblate alike. Examining the implications of these terms will further clarify the Camaldolese spirit and charisms and demonstrate their applicability to the lives of oblates as well as monks.

The first, cœnobium, refers both to "a style of [communal] life having spiritual value" and to "a place, namely a monastery."[24] Camaldolese oblates seek to add greater depth and commitment to their spiritual lives, and they find their ability to do so is enhanced by their affiliation with a single monastic community. Stability is a unique Benedictine charism, emphasizing the benefits derived from a life-long association with not simply a particular religious order but with a specific monastery within that order. Camaldolese oblates regard Big Sur's New Camaldoli Hermitage or Berkeley's Incarnation Monastery as their spiritual home, one to which they re-

20. Thomas Matus, *The Mystery of Romuald and the Five Brothers: Stories from the Benedictine and Camaldolese* (Big Sur, Hermitage Books, 1994).

21. Matus, *Mystery*, 158.

22. Merton, *Silent*, 155.

23. Matus, *Mystery*, 78–161.

24. Sweringen, *Camaldolese*, 11.

turn periodically for spiritual direction, retreat, or the opportunity to withdraw briefly from the distractions of their day-to-day lives and to be alone with God.

This aloneness with God leads to a consideration of the second aspect of the threefold good: solitude. Initially these two terms—cœnobium and solitude—may appear antithetical, but they are, in actuality, closely related. Romuald's conception of an "organized eremiticism"[25] provided the structure and discipline lacking in the life of the hermits of his day, envisioning, as it did, individual hermitages clustered around a central church where monks gathered daily for prayer. The "Introduction" to the Camaldolese *Constitutions* states, "The Camaldolese hermitage is the special fruit of St. Romuald's broad and varied monastic experience as reformer and founder. The hermitage retains aspects of cenobitic living, at the same time offering the possibility of greater solitude and freedom in the inner life . . ."[26] Complementariness, therefore, rather than antithesis is implied. In a letter to the chaplain, one oblate who shares this perception writes: "I am particularly drawn to the Camaldolese spiritual tradition because of its blend of the cenobitic and anchoritic monastic traditions. In some ways, it seems to me that the life of a layperson is similar. At least I see my spiritual life as having similar dimensions."[27] This balanced approach is symbolically displayed in the traditional Camaldolese design of two doves, one on either side of a central chalice, poised to drink from the same cup. This design is replicated on the oblate medallion.

Since solitude and silence are emphasized in the Camaldolese tradition, comparatively few group retreats are scheduled for oblates. Oblates and retreatants maintain their seclusion in individual hermitages, even taking their meals in private. While they are free to walk the public areas of the monastery grounds, to visit the bookstore or attend liturgical prayer in the church, they need not leave their cells unless they care to do so. Oblates meet in groups rather seldom, semi-annually in Los Angeles and San Francisco for one-day retreats with the oblate chaplain, and twice on their own. Many attend a weekend preached retreat, but only a few of these are offered annually. It is much more common for oblates to make private, relatively solitary retreats. The historic importance of solitude, which has "the Romualdian stamp on it," is much more emphasized than in most monastic spiritualities. It is not, however, a solitude devoid of the *koinonia* that is the mark of a community, joined in a "fellowship network of oblates, monks

25. Belisle, *Primitive*, 417.

26. Camaldolese, *Constitutions*, no. 2.

27. The anonymous quotations of oblates cited herein are taken from correspondence to the oblate chaplain and are used with permission.

and nuns." Indeed, "Romuald's aim from the beginning was to gather disparate elements into a shared solitude."[28]

While this focus on solitude is dominant in the writings attributed to St. Romuald and has continued to be stressed down to the present time, solitude does not imply a withdrawal from the corporate work of the Church. The demands of hospitality and the obligations of charity insure that neither monks nor oblates are absolved from an abiding concern for the needs of others.

Supporting cœnobium and solitude, and testifying to this communal obligation, the third good—*evangelium paganorum*—calls for a "radical witness for the gospel" that may take "a variety of forms."[29] While the term, as originally employed, implied the probability of the ultimate witness of martyrdom for monks who ventured into pagan territories, over the centuries it has been modified to cover a diversity of activities that contribute to human welfare. As the scope of missionary activity has lessened, the context for understanding and interpreting this third good has become broader and more inclusive. The work of evangelization is perceived as readily adaptable to the variety of vocations represented in the lives of Camaldolese oblates.

Camaldoli's current Prior General, Emanuele Bargellini, has asserted that *evangelium paganorum* does not signify a particular place.[30] Therefore, the radical witness for the gospel that is its impetus can be effectively realized outside the walls of the monastery as well as within them. Bargellini also makes clear that this third good is not to be understood solely as external evangelical activity, but must be as well the expression of the "interior dimension of the full love of Christ"[31] that inevitably finds its best expression in ministry.

As the oblate program continues to expand, so do the dimensions of ministry. The association of monks and oblates necessarily lead to a broader dissemination of Camaldolese spirituality through the experiences of ministry to which oblates feel called by virtue of their sharing in this ancient and fruitful monastic tradition. Just as the monk's spiritual growth involves a progressively deeper realization in his own life of the implications of the threefold good, so too can the oblate attain Christian maturity by following the same path. Some will find their greatest fulfillment in community and shared ministry. Others, drawn increasingly to contemplative prayer, will be

28. Belisle, *Romualdian*, tape 4. Thomas Merton has also stressed, "fraternal charity is by no means excluded from the eremitical life." See Merton, *Silent*, 161.

29. Sweringen, *Camaldolese*, 61.

30. Cited in Sweringen, *Camaldolese*, 88–89.

31. Sweringen, *Camaldolese*, 89.

called to solitude and a more interior ministry. Both paths of service extend and complement the evangelical dimension that is the culmination of the threefold good.

Oblates extend the charism of the monastic community into the larger society through their presence and interaction with others in home, parish, or workplace. They can thereby be described as objectifying—even incarnating—the third good in the world beyond the confines of the monastery. They can accomplish this evangelical mission in a number of ways:

- through the services they render in their various professions and occupations, such as doctor, nurse, attorney, or teacher;
- through the services they render, as part of the *Rule*, to their parish or local community;
- through a Benedictine approach to work as a form of prayer that shares in the creative and redemptive work of God;
- through a centered, contemplative way of life that offers an alternative response to the stress and pressures of twenty-first-century lifestyles.

Specific applications of these four points will illustrate the scope and diversity of the oblates' response to the evangelical dimension of their Camaldolese spirituality. One oblate's observations exemplify the first point's emphasis on the need to incorporate that spirituality into her approach to her profession as follows:

> For several years I had been feeling restless in my practice as a clinical psychologist. After over twenty years as a clinician, it had seemed to me that helping people build their egos and function "better" in this culture isn't always truly helpful to them. Sometimes traditional therapy fosters an emotional dependency and reinforces societal messages that are narcissistic, avaricious, acquisitive, and keep people pathologically self-centered and blaming others—especially their families—for their difficulties. The positive "strokes" from a therapist can be addictive and can keep people in a childlike state. . . . It has become more and more clear to me that many of the people I know and work with need a radical reorientation to life. They feel empty no matter how much praise and material possessions they have. The work I want to do is countercultural. The life I want to live personally and professionally must integrate my spirituality. I am on a path of discernment about how that might work.

Another oblate's "path of discernment" led him, over a ten-year period, from a workaholic existence as an academic, dominated by "success and hubris," to a countercultural grounding in the Gospels and the *Rule*.

> It is in these writings that my life has taken shape. . . . Whereas the gospels provide the message for life, the *Rule* gives me the tools for understanding

the message. Recognizing the combined power of the gospels and the *Rule* did not come in a flash of enlightenment. It appeared through years of hard work and dedication to my practice. Even so, in the ten years I have been following the *Rule.* . . I continue to fail daily in my attempt to live the message of the gospels. Nonetheless, it is the *Rule* that encourages me to start each day in hope of fulfilling the commandment that Christ left. I know that only through a simple and disciplined life, the basic doctrine of the *Rule*, will the message of the gospels become part of my daily routine. Living the oblate version of the *Rule* is only possible if one believes that there is nothing greater than God, or as St. Benedict says, preferring nothing to Christ. One has to believe that in God, all things are possible. When matched against God, all things of this world, money, publications, honors, awards, etc., are simply insignificant.

This self-perception of the oblate as countercultural is pervasive. Oblates recognize that their worldview and their relationships with others have been profoundly altered by the oblate experience. One oblate, an attorney, writes, "a life of prayer [has] made me a more sensitive listener, more aware of the inner needs and inner personalities of everyone with whom I come into contact, especially my clients." Another, a college professor, reflects on the strength he has been given "to bring the contemplative dimension" to his students' often stressful and hectic lives. He recounts being approached by both students and fellow faculty for "advice on how to bring more peace, stability and silence into their lives."

Many oblates' experiences reveal this kind of impact on others around them. It is often most obvious in the testimony of those oblates whose primary ministry extends to their parish or local community where the emphasis is explicitly on evangelization. One oblate on the staff of a large (four thousand families) California parish has as her primary responsibility directing the RCIA program, which prepares prospective adult converts for entrance into the Church. The use of Scripture-based catechesis and the introduction of catechumens and candidates to a wide variety of prayer experiences, both personal and liturgical, form the basis of her efforts. Working with an extensive team of parish volunteers, she has wielded the group into a cohesive and dedicated cadre that functions effectively to contribute to the vitality and vigor of parish life. The result is an ongoing and abundant infusion of well-prepared converts into the Church, many who subsequently take on leadership roles in the parish. Informal aspects of her ministry also reflect her oblate formation. She sponsors a Benedictine spirituality group that meets monthly, as well as a weekly meditation group for women.

Grounded in the Benedictine tradition of *labora* [work] as *ora* [prayer], another oblate writes, "With God's help I have tried to make work into prayer, or rather, I should say, God has made much of my work prayer, and will continue to do so as long as I do not interfere." A nurse supervisor, broadly experienced in overseeing her hospital's professional programs, has a similar approach to her work.

> As an oblate, I have come to know that God has some unique "work" for me to do, and that my mission is to fulfill God's purpose in my life in whatever situation I am in, whether it be relating to people at work, at home, in community, or in any circumstance in the passage of life. As I meet people, I deliberately . . . open myself to the gift they may have for me . . . to be a vessel for God's work in their lives as well.

This openness to others, whether encountered in the workplace or elsewhere, may well flow from the response to the call to hospitality that marks Camaldolese Benedictine spirituality. Oblates have been warmly accepted and welcomed into the family of New Camaldoli as brothers and sisters of the monastic community. In turn, they are called to go out and be sources of welcome and acceptance to others, especially to those others who are strangers, outsiders perceived as "alien." Oblates who respond to this call can be a bridge between the monastery and the world. They can also be the leaven in society for those who are excluded and rejected. As one oblate writes,

> I think the single most important concept the *Rule* helped me to understand is that we are all made in God's image. In the *Rule* this is translated in chapter 54—"The Reception of Guests." "All who arrive as guests are to be welcomed as Christ, for he is going to say, 'I was a stranger and you welcomed me.'" I sometimes forget that the homeless, the physically challenged, the mentally disabled, or most important to daily life, the co-worker who makes me miserable are also made in the image of God. Again, it is my daily practice of the *Rule* that teaches me that God is in each and every one of us, and that we are all important to God's plan.

The repercussions in the life of the oblate who embraces this call to a broader hospitality will be profound, resulting in a welcoming attitude to all in life, especially what is new and unfamiliar. A contemplative approach to life means accepting life as it comes. An oblate observes, "only by accepting the fact that I have little control of my life am I able to let go of my ego. . . . Having no assumption about God's will allows me to try and find God in the everyday and in everybody." This receptivity is very different for people who live in the world rather than in a monastery, but it is at the heart of contemplation. It also reflects a committed ecumenical attitude that respects religious and philosophical diversity.

The emphasis on ecumenism, so prominent in the history of the establishment of the oblate program in the United States, is also characteristic of contemporary Camaldolese spirituality both here and abroad. Monks at Camaldoli regularly schedule "theological and spiritual conferences and seminars open to the full range of contemporary cultures . . . engaging in ecumenism with other Christian bodies and dialogues with all faiths, especially with Judaism, Buddhism, and Hinduism."[32] Here in California, the close relationship with the Anglican monastic community in Berkeley and the activities of the aforementioned Four Winds Council at Big Sur are only two instances of how these communities zealously carry on the tradition of reaching out to those of other faiths in fraternal charity.

Because many Camaldolese oblates are not Roman Catholics, a shared ecumenical outlook is not only inevitable, but also warmly embraced. Appreciation and respect for other traditions are fostered by friendships formed among oblates from different backgrounds and religious affiliations. This viewpoint is inevitably reflected in their interactions with others in their own communities, helping to create greater tolerance and to lessen prejudice in the larger society.

Another traditional value that is also characteristic of contemporary Camaldolese spirituality is a heightened concern for the ecological health of our planet. Such ecological concerns are familiar to historians of Camaldoli who recall the eleventh-century monks who "formed the first Italian 'forestry code,'" legislating the conservation of what is now that area's extensive national park.[33] In this country the involvement of the Big Sur monks in the Four Winds Council echoes that concern today, as they, in association with other groups who occupy these beautiful but fragile coastal lands, work tirelessly to preserve them. Resident oblates especially have contributed to the enhancement of the monastic property, but even those whose visits to Big Sur are brief return home imbued with a deeper sensitivity to the needs of their environment and the responsible use of the planet's resources.

While Camaldolese Benedictine oblates share a spiritual tradition and are committed to many of the same values, they resist any description that pretends to be wholly inclusive. The celebration of diversity among them extends to almost every category and classification, including race, gender, age, profession, and lifestyle. Some live in community, and at present a group of oblates is exploring ways creatively to combine solitude with a communal lifestyle. The eremitical life has attracted a number of oblates

---

32. Salvatore Frigerio, *Camaldoli: Historical, Spiritual, and Artistic Notes.* First Eng. ed. trans. and rev. Thomas Matus (Camaldoli, Pazzini, 1997) 61.

33. See Frigerio for a history of the monks' rules for protecting the forest. Also see Giuseppe Cacciamani, *L'Antica Foresta di Camaldoli; Storia e Codice Forestale* (Camaldoli, Edizioni Camaldoli, 1965).

who are beginning to approach the Camaldolese for help. Initially Thomas Merton encouraged the Camaldolese in the United States to witness to this dimension of religious life, and perhaps one of Camaldoli's contributions in the future may be to facilitate this movement in the Church, sharing its thousand years of experience of living out the eremitical vocation. One oblate, a religious of another order, writes about the experience of living as a hermit, guided by the Camaldolese spirit:

> As a hermit, I have, of course, continued my close relationship with my own
> . . . community, and received their invaluable support. What I cannot find
> among them is a deep, experiential understanding of life in solitude. As a
> Camaldolese oblate I have found the missing piece. Just knowing others who
> are living a vowed contemplative life in solitude, in a communal setting, has
> been an ongoing confirmation of my call. Living alone I have the challenge
> of preserving a healthy balance in my life and of being consistently faithful
> to my commitment. . . . Being associated with a larger group that shares a
> call to contemplative solitude and faces similar challenges is extremely help-
> ful. Visiting the Hermitage every month, participating in the liturgy, talking
> with some of the monks, and simply being among others with a common
> vision renews my own commitment. Human relationship is essential in
> everyone's life, even in a hermit's life. There is a need to feel connected and
> supported, even a need to support others. That can be realized in so many
> ways, not the least of which is prayer. Being an oblate places one in the midst
> of a network of praying people and intensifies the realization that "we are
> one in Christ." That knowing of our unitive relationship with all is a foun-
> dation of the solitary life.

There are a "myriad ways [the] 'inner dimension of the full love of Christ' can be expressed."[34] Randy Sweringen points out that oblates will need "to personally discern their particular living arrangement and bal- ance" of the three goods of community, solitude and ministry.[35] Unity in diversity will continue to be the mark of Camaldolese spirituality as monk and oblate alike strive to achieve self-fulfillment in service to Christ.

The focus of this chapter has been the flow of life and charism from the Camaldolese monastic community to the oblates. In turn, the oblates have responded to the challenge of interpreting and applying the ideals of the threefold goods of community, solitude, and evangelization to fit their own circumstances. In their work situation, through their labor and prayer, sharing their gospel values, and persevering in the contemplative life in the marketplace, they continue the work of creation and redemption. Oblates who have experienced the hospitality of the monastic community have then

34. Sweringen, *Camaldolese*, 90, quoting Bargellini.
35. Sweringen, *Camaldolese*, 107.

gone forth to exercise this dimension of the charism in their own lives to whomever they encounter, extending the Camaldolese outreach in the world. However diverse their lifestyles, they are united in purpose.

> Oblate spirituality seeks above all else a loving union with God through a full, prayerful life: a life which is at the same time both deeply interior and outwardly expansive in love and service of neighbor. It is a spirituality which is particularly nurtured through solitude and silence as well as through warm community.[36]

36. *Oblate Rule,* 4

Concluding Remarks:
Camaldoli's Recent Journey and Its Prospects

Emanuele Bargellini, Prior General
Translated by Peter-Damian Belisle

Drawn up by a special study commission with the direct contribution of the entire Camaldolese Congregation during 1966–69 and approved by the General Chapter of 1969, the *Constitutions* of the Camaldolese Benedictines express decades worth of renewal undertaken by the Congregation. They followed a working model already begun by Vatican Council II: to involve community members as much as possible by encouraging their contributions and to overcome decisively the serious tensions of the '50s and '60s that had wounded mutual trust and fraternal communion.

The council's standards of renewal were a consistent and sure guide for drawing up the new text. Camaldolese sources could be reread under more precise historical and theological hermeneutical standards, and reinserted in their spiritual matrix formed by earlier patristic and monastic tradition. With its great pastoral documents and climate of openness and evangelical confidence toward the complex reality of the modern world, the council was a second point of reference. The phrase "Camaldoli, a community in dialogue" could summarize the energy animating the Congregation during the second half of the twentieth century. With its own roots and historical memory, the dialogue has ended up feeling the need to rethink the present and project itself into the future with the new spirit animating the Church.

From the sixteenth century down to our own days, the development of the hermitage/monastery dialectic has underlined an emblematic point of this journey, as though it were the problem par excellence of Camaldolese history. The hermitage/monastery relationship stands at the heart of Camaldolese monastic experience. Inherited by St. Romuald, mostly through ancient eastern monasticism, it expresses a constitutive tension of monastic life focused around two polarities: community/individual and unity/pluralism. Repeated tensions and ideological ruptures changed their traditional complementariness. The way of dealing with this knotty issue while drawing up the *Constitutions* represented a significant example of the long, painful, and patient dialogue with the Congregation's spiritual and historical roots, and among its members. The foundation laid in that decisive passage rendered possible further excavations of the problematic and the drafting of a definitive constitutional text in the 1993 General Chapter that is revealing itself susceptible to significant ongoing enrichment.[1] It is an authoritative text that orients the monk's journey, showing a precise layout for Camaldolese monastic identity, and also an open, dynamic text, since it is the whole spiritual and institutional foundation of the *Constitutions*.

The great conciliar documents *Dei Verbum, Lumen Gentium, Sacrosanctum Concilium, Unitatis Redintegratio* and *Gaudium et Spes*—together with all the sources of the tradition—have constituted the woof on which the spiritual and institutional horizon of the *Constitutions* has been restructured, as well as the daily life within Camaldolese communities and their relations with the local church and the various societies in which they exist.

A simple and participative communal lifestyle has taken shape—truly centered on the word of God in studies, communal and personal prayer (*lectio divina* and *collatio*), a profound restructuring of communal liturgy mindful of the community's needs and hospitality toward guests, and a decisive entrance into both an ecumenical dialogue and an interreligious dialogue (with particular reference to the Jewish-Christian dialogue). The general setup for initial formation of new members, as well as for ongoing formation of the community, also has a new foundation coherent with the general, open horizon stemming from the renewal.

With these *Constitutions*, then, began a new Camaldolese self-awareness of its own identity that has continued throughout successive decades the work of building up and interiorizing through the lived experience of the community. The *Constitutions* have continued to refashion their own features: some born of very different cultural and ecclesial contexts (U.S.A., India, Brazil, and Italy), others changed in composition, and still others

---

1. Article 3 reads: "The Camaldolese Congregation consists of hermitages and monasteries. The characteristic element of the Camaldolese tradition is the unity of the monastic family in the threefold good: communion/solitude/preaching the gospel (this would offer the threefold advantage: the community life, which is what novices want; golden solitude, for those who are mature and who thirst for the living God; and the preaching of the gospel to the pagans, for those who long to be freed from this life in order to be with Christ). Matus, *Mystery*, 95. This spiritual patrimony makes the Prior and community responsible for paying attention to individuals so that, as much as possible, the external form of life corresponds to the actual interior circumstances."

ended. The foundation of New Camaldoli Hermitage in Big Sur, California, has now existed over forty years (1958). It has established its own identity as a Camaldolese hermitage offering the opportunity for much solitude, but is also open to the cenobitical dimension (Incarnation Monastery in Berkeley, California) and to spiritual hospitality toward guests in the traditional Camaldolese model of the Benedictine mold. New Camaldoli is a new offering on the American monastic scene.

Thomas Merton had already caught a glimpse of it as he followed the pre-foundation phase 1953–56 with great personal interest. In a letter to Prior General Anselm Giabbani, he wrote enthusiastically, "I am convinced that the Church in America needs Camaldoli, needs the eremitical life . . ." (May 4, 1953).[2] Speaking of his possible personal role in the foundation, he observed, "But I need not tell you how deeply my heart is engaged in the project of a Camaldolese foundation in America, even though I may have no visible hope of ever having anything to do with it when it is made." Many pressures arising from within the Trappist Order and the Roman Curia, in fact, blocked his every attempt to shift to the Camaldolese in the United States. Faithful to his contemplative, eremitical ideal (even in his unreservedly embraced obedience), Merton wrote to Giabbani at last, "I pray that you consider me at least a hermit in spirit, a secret and hidden Camaldolese, a Camaldolese in God's eyes alone" (March 26, 1956).[3] From forty years' distance, the prospect for New Camaldoli Hermitage and Incarnation Monastery still remains a further refashioning of the Romualdian-Camaldolese charism in the contexts of the American Church and the multifaceted American society. Perhaps Merton's bold affirmation is even truer today than forty years ago: "I am convinced that the Church in America needs Camaldoli."

The process has also continued in Italy, experiencing intense phases of vitality and moments of crisis requiring new clarifications and deepening of the basic orientations to which the Camaldolese have remained faithful. New prospects and challenges have manifested themselves. The General Chapter of 1999 has singled out two images to express the inner tension in which the Camaldolese Congregation should persevere: a *building site* and *workshop* where monks and nuns are together painting the icon of St. Romuald for our time. Indeed, one of the more interesting aspects of our postconciliar journey has been the progressive renewal of fruitful collaboration and interaction between monks and nuns in various communities both inside and outside Italy.

2. Archives of Camaldoli.
3. Ibid.

The Camaldolese journey during these decades has constantly kept in mind two reference parameters among others: the ecclesiology of communion and the dynamic vision of reality particular to modern culture. These two elements have corresponded well on the cultural and theological levels with the acknowledged dynamism of the Romualdian-Camaldolese charism, its communal tension with the centrality of the person, and the flexibility of its institutional structures.

In this context, I am referring to some actual, present challenges that we seem destined by our tradition to confront. I refer particularly to two phenomena that are only seemingly distant from each other and are emerging more and more: the new "spontaneous eremitism" that is searching for an ecclesial space[4] and the new "urban cenobitism."[5] Both find it difficult to be "at home" in the traditional monastic institutions—including the Camaldolese—that have also expressed for centuries these two aspects of maturing monasticism and have certain experience of their own. It is not a question of confronting new competitors on a market already too weak. These two phenomena pose stinging questions in a sometimes confusing manner and express spiritual urgencies emerging from the torn fabric of our society and Church. It is true that before they are organized spaces, the cœnobium and hermitage are places of the Spirit and as such, places to cultivate in the depths of one's conscience.

But it is also true that, in order to live as human beings, our interior dimensions also need structures to define and sustain them. Traditions and monastic communities should let themselves question and share the fruit of their own experience in a dialogue between traditional monasticism and the new offshoots—each enriching the other. Just as it is not enough to have a long history behind one to be "rooted in living tradition," so it is not sufficient today simply to appear on the ecclesial scene in order to be "new." It is not enough to live in a venerable hermitage within a well-defined structure to "be a hermit." It is not enough to live in a city to be "urban" monks or nuns, capable of creative and prophetic dialogue in the modern world. The history of eremitical experience and Camaldolese urbanization from 1200 to 1330 has shown that, in order to be creative, changes of place require many other cultural and spiritual conditions.[6]

---

4. See, for example, the experience and witness of E. Romano, *A Way of Desert Spirituality—The Rule of Life of the Hermits of Bethlehem of the Heart of Jesus* (New York, Alba House, 1997).

5. Significant examples are the *Fraternités monastiques de Jérusalem* present in France, Italy, and other European countries.

6. See C. Caby, *De l'Érémitisme Rural au Monachisme Urbain. Les Camaldules en Italie à la fin du Moyen Âge* (Rome, École Française de Rome, 1999).

The hermitage and the city express two cultural and spiritual worlds, two paths, or better, two dimensions of each spiritual path. To rediscover them in a new way could place us in the position of interacting and collaborating in the fulfillment (maturation) of these two new needs of our time. Small but serious signs fixed in these directions already exist in Camaldolese communities. These are seeds worth our attention and support for strengthening the life of our Congregation and better qualifying its service to the Church and to men and women of our day. The past and future once again intersect with our present.

Our public document of the 1999 General Chapter's work affirms:

> Camaldolese identity reveals itself more than ever as a dynamic balance of various spiritual and structural elements in a fruitful tension: the conscious utilization of one's own experience united with a warm welcome of the other's; the inner search open to joining to the masculine and the feminine that exceptional charism that knows the unity of solitude and communion, rootedness and breathing universally, historical memory and an openness to the present and future, spiritual foundation and the richness of expression.

> Reflecting on a millennium of Camaldolese history, on the events of these last decades, and on the interior structure of the Camaldolese spiritual journey—well expressed symbolically in the *triplex bonum* of St. Bruno Boniface (Camaldolese, Constitutions, #3)—a very important given stands out: the tension between different polarities and the search for ever-delicate and moveable balances between them is a structural given of the Romualdian-Camaldolese monastic identity.[7]

Perhaps the course of these reflections has allowed us a glimpse of a certain real consistency to this affirmation and its timeliness. Such a perspective can convey vital energy to a little Congregation like the Camaldolese that lives, humbly and joyfully, the tension between a rich spiritual inheritance reaching back a long way and the inner attraction to an always greater truth and freedom that can only come from the Lord.

---

7. E. Bargellini, ed., *Camaldoli ieri e oggi—l'identità camaldolese nel nuovo millennio* (Camaldoli, Edizioni Camaldoli, 2000) 6.

Bibliography for the Study of Camaldolese History and Spirituality

Compiled by Peter-Damian Belisle

Abbaye de Saint Michel de Cuxa. *Cuxa*. Lyons: Lecuyer, 1984.

Acampora, Vincenzo. *Guide Historique-Artistique Illustré des Camaldules de Naples*. Naples: Lubrano, 1911.

Agnoletti, E. *San Sepolcro nel periodo degli abati (1012–1521)*. Sansepolcro, 1976.

Alberigo, Giuseppe. *Christian Unity; the Council of Ferrara-Florence, 1438/39–1989*. Leuven: University Press, 1991.

_____. *Les Conciles Œcumeniques*. 3 vols. Traduction par Jacques Mignon. Paris: du Cerf, 1994.

Allchin, A.M., ed. *Solitude and Communion*. Oxford: SLG Press, 1977.

Anon. "Il Beato Paolo Giustiniani; Breve profilo storico e spirituale del fondatore Della Congregazione degli Eremiti Camaldolesi di Monte Corona." *Vita Monastica* 205 (1997) 59–79.

_____. "Bibliografia su S. Pier Damiano (1950–1970)." *Studi su S. Pier Damiano* 5 (1970) xxi–xxxi.

_____. *Breve Guida Storica dell'Eremo di Fonte Avellana*. Castelbolognese: Grafica Artigiana, 1981.

_____. "Les Camaldules." *Revue Benedictine*. Maredsous, 1887, 356–63.

_____. *Cenni Storici del Sacro Eremo di Camaldoli*. Firenze, 1864.

_____. *De S. Joanne Laudensi . . . .* Antuerpiae: Vander Plassche, 1750.

_____. *Monte Rua: L'Eremo e gli Eremiti; Cenni di storia e di spiritualità*. Cadoneghe (Pd): Valentini, 1992.

_____. *L'Ordine Camaldolese*. Firenze, 1864.

_____. *Il Sacro Eremo di Camaldoli*. Genova: Marconi, 1956.

_____. *La Vita del Padre Don Emiliano, Eremita Recluso Camaldolese della Congregazione di Monte Corona*. Perugia: Carlo Baduel, 1792.

Anson, Peter F. *The Call of the Desert: the Solitary Life in the Christian Church*. London: SPCK, 1964.

Antonelli, A. "Il monastero di Santa Maria 'de Rotis' a Matelica." *Studia Picena* 54 (1989) 43–58.

Arcopinto, M. *Camaldoli di Napoli, Memorie Complete*. Napoli: D'Agostino, 1955.

Arrighi, Gino. "Un epistolario di Ambrogio Traversari (cod. 540 della Biblioteca Capitolare Feliniana di Lucca)." *Vita Monastica* 168–69 (1987) 146–53.

Arseni, Carlo. "Fonte Avellana e Cagli durante il priorato di S. Albertino." *Sant' Albertino e il Suo Tempo (XIII Secolo)*. Fonte Avellana, 1994, 311–36.

Asher, Charles. *The Contemplative Self.* Big Sur: Hermitage Publications, n.d.

Babb, Warren, trans., *Hucbald, Guido, and John on Music: Three Medieval Treatises.* New Haven: Yale University Press, 1978.

Baldelli-Cherubini, S. "I manoscritti della biblioteca fiorentina di Santa Maria degli Angeli attraverso i suoi inventari." *La Bibliofilia* 74 (1972) 9–47.

Barbieri, E. "La fortuna della 'Bibbia vulgarizata' di Nicolò Malerbi." *Aevum* 63 (1989) 419–500.

Bargellini, Emanuele. "Bibbia e spiritualità monastica." *Vita Monastica* 75 (1963) 179–92.

_____. *Camaldoli: a Community in Dialogue.* Camaldoli, 1993.

_____. *Camaldoli comunità in dialogo. La nuove Costituzioni monastiche del 1968–69 in dialogo con le proprie radici e con il Concilio Vaticano II.* Not yet published.

_____. "L'identità camaldolese davanti al nuovo millennio." *Camaldoli Ieri e Oggi; l'identità camaldolese nel nuovo millennio.* A.c. Emanuele Bargellini. Camaldoli: Edizioni Camaldoli, 2000, 7–27.

_____. "Camaldoli tra oriente e occidente." *Monaci e missione.* A.c. E. Farrugia e I. Gargano. Verucchio: Pazzini, 1999, 31–48.

_____. "Chiesa e vita monastica." *Vita Monastica* 79 (1964) 183–90.

_____. *La dimensione sabbatica dell'esistenza nella vita del monaco.* Camaldoli: Edizioni Camaldoli, 1998.

_____. "L'imitazione di Cristo nella tradizione monastica." *Vita Monastica* 83 (1965) 179–85.

_____. "Monachesimo e vita religiosa dal Concilio Vaticano II ad oggi: rinnovamento e prospettive." *Firmana* 15 (1997).

_____. "Oblati e Monaci: quale cammino per il futuro?" *Monaci E Oblati Camminare Insieme.* A.c. G. Tamburrino e G. Pirolo. Praglia: Scritti Monastici, 1997, 61–80.

_____. "La Preghiera dell'eremita: Solitudine o Comunione?" *Vita Monastica* 110–11 (1972) 178–99.

_____. "La Preghiera nella tradizione monastica." *Vita Monastica* 71 (1962) 176–85.

_____. "San Benedetto tra passato e presente." *Vita Monastica* 205 (1997) 39–58.

_____. Tommaso e Somigli, Costanzo. *Ambrogio Traversari Monaco camaldolese; la figura e la dottrina monastica.* Camaldoli: Edizioni Camaldoli, 1986.

Bartoletti, Domenico. *L'Eremo di Montecucco; la civiltà eremitica e monastica sull' Appennino dell'Alta Umbria.* Gubbio: Donati, 1987.

_____. Romualdo. *San Romualdo: Documenti e Studi Recognizione Sepolcro.* Fabriano, 1981.

_____. *San Romualdo: Vita Iconografica.* Camaldoli: Edizioni Camaldoli, 1984.

Basilio da Vicenza, Fra. *Sommario della Storia Eremitica Camaldolese; Eremo di San Bernardo in Gussago di Brescia.* Brescia, 1996.

Batteli, Guido. "Una dedica inedita di Ambrogio Traversari all'infante Don Pedro di Portogallo, Duca di Coimbra" *La Rinascità* II (1939) 613–16.

Belisle, Peter-Damian. *Camaldolese Artists*. Big Sur: Hermitage Tapes, 1995.

_____. "Il dialogo ecumenico nello spirito delle Beatitudini." *Presenza pastorale* 11 (1993) 61–72.

_____. "The *Hermit* Archetype Within the Monastic Spiritual Journey." *Word & Spirit: A Monastic Review* 15 (1993) 41–50.

_____. "Primitive Romualdian/Camaldolese Spirituality." *Cistercian Studies Quarterly* 31:3 (1996) 413–29.

_____. *Romualdian/Camaldolese Benedictine Spirituality*. Big Sur: Hermitage Tapes, 1995.

Bellosi, Luciano. "Da Spinello Aretino a Lorenzo Monaco." *Paragone Arte* 31 (1965) 18–43.

_____. "Lorenzo Monaco." *I Maestri del Colore*. Milano: Fratelli Fabbri, 1965.

Belogi, M. *Monte Giove un eremo camaldolese a Fano*. Fano, 1996.

Benvenuti Papi, A. and Pirillo, P. "'Lo Sermon de la Pazzarella.' Vallombrosani e Camaldolesi nella Valdorcia medievale." *La Val d'Orcia nel medioevo e nei primi secoli dell'età moderna*. A.c. A. Cortonesi. Roma: 1990, 59–82.

Berschin, Walter. *Greek Letters and the Latin Middle Ages from Jerome to Nicholas of Cusa*. Washington: The Catholic University of America Press, 1988.

Bianco, M. G. "La '*Vita Romualdi*' e la '*Vita Antonii*': motivi letterari tra continuità e innovazione." *Le Abbazie delle Marche, Storia e Arte (Italia Benedettina 12)*. Cesena: CSBI, 1992, 209–32.

Biblioteca Cardinale Gaetano Cicognani. *Studi su S. Pier Damiano*. Faenza: Lega, 1970.

Billi, Ildebrando. "La vocazione di S. Romualdo." *Camaldoli* 29 (1952) 51–56.

Biron, Reginald. *St. Pierre Damien (1007–1072)*. Paris: Lecoffre, 1930.

Blum, Owen J. "Alberic of Monte Cassino and a Letter of St. Peter Damian to Hildebrand." *Studi Gregoriani* 3 (1956) 291–98.

_____. "The Monitor of the Popes: St. Peter Damian." *Studi Gregoriani* 2 (1947) 459–76.

_____. *St. Peter Damian: His Teaching on the Spiritual Life*. Washington: The Catholic University of America Press, 1947.

Blumenthal, Uta-Renate. *The Investiture Controversy: Church and Monarchy from the Ninth to the Twelfth Century*. Philadelphia: University of Penn. Press, 1988.

Boaga, Emanuele. "La soppressione della Congregazione Avellanita e la sua unione con Camaldoli (1569)." *Fonte Avellana Nella Società Dei Secoli XV e XVI*. Fonte Avellana, 1980, 161–72.

Bonaventura di Fano. "Constitutiones (1328)." *Annales Camaldulenses* VI, App., col. 272–87.

Bordeaux, Paul. *Recherches historiques sur le Couvent des Camaldules de Grosbois a Yerres*. Fontenay-le-Comte, 1923.

Borghesi, B. "Memorie del Monastero Camaldolese di San Benedetto di Savignano." *Atti e Memorie della Regia Deputazione di Storia Patria per le Province di Romagna* 1 (1862) 1–56.

Boskovits, Miklos. "Su Don Silvestro, Don Simone e la *Scuola degli Angeli.*" Paragone 265 (1972) 35-61.

Bossi, Paolo e Ceratti, Alessandro. *Eremi camaldolesi in Italia: luoghi, architettura, spiritualità.* Milano: Gemelli, 1993.

Bottacioli, Pietro. *Pellegrini Sulle Strade di Romualdo e di Francesco.* Gubbio: GESP, 1999.

Bracci, N. *Memorie per servire alla storia dell'abbazia di S. Stefano di Cintoia o Castrum Cintoriae.* Pisa, 1855.

Brooke, Christopher N.L. The Medieval Idea of Marriage. Oxford: Clarendon, 1989.

Brown, Raphael. *St. Romuald's Brief Rule for Hermit Novices.* Big Sur: Hermitage Books, n.d.

Brucker, G. A. "Monasteries, Friaries and Nunneries in Quattrocento Florence." *Christianity and the Renaissance. Image and Religious Imagination in the Quattrocento.* Ed. Verdon. New York: SUNY, 1990, 41–62.

Brunetti, Manlio. *S. Albertino, Priore di Fonte Avellana (sec. XIII).* Fonte Avellana: Centro di Studi Avellaniti, 1994.

_____. "Caratteristiche strutturali ed ermeneutiche della nuova biografia di S. Albertino." *Sant'Albertino e il Suo Tempo (XIII Secolo).* Fonte Avellana, 1994, 295–310.

Bruni, B. "La chiesa ed il convento di Santa Maria degli Angeli in Bologna." *Strenna Storica Bolognese* 11 (1961) 59–90.

Bruno di Querfurt, Saint, e Pierre Damien, Saint. *Textes Primitifs Camaldules.* Trans. L. A. Lassus. Namur: Du Soleil Levant, 1962.

Bruno di Querfurt, Saint, *Vita dei Cinque Fratelli e Lettera a Re Enrico.* Trans. Bernardo Ignesti. Camaldoli: Edizioni Camaldoli, 1951.

_____. *Passio Sanctorum Benedicti et Johannis ac Sociorum Eorundem.* Ed. Wojciech Ketrzynski, in *Monumenta Poloniae Historica* VI, 388–428, Cracow, Polski, 1893.

Bruno-Boniface of Querfurt, Saint. *The Life of the Five Brothers.* Trans. Thomas Matus, in *The Mystery of Romuald and the Five Brothers.* Big Sur: Source Books/Hermitage Books, 1994.

Buffadini, Antonio. *Camaldoli nel Casentino in Fiamme; diario di Guerra . . . (Giugno-Settembre, 1944).* Arezzo: Barbera, 1946.

Bussinello, Albano. *Su la Rocca di Garda; Ricordo dell'Eremo di Garda.* Verona: Nigrizia, 1923.

Caby, Cécile. "Bernardino Gadolo ou les débuts de l'historiographie camaldule." *MEFRM* 109:1 (1997) 225–68.

_____. "Conversi, commissi, oblati et devoti: les laics dans les établissements camaldules (XIII–XVs.)" *Les mouvance laïques des orders religieux.* Saint-Étienne, 1996, 51–65.

_____. "Culte monastique et fortune humaniste: Ambrogio Traversari, *Vir illuster* de l'ordre camaldule." *MEFRM* 108 (1996) 321–54.

_____. "Du monastère à la cite. Le culte de saint Romuald à la fin du Moyen Âge." *Revue Mabillon* 6 (1995) 137–58.

_____. "Érémitisme et *inurbamento* dans l'ordre camaldule à la fin du Moyen Âge." *Médiévales* 28 (1995) 137–58.

_____. *De L'Érémitisme Rural au Monachisme Urbain: Les Camaldules en Italie à la fin du Moyen Âge.* Rome: École Française de Rome, 1999.

_____. "La sainteté féminine camaldule au moyen âge: autour de la b. Gherardesca de Pise." *Hagiographica* 1 (1994) 235–69.

Cacciamani, Giuseppe M. *L'Antica Foresta di Camaldoli; Storia e Codice Forestale.* Camaldoli: Edizioni Camaldoli, 1965.

_____. *Atlante Storico-Geografico Camaldolese con 23 tavole (secoli X–XX).* Camaldoli: Edizioni Camaldoli, 1963.

_____. "Camaldolesi" and "Camaldoli." *Dizionario degli Istituti della Perfezione* II, col. 1718–28.

_____. *Camaldoli, Citadella di Dio.* Roma: Edizioni Paoline, 1968.

_____. "Camaldoli e Fonte Avellana ai tempi di S. Bernardo." *Camaldoli* 34–35 (1953) 159–63.

_____. "Un falso nelle antiche Costituzioni del Sacro Eremo di Camaldoli." *Camaldoli* 33 (1953) 74–77.

_____. "Le fondazioni eremitiche e cenobitiche di S. Pier Damiani. Inizi della congregazione di S. Croce di Fonte Avellana." *Ravennatensia* V (1976) 5–33.

_____. *I Grandi Avellaniti.* Camaldoli: Edizioni Camaldoli, 1962.

_____. "Note storiche su la Scuola e il Museo dell'abbazia camaldolese di Sant' Apollinare in Classe a Ravenna." *Ravennatensia* II (1971) 397–421.

_____. "La povertà nell'insegnamento di S. Romualdo." *Vita Monastica* 87 (1966) 206–16.

_____. "La Reclusion dans l'Ordre Camaldule." *Revue d'Ascétique et de Mystique* 151 (1962) 137–54, 273–87.

_____. *Reclusion in the Camaldolese Order.* Big Sur: Hermitage Books, n.d.

_____. *La Reclusione presso L'Ordine Camaldolese.* Camaldoli: Edizioni Camaldoli, 1960.

_____. *Storia del Conclave di Papa Gregorio XVI (15 decembre, 1830–2 febbraio, 1831).* Fano: Edizioni Camaldoli, 1960.

_____. "Gli studi umanistici nel pensiero di Ambrogio Traversari." *Ravennatensia* III (1972) 377–96.

_____. *Un contributo alle celebrazione in onore del Beato Angelo di Gualdo Tadino: note storiche con brevi osservazioni intorno all'abbazia camaldolese di San Benedetto, e al Beato Angelo.* Pergola: Edizioni Camaldoli, 1961.

Caciolli, L. "Codici di Giovanni Aurispa e di Ambrogio Traversari negli anni del Concilio di Firenze." *Firenze e il concilio del 1439.* A.c. P. Viti. Firenze, 1994, 599–647.

Calati, Benedetto. *Comunione e libertà; il monachesimo di S. Pier Damiani (sec. XI).* Camaldoli: Edizioni Camaldoli, 1995.

_____. "Dalla *lectio* alla *meditatio*; la tradizione benedettina fino a Ludovico Barbo." *Riforma della Chiesa, Cultura e Spiritualità nel Quattrocento Veneto (Italia Benedettina 6).* Cesena, 1984, 45–58.

_____. "Il *De Perfectione monachorum* di S. Pier Damiano e il contributo di Pomposa alla riforma monastica del sec. XI." *Analecta Pomposiana* I (1965) 21–36.

_____. "Fonte Avellana da Eremo a Cenobio." *Sant'Albertino e il Suo Tempo (XIII Secolo)*. Fonte Avellana, 1994, 13–23.

_____. "Pierre Damien." *Dictionnaire de Spiritualité* XII, col. 1551–74.

_____. *Il Primato dell'Amore*. Parma: Edizioni Camaldoli, 1989.

_____. "Rodolphe (bienheureux)." *Dictionnaire de spiritualité* XIII, Paris, 1988, col. 843–46.

_____. *Sapienza Monastica; saggi di storia, spiritualità e problemi monastici*. A.c. di Allesandra Cislaghi e Giordano Remondi. Roma: Studia Anselmiana, 1994.

_____. "La spiritualità camaldolese nel periodo della Riforma." *Eremiti e Pastori della Riforma Cattolica nell'Italia del'500*. Fonte Avellana, 1983, 181–98.

_____. "La spiritualità del Quattrocento e la tradizione camaldolese." *Ambrogio Traversari nel VI Centenario della Nascita*. Firenze, 1988, 27–48.

_____. "Spiritualità monastica." *Vita Monastica* 56 (1959) 3–48.

_____. "Vita attiva e vita contemplativa . . . la tradizione patristica nella primitiva legislazione camaldolese." *Camaldoli* 6 (1952) 10–24, 83–90; 7 (1953) 48–57; 8(1954) 66–77.

_____ e Gargano, Innocenzo. "Introduzione Generale." *Opere di Pier Damiani*. I. A.c. G. I. Gargano e N. D'Acunto. Roma: Città Nuova, 2000, 7–41.

_____ e Leipold, Winfried. "Giustiniani, Paolo, beato." *Dizionari degli Istituti de Perfezione* IV, col. 1367–69.

Camaldolese Congregation of the Order of Saint Benedict. *Constitutions and Declarations . . .* Camaldoli, 1985.

_____. *Oblate Rule of the Camaldolese Benedictine Monks*. Big Sur: Hermitage Books, n.d.

Camaldolese Hermits of Monte Corona. *The Constitutions of the Congregation of the Camaldolese Hermits of Monte Corona*. Bloomingdale: Holy Family Hermitage, 1994.

_____. *Customs of the Congregation of the Camaldolese Hermits of Monte Corona*. Bloomingdale: Holy Family Hermitage, 1989.

Camaldoli Ieri e Oggi: l'identità camaldolese nel nuovo millennio. A.c. Emanuele Bargellini. Camaldoli: Edizioni Camaldoli, 2000.

Campana, Paolo. *L'Antica Abbazia dei Santi Ippolito e Lorenzo di Faenza; I Suoi Abbati e gli Abbati Generali Camaldolesi*. Faenza, 1987.

Cannata, Pietro e Tabacco, Giovanni. "Romualdo." *Bibliotheca Sanctorum* XI. Roma: Città Nuova, 1968, col. 365–84.

Capitani, Ovidio. "San Pier Damiani e l'istituto eremitico." *L'Eremitismo in Occidente Nei Secoli XI e XII*. Milano: SEVEP, 1965, 122–63.

Capogrossi, V. *L'Eremo delle Grotte di Cupramontana e i frati bianchi*. Ancona, 1963.

Castagnizza, Giovanni da. *Historia della vita de S. Romualdo, Padre e Fondatore dell'Ordine Camaldolese*. Firenze: Insegna della Stella, 1671.

Castelli, Patrizia. "*Lux Italiae*: Ambrogio Traversari Monaco Camaldolese; idee e imagini nel Quattrocento fiorentino." *La Colombaria* 47 (1982) 39–90.

_____. "Marmi policromi e bianchi screziati." *Ambrogio Traversari nel VI centenario della nascità*. Firenze, 1988, 211–24.

Cataluccio, M. Elena Magheri e Fossa, Ugo. *Biblioteca e Cultura a Camaldoli del Medioeva all'umanesimo*. Roma: Editrice Anselmiana, 1979.

Cavalli, Armando. *Vita di S. Pier Damiano*. Faenza, 1938.

Centro di Studi Avellaniti. *La Preparazione della Riforma Gregoriana e del Pontificato di Gregorio VII*. Fonte Avellana, 1985.

Ciampelli, Parisio. *Guida Storica Illustrata di Camaldoli e Sacro Eremo*. 3e. Bagno di Romagna: Vestrucci e Figlio, 1939.

_____. *Il trionfo della grazia divina nel cuore di D. Crocifissa Veraci, Religiosa professa della Congregazione Camaldolese nel Monastero di Pratovecchio in Casentino*. Bagno di Romana: Vestrucci, 1928.

Ciaranfi, Anna Maria. "Lorenzo Monaco Miniatore." *L'Arte* XXV (1932) 285–317, 379–99.

Ciardi Dupré Dal Poggetto, M. G. "Proposte per Don Bartolomo della Gatta 'miniatore singularissimo.'" *Miniatura* 2 (1989) 65–87.

Cinci, A. *La Badia dei Camaldolesi*. Volterra, 1884.

Congregation of Camaldolese Hermits of Monte Corona. *Program of Formation*. Frascati, 1994.

Congregazione Camaldolese dell'Ordine di San Benedetto. *Regola di S. Benedetto; Costituzioni e Dichiarazioni*. Camaldoli, 1985.

Conigliello, Lucilla. *Da Antiveduto della Gramatica a Venanzio L'Eremita; Nuovi dipinti caravaggeschi a Camaldoli*. Firenze: Franco Cantini, 1995.

Consortini, L. *La Badia dei SS. Giusti e Clemente presso Volterra. Notizie storiche e guida del tempio e del cenobio*. Lucca, 1915.

Constable, Giles. *Monks, Hermits and Crusaders in Medieval Europe*. London: Variorum, 1988.

Contardi, Emilio. "Camaldoli: Dalla Soppressione al Post-Concilio." unpub.

Corcoran, S. Donald. "Reflections on the Monastic Spiritual Journey." *Word and Spirit* 15 (1993) 12–28.

Cortesi, G. "L'abate Pietro Canneti bibliofilo e bibliografo (1659–1730)." *Felix Ravenna* 59 (1952) 31–80.

Costadoni, Anselmo. *Annales Camaldulenses Ordinis Sancti Benedicti*. 9v. Venezia, 1755–73.

_____. "Memorie della Vita di D. Giambenedetto Mittarelli abate e generale de'-Camaldolesi." *Nuova raccolta d'opuscoli scientifici e filologici* XXXIII. Venezia, 1779.

Cousin, Patrice. *Precîs d'Histoire Monastique*. Turnhout: Desclée, 1956.

Cowdrey, H.E.J. *The Cluniacs and the Gregorian Reform*. Oxford: Clarendon, 1970.

_____. *Pope Gregory VII 1073–1085*. Oxford: Clarendon, 1998.

Croce, Giuseppe M. "I Camaldolesi nell'Età Contemporanea—Declino, metamorfosi e rinascità di un movimento monastico (1830-1950)." *Il Monachesimo in Italia tra Vaticano I e Vaticano II (Italia Benedettina 15)* Cesena: CSBI, 1995, 87–142.

_____. "I Camaldolesi nel Settecento: tra la *rusticitas* degli eremiti e l'erudizione dei cenobiti." *Settecento Monastico Italiano (Italia Benedettina 9)*. Cesena: CSBI, 1990, 203–70.

_____. "Un courant eremitique à travers L'Europe Moderne: Les Congregations de Camaldules du XVI au XVIII Siècle." *Naissance et Fonctionnement des Reseaux Monastiques et Canoniaux*. Saint-Étienne: CERCOR, 1991.

_____. "Monaci ed Eremiti Camaldolesi in Italia dal Settecento all'Ottocento. Tra Soppressioni e Restaurazioni (1769–1830)." *Il Monachesimo Italiano dalle Riforme Illuministiche All'Unità Nazionale (1768–1870) (Italia Benedettina 11)*. Cesena: CSBI, 1992, 199–306.

_____. "La Nazione Napolitana degli Eremiti Camaldolesi di Monte Corona (1577–1866)." *Campania Sacra* 18/2 (1987) 175–252.

Crossara, Fulvio. *Le "Constitutiones" e le "Regulae de Vita Eremitica" del B. Rodolfo; Prima Legislazione Camaldolese nella Riforma Gregoriana*. Roma: S. Pio X, 1970.

_____. "Rodolfo, abate camaldolese, beato." *Bibliotheca Sanctorum* XI. Roma, 1968, col. 277–84.

Cuniberti, Nicolao Martino. *I Monasteri del Piemonte (Notizie storiche di circa 1300 Monasteri)*. Chieri: Bigliardi, 1970.

Cushing, Kathleen G. *Papacy and Law in the Gregorian Revolution: The Canonistic Work of Anselm of Lucca*. Oxford: Clarendon, 1998.

Czortek, A. *Un'abbazia, un comune: Sansepolcro nei secoli XI–XIII*. Città di Castello, 1997.

D'Acunto, Nicolangelo. "Linee di sviluppo della santità e dell'agiografia benedettina nelle Marche (secoli XI-XIV)." *Sant'Albertino e il Suo Tempo (XIII Secolo)*. Fonte Avellana, 1994, 153–75.

_____. "Riflessioni sulla tematica del lavoro nella vita e nell'opera di San Pier Damiani." *Il Lavoro nella Storia della Civiltà Occidentale* II. Fonte Avellana, 1993, 67–87.

Dal-Gal, Girolamo. *Nel Silenzio dell'Eremo; Il P. Don Mariano Da Fermo, Maggiore degli Eremiti di Monte Corona (1775–1854)*. Frascati, 1943.

D'Allerit, Odette. "Alle origini dell'Ordine Camaldolese. S. Michele di Cuxa." *Vita Monastica* 64 (1961) 31–43.

Dalla Torre, Paolo. "L'Opera Riformatrice ed Amministrativa di Gregorio XVI." *Gregorio XVI: Miscellanea Commemorativa* II, 29–121.

D'Ancona, P. "Don Simone camaldolese miniatore fiorentino dalla fine del sec. XIV." *La Bibliofilia* 16 (1914) 1–4.

Decarreaux, Jean. "Un Moine Helleniste et Diplomate: Ambroise Traversari." *Revue des Etudes Italiennes*. Nouvelle serié, IV (1957) 101–43.

Della Santa, Mansueto. "Aspetti della spiritualità romualdina." *Camaldoli* 39 (1954) 150–61.

_____. *Ricerche Sull'Idea Monastica di San Pier Damiano*. Camaldoli: Edizioni Camaldoli, 1961.

Del Migliore, F. L. "Monastero di S. Maria degli Angeli." *Firenze città nobilissima illustrata . . .* Firenze, 1684, 324–41.

De Luca, Giuseppe. "La storia della Pietà nell'Umanesimo: il Beato Paolo Giustiniani." *Letteratura di pietà a Venezia dal '300 al '600.* Firenze, 1963, 44–59.

De Marchi, A. "Identità di Giuliano Amidei miniatore." *Bollettino d'Arte* 93–94 (1995) 119–58.

De Vita, A. "Nuovi documenti sul pittore Don Bartolomeo Della Gatta." *Rivista d'arte* 8 (1917) 4–44.

Devoti, Luigi. *L'Eremo Tuscolano e la villa detta dei Fuiri.* Frascati, ATAF, 1981.

Di Meglio, Salvatore. "Testimonianze di fede dell'età umanistica." *Vita Monastica* 168–169 (1987) 112–41.

Di Nicola, A. "La soppressione dei monaci camaldolesi nell'Abruzzo Teramano." *Il monachesimo italiano dalle reforme illuministiche all'unità nazionale (1768–1870) (Italia Benedettina 11).* Cesena: CSBI, 1992, 307–26.

Dini-Traversari, Alessandro. *Ambrogio Traversari e I suoi tempi.* Firenze, 1912.

Domenicantonio, Francesco Di. "Schuster e Camaldoli: 1922–1925." *Benedictina* 27 (1980) 215–47.

_____. *Storia e spiritualità della Congregazione camaldolese degli Eremiti di Toscana dell'Unità d'Italia al Secondo Dopoguerra (1866–1951).* Roma, Tesi di laurea, 1978.

Donati, Giovanni Gualberto. *L'Ordine Camaldolese.* Arezzo: Edizioni Camaldoli, 1964.

_____. "Passaggio dal Cenobio al S. Eremo di Camaldoli; Rilievi sulla prima legislazione camaldolese (1080–1513)." *Vita Monastica* 74 (1963) 110–24.

_____. *Regime e organizzazione dei Camaldolesi dal 1080 al 1513. Note storico-giuridiche.* Tesi. Pisa, 1993.

_____. "San Romualdo e il suo Istituto in rapporto alla Confederazione Benedettina." *Vita Monastica* 72 (1963) 110–24.

Doyere, Pierre. "Eremitisme en Occident." *Dictionnaire de Spiritualité,* IV, col. 953–82.

Dressler, Fridolin. *Petrus Damiani; Leben und Werk.* Roma: Herder, 1954.

Eisenberg, Marvin. *Lorenzo Monaco.* Princeton: University Press, 1989.

_____. "Some Monastic and Liturgical Allusion in an Early Work of Lorenzo Monaco." *Monasticism and the Arts.* Ed. Verdon. Syracuse: SUNY, 1984, 271–90.

Gli Eremiti Camaldolesi di Toscana. *Guido d'Arezzo, Monaco ed eremita Camaldolese.* Prato: Giachetti, 1882.

L'Eremitismo in Occidente nei Secoli XI e XII. Miscellanea del Centro di Studi Medioevali IV. Milano: Società Editrice Vita e Pensiero, 1965.

Ernetti, Pellegrino. "La riforma musicale di Guido Monaco Pomposiano." *Analecta Pomposiana* I (1965) 130–41.

Faldon, Nilo. *Rua di Feletto.* Veneto: TIPSE, 1977.

Farulli, Gregorio, pseud. Niccolo Castrucci. *Vita del Beato Ambrogio Traversari da Portico di Romagna.* Lucca, 1722.

Filippetti, Bonifacio. "Appunti sulla fisionomia spirituale e giuridica della comunità camaldolese." *Vita Monastica* 102 (1970) 159–72.

_____. "Monachesimo integrale." *Vita Monastica* 74 (1963) 125–39.

Fisher, Duncan. "Liminality: The Vocation of the Church (II)—the Desert Image in Early Medieval Monasticism." *Cistercian Studies Quarterly* 25 (1990) 188–218.

Flîche, Augustin. *La Réforme Grégorienne.* 3v. Paris: Champion, 1924.

Font, François. *Histoire de L'Abbaye Royale de Saint-Michel de Cûxa.* Perpignan: Comet, 1881.

Fornaciari, Roberto. *Monachesimo-Missione-Martirio; Bruno-Bonifacio di Querfurt dall'Eremo del Pereo a Kiev.* Tesi. Roma: Gregorianum, 1994.

Fornasari, Giuseppe. *Medioevo riformato del secolo XI: Pier Damiani e Gregorio VII.* Napoli: Liguori, 1996.

_____. *"Pater Rationabilium Eremitarum:* tradizione agiografica e attualizzazione eremitica nella *Vita Beati Romualdi" Fonte Avellana nel Suo Millenario. 2. Idee, figure, luoghi.* Fonte Avellana, 1983, 25–103.

Fortunio, Agostino. *Historiarum Camaldulensium, libri tres.* Florentiae, 1575.

_____, pars posterior. Florentiae, 1579.

_____. "Vita Ambrosii Camaldulensium generalis Antistitis, & luculentissimi Interpretis Graeci." *Historiarum Camaldulensium, libri tres.* Florentiae, 1575, 321–400.

Foschi, U. "San Pietro in Vinvoli e la sua storia." *Bollettino economico della Camera Di Commercio di Ravenna* 17 (1962) 292–99.

_____. "La Badia di Santa Maria d'Urano in Bertinoro." *Studia Romagnoli* 15 (1964) 41–72.

Fossa, Ugo. "I Camaldolesi e il vescovo Guglielmino. *La Battaglia di Campaldino e La società toscana del'200.* Tavernelle Val di Pesa, 1994, 196–215.

_____. "Camaldolesi." *La Sostanza dell'Effimero; gli abiti degli Ordini religiosi in Occidente.* A.c. Giancarlo Rocca. Roma: Edizioni Paoline, 2000, 142–45.

_____. "La storiografia camaldolese sul Traversari dal Quattrocento al Settecento." *Ambrogio Traversari nel VI centenario della nascità.* Firenze, 1988, 121–46.

_____. "Una biografia inedita di Ambrogio Traversari in un codice della Biblioteca Comunale di Cortona." *Vita Monastica* 168–69 (1987) 142–45.

_____ e Cataluccio, M. Elena-Magheri. *Biblioteca e Cultura a Camaldoli del Medioevo all'Umanesimo.* Roma: Editrice Anselmiana, 1979.

Franceschi, Paolo. *Venezia, San Michele in Isola; guida Pratica Illustrata.* Venezia: Stamperia de Venezia, 1992.

Franke, Walter. *Romuald von Camaldoli und seine Reformatätigkeit zur Zeit Ottos III.* Berlin: Emil Ebering, 1913.

Frigerio, Salvatore. *Ambrogio Traversari, un monaco e un monastero nell'umanesimo fiorentino.* Camaldoli: Edizioni Camaldoli, 1988.

_____. *Camaldoli: Note Storiche, Spirituali, Artistiche.* Camaldoli: Edizioni Camaldoli, 1991.

_____. "L'Hodoeporicon di Ambrogio Traversari: un viaggio tra due epoche." Opuscoli di Primarno no. 33. Arezzo, 1987.

_____ e Peters, Arno. *Dalle carte di Fra Mauro alla carta di Peters; la riscoperta del 'nuovo mondo.'* Camaldoli: Edizioni Camaldoli, 1993.

Gain, B. "Ambroise Traversari (1386–1439) lecteur et traducteur de saint Basile." *Rivista di storia e letteratura religiosa* 21 (1985) 56–76.

Gargano, Innocenzo. "I camaldolesi e la teologia oggi." *Camaldoli Ieri e Oggi: l'identità camaldolese nel nuovo millennio.* A.c. Emanuele Bargellini. Camaldoli: Edizioni Camaldolese, 2000, 55–81.

_____. *Camaldolesi nella Spiritualità italiana del Novecento.* Roma: EDB, 2000.

_____. "Camaldoli e la vocazione ecumenica." *Vita Monastica* 152 (1983) 97–106.

_____. "Introduzione." *Sapienza Monastica: Saggi di Benedetto Calati.* Roma: Studia Anselmiana, 1994, 15–65.

_____. "Per un ecumenismo monastico." *Vita Monastica* 98 (1969) 178–92.

_____. "La Svolta di Camaldoli: Un punto nodale della spiritualità monastica in Italia." *Vita Monastica* 207 (1997) 3–84.

_____ e Calati, Benedetto. "Introduzione Generale." *Opere di Pier Damiani* I. A.c. G. I. Gargano e N. D'Acunto. Roma: Città Nuova, 2000, 7–41.

Garin, Eugenio. "Presentazione." *Hodoeporicon di Ambrogio Traversari.* Firenze: Le Monnier, 1985, vii–xii.

Gasparrini, Enrico Filippo. *Camminiamo Con La Croce.* Fano, 1987.

_____. *Paolo Tarcisio Generali.* Rimini: Ramberti, 1977.

Gentili, G. "L'antico scomparso eremo di S. Maria di Camaldoli presso Bologna." *Strenna Storica Bolognese* 14 (1964) 117–35.

Gerardo I. "Constitutiones Camaldulenses a 1279." *Annales Camaldulenses* VI, App., col. 240–55.

Ghini, Emanuela. *Oltre Ogni Limite; Nazarena monaca reclusa 1945–1990.* Monferrato: Edizioni Pemme, 1993.

Giabbani, Anselmo. *Camaldolesi; Le Figure più Espressive dell'ordine viste da S. Pier Damiano, Dante, Petrarca, ecc.* Camaldoli, 1944.

_____. *Catechismo Camaldolese seu Medulla Camaldulensis Doctrinae.* Camaldoli: Edizioni Camaldoli, 1951.

_____. *L'Eremo: Vita e Spiritualità Eremitica nel Monachesimo Camaldolese Primitivo.* Brescia: Morcelliana, 1945.

_____. *Menologio Camaldolese.* Roma: S. Gregorio al Celio, 1950.

_____. "Problemi dell'eremitismo." *Vita Monastica* 90 (1967) 137–46.

_____. "Profilo spirituale di Ambrogio Traversari." *Vita Monastica* 168–69 (1987) 19–29.

_____. "Spirito camaldolese." *Vita Monastica* 58 (1959) 99–106; 60 (1960) 21–31.

_____. "Lo spirito della regola di S. Benedetto e la vita monastico-eremitica secondo S. Pier Damiano." *Benedictina* I (1974) 135–56.

Gibelli, Alberto. *L'Antico monastero dei SS. Andrea e Gregorio al Clivio di Scauro sul Monte Celio; I suoi abbati, I castelli e le chiese dipendenti dal medisimo.* Faenza, 1892.

_____. *Memorie Storiche della Congregazione Camaldolese Posteriori agli Annali della stessa (1765–1873).*

_____. *Memorie Storiche ed Artistiche dell'Antichissima Chiesa Abbaziale dei SS. Andrea e Gregorio al Clivio di Scauro sul Monte Celio.* Roma, 1888.

_____. *Monografia dell'Antico Monastero di S. Croce di Fonte Avellana; I Suoi Priori ed Abbati*. Faenza, 1895.

Gigante, A. "A. Traversari interprete di Diogene Laerzio." *Ambrogio Traversari nel VI centenario della nascità*. Firenze, 1988, 367–459.

Gill, Joseph. *The Council of Florence*. Cambridge: University Press, 1959.

_____. *Personalities of the Council of Florence and other Essays*. New York: Barnes & Noble, 1964.

Giovanni di Lodi, S. *Vita di San Pier Damiani*. Roma: Città Nuova, 1993.

Giustiniani, Paolo, B. *Eremiticae vitae regula*. Camaldoli, 1516, abridged.

_____. *Preghiera e Perseveranza*. Monte Rua, 1983.

_____. *Regola Della Vita Eremitica*. Seregno: San Benedetto, 1996.

_____. *Regula Vitae Eremiticae*. Camaldoli, 1520.

_____. *Rule of the Hermit Life (1520)*. Bloomingdale: Holy Family Hermitage, n.d., unpub.

_____. *Secretum Meum Mihi, o dell'Amor di Dio*. Frascati, 1941.

_____. *Trattato dell'Ubbidienza*. Padova, 1753.

_____ e Quirini, Pietro. "Epistolicum Commercium." *Annales Camaldulenses* VI, App., col. 446–611.

_____. *Lettera Al Papa; Libellus ad Leonem X [1513]*. Trans. Geminiano Bianchini. Modena: Artioli, 1995.

_____. "Libellus ad Leonem X." *Annales Camaldulenses* VI, App., col. 612–719.

Giustiniani, Paul, Bx. "De l'Institution plus parfaite de la reclusion." *Collectanea Cisterciensia* 54 (1992) 85–97.

Gori, Rinaldo. "Ambrogio Traversari (nel V Centenario della sua morte)." *Pax* VIII-9 (1939) 1–39.

Gradenigo, G. A. "Notizie storiche della chiesa e monastero di San Giovanni Battista de' Camaldolesi in Cal Maggiore fuori Chioggia." *Nuova raccolta D'opuscoli scientifici e filologici*. A.c. A. Cologerà. Venezia, 1768.

Grandi, Guido. *Dissertationes Camaldulenses*. Lucca, 1707.

Gratian. *The Treatise on Laws*. Trans. Augustine Thompson. Washington: The Catholic University of America Press, 1993.

Griffiths, Bede. "The Significance of India for Camaldolese Monasticism." *The American Benedictine Review* 40:2 (1989) 138–41.

Gronau, H. D. "The Earliest Works of Lorenzo Monaco." *The Burlington Magazine* XCII (1950) 183–88, 217–22.

Gualdo Rosa, Lucia. "Leonardo Bruni, *l'Oratio in hypocritas* e i suoi difficili rapporti con Ambrogio Traversari." *Vita Monastica* 168–69 (1987) 89–111.

Gurerrini, P. "L'Eremo Camaldolese di Gussago." *Memorie storiche della diocesi di Brescia*. Serie Seconda. Brescia, 1931, 3–14.

Hale, Robert. "Camaldolese Spirituality." *The New Dictionary of Catholic Spirituality*. Collegeville: The Liturgical Press, 1993, 107–10.

_____. "Dimensione profetica della vita monastica." *Vita Monastica* 120–21 (1975) 40–74.

_____. "Fr. Cyprian Vagaggini, O.S.B. CAM." *The American Benedictine Review* 50:2 (1999) 214–15.

_____. "La *koinonia* aperta della vita monastica." *Vita Monastica* 126 (1976) 128–62.

_____. *Love on the Mountain: the Chronicle Journal of a Camaldolese Monk.* Big Sur: Source Books/Hermitage Books, 1999.

_____. "Monachesimo e urbanizzazione." *Vita Monastica* 98 (1969) 155–77.

_____. "Il monaco e il mondo." *Vita Monastica* 106 (1971) 182–92.

_____. "New Camaldoli Before the Monks: Some Data and References." Big Sur, 1989, unpub.

_____. "Some Notes about the Early Years of New Camaldoli." Big Sur, 1988, unpub.

_____. "Some Notes Regarding the Camaldolese Residence of Incarnation Priory, 1978–1988." unpub.

Hales, Edward Elton. *Pio Nono: A Study in European Politics and Religion in the Nineteenth Century.* New York: P. J. Kenedy, 1960.

_____. *Revolution and Papacy 1769–1846.* New York: Hanover House, 1960.

Hamilton, Bernard. "The City of Rome and the Eastern Churches in the Tenth Century." *Orientalia Cristiania Periodica* XXVII (1961) 5–26.

_____. "The Monastery of S. Alessio and the Religious and Intellectual Renaissance in Tenth-Century Rome." *Studies in Medieval and Renaissance History* II. Lincoln, Nebraska, 1965, 265–310.

_____. "The Monastic Revival in Tenth-Century Rome." *Studia Monastica* IV (1962) 35–68.

_____. "*Orientale Lumen et Magistra Latinitas*: Greek Influences on Western Monasticism (900–1100)." *Le Millénaire du Mont Athos, 963–1963. Etudes et Mélanges* I, Chevetogne, 1963, 181–216.

_____. "S. Pierre Damien et les mouvements monastiques de son temps." *Monastic Reform, Catharism and the Crusades.* London: Variorum, 1979.

Hiley, David. *Western Plainchant, a Handbook.* Oxford: Clarendon, 1993.

Holmes, George. *The Florentine Enlightenment 1400–1450.* Oxford: Clarendon, 1969.

Holy Cross Convent. *The Camaldolese Nuns.* Dallas, Texas, n.d.

Holy Family Hermitage. *Alone With God.* McConnelsville, Ohio: Holy Family Hermitage, 1960.

Howe, John. *Church Reform and Social Change in Eleventh-Century Italy: Dominic of Sora and His Patrons.* Philadelphia: University of Pennsylvania Press, 1997.

Huant, Ernest. *Othon III . . . La merveille du monde; Renovateur de l'"Universalisme Romain, Unificateur de l'Europe de l'An 1,000.* Paris: Editions Tequi, 1971.

Hunt, Noreen, ed. *Cluniac Monasticism in the Central Middle Ages.* Hamden, Conn.: Archon, 1971.

_____. *Cluny Under Saint Hugh 1049–1109.* Notre Dame: University Press, 1968.

Hyland, William Patrick. *John-Jerome of Prague (ca. 1368–1440): A Study in Late Medieval Monastic Intellectual Life.* Thesis. Cornell University, 1992, unpub.

_____. "John-Jerome of Prague: Portrait of a Fifteenth-Century Camaldolese." *American Benedictine Review* 46:3 (1995) 308–34.

_____. "John-Jerome of Prague and Monastic Reform in the Fifteenth Century." *American Benedictine Review* 47:1 (1996) 58–98.

Ignesti, Bernardo. "Ambrogio Traversari asceta e mistico." *Vita Monastica* 66 (1961) 112–22.

_____. "Ambrogio Traversari: letterato, Monaco, diplomatico." *Studium* 35 (1939) 563–72.

_____. "Coluccio Salutati e i Camaldolesi." *Vita Monastica* 168–69 (1987) 55–88.

_____. *Fiori della Foresta; San Pier Damiano racconta.* Milano: Vita e Pensiero, 1963.

_____. "Lettere ed arti in S. Maria degli Angeli." *Vita Monastica* 168–69 (1987) 45–54.

_____. *San Pier Damiano e I Suoi Discepoli.* Siena: Cantagalli, 1972.

Ioannes Lodensis, St. *Vita B. Petri Damiani.* PL 144, col. 113–80.

Iwanczak, W. "Entre l'espace ptolémaïque et l'empirie: les cartes de Fra Mauro." *Médiévales* 18 (1990) 53–68.

Jedin, H. "Contarini und Camaldoli (1511–1523)." *Archivio per la storia della pietà* 3 (1959) 51–117.

John of Lodi, Saint. *The Life of Peter Damian.* Trans. Belisle. Big Sur, 1994, unpub.

Jones, P. J. "A Tuscan Monastic Lordship in the Later Middle Ages: Camaldoli." *The Journal of Ecclesiastical History* V (1954) 168–83.

Kaisserlian, Giorgio. *Martino Pinese.* Arezzo: Editrice Gemelli, 1965.

Kanter, Laurence B., ed. *Painting and illumination in early Renaissance Florence 1300–1450.* New York: The Metropolitan Museum of Art, 1994.

Kloczowski, Jerzy. "L'Eremitisme dans les territoires slaves occidentaux." *L'Eremitismo in Occidente Nei Secoli XI e XII.* Milano: SEVEP, 1965, 330–54.

_____. "La Vie Monastique en Pologne et en Bohême aux XI-XII Siècles (Jusqu'à La Moitié du XII Siècle)." *Il Monachesimo e La Riforma Ecclesiastica (1049–1122).* Milano: Vita E Pensiero, 1968, 153–69.

Kristeller, Paul Oskar. *Medieval Aspects of Renaissance Learning: Three Essays.* New York: Columbia University Press, 1992.

_____. *Renaissance Thought and Its Sources.* New York: Columbia University Press, 1979.

Kurze, Wilhelm. "Campus Malduli: Die Frühgeschichte Camaldolis." *Quellen und Forschungen aus Italienischen Archiven und Bibliotheken* 44 (1964) 1–34.

_____. "Monasteri e comuni in Toscana." *Il monachesimo italiano nell'età comunale* (Studia Benedettina 16). Cesena: CSBI, 1998, 507–28.

_____. "Monasteri e nobiltà nella Toscana Medievale." *Le Vie Europee dei Monaci: Civiltà Monastiche tra Occidente e Oriente.* Verona: Gabrielli, 1998, 47–65.

_____. "Zur Geschichte Camaldolis im Zeitalter der Reform." *Il Monachesimo e La Riforma Ecclesiastica (1049–1122).* Milano: Vita e Pensiero, 1968, 399–412.

Kuttner, Stephan. *Gratian and the Schools of Law 1140–1234.* London: Variorum, 1983.

Lacko, M. "Camaldolese Hermits in Slovakia." *Slovak Studies* 5 (1965) 99–203.

Lasinio, E. "Appunti su Fontebuono." *Rivista Storica Benedettina* 5 (1910) 560–70.

Lassus, M-A (Louis Albert). "L'Amour e l'amitié chez les premiers ermites camaldules." *Revue d'Ascétique et de Mystique* 39 (1963) 302–18.

_____. "Chi è San Romualdo?" *Vita Monastica* 193 (1993) 147–51.

_____. "Essai sur la mariologie de Saint Pierre Damien, précurseur de S. Bernard." *Collectanea Cisterciensia* 45 (1983) 37–56.

_____. "Notes pour une histoire des Ermites Camaldules de France (1626–1792)." *Revue Bénédictine* 37 (1967) 174–93.

_____. "L'œuvre legislative du Bienheureux Giustiniani concernant la très sainte institution des reclus Camaldules." *Collectanea Cisterciensia* 54 (1992) 80–84.

_____. *Saint Romuald de Ravenne, l'ermite-prophete*. Paris: Editions Sainte-Madeleine, 1991.

_____. *Saint Pierre Damien: l'homme des deserts de Dieu*. Paris: OEIL, 1986.

Leclercq, Jean. *Alone with God*. New York: Farrar, 1961.

_____. *Aux Sources de la Spiritualité, Etapes et Constantes*. Paris: du Cerf, 1964.

_____. "Le Bx Paul Giustiniani et les ermites de son temps." *Problemi di Vita Religiosa in Italia nel Cinquecento*. Padova: Antenore, 1960.

_____. "La crise du monachisme aux XI et XII siècles." *Bullettino dell' Istituto Storico Italiano Per Il Medio Evo* (Archivio Muratoriano) 70 (1958) 19–41.

_____. *La Dottrina del Beato Paolo Giustiniani*. Frascati, 1953.

_____. "Giustiniani (Paul)." *Dictionnaire de Spiritualité* VI, col. 414–17.

_____. "Pier Damiani: Fonti e Temi." *Momenti e Figure di Storia Monastica Italiana*. A.c. Valerio Cattana (Italia Benedettina XVI). Cesena: CSBI, 1993, 305–67.

_____. *Saint Pierre Damien, Eremite et Homme D'Eglise*. Roma: Edizioni di Storia e Letteratura, 1960.

_____. *San Pier Damiano, Eremita e uomo di Chiesa*. Brescia: Morcelliana, 1972.

_____. "San Romualdo e il Monachesimo Missionario." *Momenti e Figure di Storia Monastica Italiana*. A.c. Valerio Cattana (Italia Benedettina XVI). Cesena: CSBI, 1993, 259–74.

_____. *Temoins de la Spiritualité Occidentale*. Paris: du Cerf, 1965.

_____. *Un Humaniste Ermite Le Bienheureux Paul Giustiniani (1476–1528)*. Roma: Edizioni Camaldoli, 1951.

_____. *Un Umanista Eremita Il Beato Paolo Giustiniani (1476–1528)*. Frascati: Sacro Eremo Tuscolano, 1975.

Leipold, Winfried, "Eremiti camaldolesi di Monte Corona." *La Sostanza dell'Effimero; gli abiti degli Ordini religiosi in Occidente*. A.c. Giancarlo Rocca. Roma: Edizioni Paoline, 2000, 215–17.

_____ e Cacciamani, G. "Giustiniani, Paolo, Beato." *Dizionario degli Istituti di Perfezione* IV, col. 1367–69.

Leonardi, Nazzareno. *L'Eremo Camaldolese di Rua Nelle Bregonze*. Thiere: Euro-Grafica S.p.A., n.d.

Levi D'Ancona, Mirella. *I Corali del Monastero di Santa Maria degli Angeli e le loro Miniature Asportate*. Firenze: Centro Di, 1995.

_____. "Don Silvestro dei Gherarducci e Maestro delle Canzoni." *Rivista d'Arte* 32 (1957) 3–37.

_____. *The Illuminators and Illuminations of the Choir Books from Santa Maria degli Angeli and Santa Maria Nuova in Florence*. Firenze: Centro Di, 1994.

_____. *Miniatura e miniatori a Firenze dal XIV al XVI secolo*. Firenze, 1962.

_____. "La miniatura fiorentina tra Gotico e Rinascimento." *La Miniatura italiana tra Gotico e Rinascimento* I. Ed. Sesti. Firenze, 1985, 451–64.

_____. *The Reconstructed 'Diuno Domenicale' from Santa Maria degli Angeli in Florence.* Firenze: Centro Di, 1995.

Leyser, Henrietta. *Hermits and the New Monasticism: A Study of Religious Communities in Western Europe 1000–1150.* New York: St. Martin's, 1984.

Linnacher, Arturo. "Il Tempio degli Scolari." *La Rotonda del Brunelleschi.* Firenze: Esuvia, 1992, 58–66.

Little, Lester K. "Personal Growth in Peter Damian." *Order and Innovation in the Middle Ages: Essays in Honor of Joseph R. Strayer.* Ed. Jordan. Princeton: University Press, 1976, 317–41.

_____. *Religious Poverty and the Profit Economy in Medieval Europe.* Ithaca: Cornell University Press, 1978.

Lohmer, Christian. *Heremi conversatio; studien zu den monastischen Vorschriften des Petrus Damiani.* Münster: Aschendorff, 1991.

Longhi, R. "Il 'Maestro di Pratovecchio.'" *Paragone* 35 (1952) 10–37.

Lucchesi, Giovanni. "Clavis S. Petri Damiani (1970)." Rev. reprint from *Studi su San Pier Damiano.* Faenza, 1970, 1–215.

_____. "Giovanni da Lodi il Discepolo." *San Pier Damiano nel IX Centenario Della Morte (1072–1972)* IV. Cesena: Centro Studi e Ricerche, 1978, 7–66.

_____. "Per una vita di San Pier Damiani; Componenti cronologiche e topografiche." *San Pier Damiano nel IX Centenario Della Morte (1072–1972)* I: 13–179; II: 13–160.

_____. "I Viaggi di S. Pier Damiani." *Atti del Convegno di Studi nel IX Centenario della Morte.* Faenza, 1972, 71–91.

Lugano, Placido. *La Congregazione Camaldolese degli Eremiti di Montecorona.* Frascati: Sacro Eremo Tuscolano, 1908.

_____. *L'Italia Benedettina.* Roma: Ferrari, 1929.

Lumini, U. *Abbazia di San Zeno in Pisa.* Pisa, 1972.

Mabillon, Jean. *Acta Sanctorum Ordinis S. Benedicti*, Saculum Quintum, Venetiis, 1733.

Maetzke, A. "Don Bartolomeo della Gatta abate di San Clemente in Arezzo, Miniatore, architeto, pittore e musico." *Nel raggio di Piero. La Pittura nell' Italia centrale nell'età di Piero della Francesca.* Venezia, 1992, 125–39.

Manfredi, A. "Traversari, Parentucelli e Pomposa: ricerche di codici al servizio Del concilio fiorentino." *Ambrogio Traversari nel VI centenario della nascità.* Firenze, 1988, 165–87.

Manneschi, Eugenio. *Le Origini e le vicende storiche del Patrimonio del Monastero di Camaldoli.* Camaldoli, 1993.

Martini, A. "The Early Work of Bartolomeo della Gatta." *The Art Bulletin* 42 (1960) 133–41.

Martino III. "Constitutiones Camaldulensis a 1253." *Annales Camaldulenses* VI, App., col. 1–65.

Massa, Eugenio. *L'Eremo, la Bibbia e il Medioevo in Umanisti veneti del primo Cinquecento.* Napoli: Liguori, 1992.

_____. "Gasparo Contarini e gli amici fra Venezia e Camaldoli." *Gaspare Contarini e il suo tempo*. Atti del convegno, 1985. Venezia, 1988, 39–91.

_____. *I manoscritti originali del Beato Paolo Giustiniani custoditi nell'eremo di Frascati*. Rome, 1967.

_____. "Paolo Giustiniani e Gasparo Contarini, la vocazione al bivio del neoplatonismo e della teologia biblica." *Benedictina* 35 (1988) 429–74.

_____. "Le prime meditazioni del Secretum di Paolo Giustiniani." *Atti del IV Convegno di Studi Umbri*. Gubbio, 1996, 301–66.

Matus, Thomas. *Alle Origini di Camaldoli: San Romualdo e I Cinque Fratelli*. Verucchio: Edizioni Camaldoli, 1996.

_____. "Bruno di Querfurt: il monaco evangelizzatore della Prussia orientale e il Maestro Romualdo di Ravenna." *Monaci e Missione*. A.c. Edward Farrugia e Innocenzo Gargano. Verruchio: Pazzini, 1999, 127–44.

_____. *The Monastic Life of the Camaldolese Benedictines*. Big Sur: Hermitage Books, 1985.

_____. *The Mystery of Romuald and the Five Brothers*. Big Sur: Source Books/Hermitage Books, 1994.

_____. *Nazarena: An American Anchoress*. New York: Paulist, 1998.

Mazzacchera, Alberto. "Soppressione degli ordini religiosi e confische dei beni Ecclesiastici nella diocesi di Cagli dopo l'Annessione." *Marche e Umbria nell'Età di Pio IX e di Leone XIII*. Fonte Avellana, 1997, 410–44.

McGinn, Bernard. *The Doctors of the Church: Thirty-three Men and Women Who Shaped Christianity*. New York: Paulist, 1998.

McManners, John. *Church and Society in Eighteenth-Century France*. II. Oxford: Clarendon, 1998.

Meneghin, Vittorino. "Il Camaldolino." *Avesa. Studi, ricerche, cose varie*. A.c. G. Peroni e B. Polverigiani. Verona, 1979, 197–212.

_____. *S. Michele in Isola de Venezia*. I. Venezia: Stamperia di Venezia, 1962.

Meoni, L. *San Felice in Piazza a Firenze*. Firenze, 1993.

Merino, Leandro. *Blessed Paul Giustiniani and his Congregation of Camaldolese Hermits of Monte Corona*. Frascati, 1968, unpub.

Merloni, Domenico. *S. Benedetto . . . S. Romualdo . . .* Fabriano, 1974, 55–110.

Merolla, L. "La dispersione dei codici di San Michele di Murano." *Il monachesimo Italiano dalle riforme illuministiche all'unità nazionale (1768–1870)* (Italia Benedettina 11). Cesena: CSBI, 1992, 685–700.

Merton, Thomas. *Disputed Questions*. New York: Farrar, 1960.

_____. *The Silent Life*. New York: Farrar, 1957.

Meysztowicz, Valerien. "La Vocation Monastique d'Otton III." *Antemurale* 4 (1958) 27–75.

Micali, Osanna Fantozzi e Roselli, Piero. *Le Soppressioni dei Conventi a Firenze*. Firenze: LEF, 1980.

Miccoli, Giovanni. "Theologie de la vie monastique chez Saint Pierre Damien (1007–1072)." *Theologie de la Vie Monastique: Etudes sur la Tradition Patristique*. Aubier, 1961, 459–83.

Mini, Tommaso. *Catalogus Sanctorum et Beatorum totius Ordinis Camaldulensis*. Florentiae, 1606.

Minnich, Nelson H. *The Catholic Reformation: Council, Churchmen, Controversies.* Brookfield, Vt.: Variorum, 1993.

Mioni, E. "I manoscritti greci di San Michele di Murano." *Italia medioevale e umanistica* 1 (1958) 317–43.

_____. "Le *Vitae Patrum* nella Traduzione di Ambrogio Traversari." *Aevum* 24 (1950) 319–31.

Mittarelli, Johanne-Benedicto. *Annales Camaldulenses Ordinis Sancti Benedicti* . . . . 9v. Venetiae, 1755–1773.

_____. *Bibliotheca codicum manuscriptorum monasterii S. Michaelis Venetiarum prope Murianum.* Venetiae, 1779.

_____. *Memorie della vita di s. Parisio monaco camaldolese e del monastero de' SS. Cristina e Parisio di Treviso.* Venezia, 1748.

Monaci ed Eremiti Camaldolesi. *Rivista Camaldolese.* Ravenna: Arti Grafiche, 1926–27.

Monetti, F. "Michele Sassetti (1762–1837) e i suoi tentativi di riforma in Piemonte." *Benedictina* 30 (1983) 501–30.

Monk-Hermits of Camaldoli O.S.B. *The Holy Rule of Saint Benedict together with the Declarations and Constitutions of* . . . Camaldoli, 1960.

Mugnotio, Andrea. *Eremi Camaldulensis descriptio.* Roma: Accoltum, 1570.

Nicoletto, Ivan. "Fisionomia attuale della Congregazione Camaldolese e prospettive." *Camaldoli Ieri e Oggi: l'identità camaldolese nel nuovo millennio.* A.c. Emanuele Bargellini. Camaldoli: Edizioni Camaldoli, 2000, 167–72.

Noonan, J. T. "Gratian slept here: the changing identity of the father of the systematic study of canon law." *Traditio* 35 (1979) 145–72.

Norcini, Pietro. *Relazioni di Camaldoli con l'Episcopio di Arezzo, Secoli XI–XVI.* Firenze: Università Degli Studi, 1974.

"Ordo Divinorum Officiorum, seu Constitutiones Veterum Monachorum Alborum Ordinis S. Benedicti." Annales Camaldulenses, VI, App., col. 352–469.

Ornam, Divadac. *Il Paraiso Verde.* Medellín: Lealon, 1977.

Ortes, G. M. *Memorie per servire alla vita del p. abate d. Guido Grandi camaldolese.* Massa, 1742.

Ostroumoff, Ivan N. *The History of the Council of Florence.* Boston: Holy Transfiguration Monastery, 1971.

Ottaviani, Enrico. *Vita di S. Albertino da Montone, Priore di Fonte Avellana.* Castel-Bolognese: TGA, 1974.

Paatz, Walter und Elisabeth. *Die Kirchen Von Florenz.* III. (Trans. Nicoletto). Frankfurt: Klostermann, 1952.

Padri Camaldolesi di S. Gregorio al Celio. *Graziano.* Roma: S. Gregorio al Celio, 1949.

_____. *Gregorio XVI: Miscellanea Commemorativa.* 2v. Roma: San Gregorio al Celio, 1948.

Pagnani, Alberico. *Storia dei Benedettini Camaldolesi: Cenobiti, Eremiti, Monache ed Oblati.* Sassoferrato, 1949.

_____. *Vita di S. Romualdo, Abbate, Fondatore dei Camaldolesi.* Fabriano, 1967.

Palazzini, Giuseppe. *S. Raniero (1100?–1180) Arcivescovo e Martire.* Urbania, 1945.

_____. "S. romualdo e le sue fondazioni tra i monti del Cagliese." *Studia Picena* 18 (1948) 61–76.

Palazzini, Pietro. "Albertino da Montone e la conferma del Suo culto." *Sant' Albertino e il Suo Tempo (XIII Secolo).* Fonte Avellana, 1994, 403–15.

_____. "Fonte Avellana e Pier Damiani." *Le Abbazie delle Marche, Storia e Arte (Italia Benedettina 12).* Cesena: CSBI, 1992, 127–58.

_____. "Note sul Card. Giulio della Rovere e la sua azione nella soppressione della Congregazione avellanita." *Fonte Avellana nella Società dei Secoli XV e XVI.* Fonte Avellana, 1980, 173–91.

_____. "S. Albertino ed il suo tempo." *Sant'Albertino e il Suo Tempo (XIII Secolo).* Fonte Avellana, 1994, 5–12.

_____. "San Pier Damiani al centro della riforma della Chiesa Marchigiana nel sec. XI." *San Pier Damiano nel IX Centenario Della Morte (1072–1972).* Cesena: Centro Studi e Ricerche, 1972, 161–232.

Pantoni, Angelo. "Un amico dei Greci: Ambrogio Traversari." *Vita Monastica* 79 (1964) 179–82.

Papadakis, Aristeides. *The Christian East and the Rise of the Papacy: the Church 1071–1453.* Crestwood, N.Y.: SVS Press, 1994.

Pappajanni, G. "L'ordine di Camaldoli e il suo archivio conservato nell'Archivio Di Stato di Firenze." *Gli archivi italiani* 3 (1921) 3–20.

Pasqui, Ubaldo. *Di Bartolomeo Della Gatta Monaco Camaldolese Miniatore Pittore e Architetto.* Arezzo, 1926.

Patrizia, Rosettani. *Lo Scriptorium di Fonte Avellana: Opus Scientiae et Artis.* Fermo: Studi e Saggi dei Quaderni dell'ASAF, 1998.

Pedrocchi, Anna Maria. *San Gregorio Al Celio; Storia di una abbazia.* Roma: Libreria Dello Stato, 1993.

Penco, Gregorio. "L'Eremitismo irregolare in Italia nei secoli XI–XII." *Benedictina* 32 (1985) 201–21.

_____. *Storia del Monachesimo in Italia dalle origini alla fine del Medioevo.* Milano: Jaca, 1983.

_____. *Storia del Monachesimo in Italia nell'epocha moderna.* Roma: Paoline, 1968.

Peter Damian, St. *Book of Gomorrah: an Eleventh-Century Treatise against Clerical Homosexual Practices.* Wilfrid Laurier University, 1982.

_____. *Letters.* 4v. Trans. Blum. Washington: The Catholic University of America Press, 1989, 1990, 1992, 1998, (2 future vols.)

_____. *The Life of Blessed Romuald.* Trans. Matus. Big Sur: Source Books/Hermitage Books, 1994.

_____. *Selected Writings on the Spiritual Life.* Trans. McNulty. London: Faber, 1959.

Petrus Damianus, S. *Opera Omnia.* PL 144-145, 1853.

_____. *Sermones.* Corpus Christianorum. Cont. Med. LVII. Cura et Studio Lucchesi. Turnholt: Brepols, 1983.

_____. *Vita Beati Romualdi.* A.c. Tabacco. Roma: Istituto Storico Italiano, 1957.

Peyretti, Enrico. "Eremi nella Vita Comune." *Vita Monastica* 199 (1995) 80–85.

Phipps, Colin. "Romuald-Model Hermit: Eremitical Theory in Saint Peter Damian's *Vita Beati Romualdi*, chapters 16–27." *Monks, Hermits and the Ascetic Tradition*. Ed. Sheils. London: Blackwell, 1985, 65–77.

Picasso, Giorgio. "L'eremitismo in occidente nei secoli XI e XII." *Vita Monastica* 71 (1962) 169–75.

Pier Damiani. *Il cammino verso la luce*. Trans. Di Meglio. Padova: EMP, 1987.

_____. *Opera Omnia*. 12v. A.c. Gargano e D'Acunto. Roma: Città Nuova, 2000–.

Pier Damiano, S. *Lettere e Discorsi*. Trans. Pasini. Siena: Cantagalli, 1956.

_____. *Scritti Monastici*. 2v. Trans. Ignesti. Siena: Cantagalli, 1959.

_____. *Vita di San Romualdo*. Trans. Matus. Camaldoli: Edizioni Camaldoli, 1988.

Pierre Damien, St. e Bruno di Querfurt, St. *Textes Primitifs Camaldules*. Trans Lassus. Namur: Du Soleil Levant, 1962.

Pierucci, A. "Rilievi sugli oblati e conversi camaldolesi." *Camaldoli* 42 (1955) 112–20.

_____Celestino. *L'Abbazia di S. Elena Dell'Esino; Memorie storiche e artistiche*. Edizioni Camaldoli, 1981.

_____. "Da 'Eremo' a 'Cenobio': l'evoluzione interna di Fonte Avellana." *Fonte Avellana nella Società dei secoli XV e XVI*. Fonte Avellana, 1980, 11–30.

_____. *Fonte Avellana: Mille Anni di Storia*. Fonte Avellana, 1983.

_____. "La più antica storia di Fonte Avellana." *Benedictina* I–II (1973) 121–39.

_____. "La riforma romualdino-camaldolese nelle Marche." *Aspetti e Problemi del Monachesimo Nelle Marche*. I., 1982, 39–59.

_____. "Rilievi sulla soppressione della Congregazione di S. Croce di Fonte Avellana (1570)." *Benedictina* 2 (1971) 278–313.

_____. "Sulle origini di Fonte Avellana." *Fonte Avellana nel suo Millenario. I. Le origini*. Fonte Avellana, 1981, 11–26.

Pilati, Dalmazio. *Chiesa dei Santi Biagio e Romualdo: Storia Arte Culto*. Fabriano: Arte Grafiche Gentile, 1996.

_____. *Ricordo di Don Carlo Maria Ghezzi, Monaco Camaldolese già vice-parroco della Chiesa dei SS. Biagio e Romualdo a 50 anni dal suo olocausto in terra di Polonia, 9 maggio 1945–9 maggio 1995*. Fabriano: Arte Grafiche Gentile, 1995.

Pirillo, P. "I Camaldolesi a Bologna nel XII e XIII secolo. Il monastero del Bosco Dei Burelli, la società cittadina e gli 'scolares ultramontane.'" *Atti e Memorie della Deputazione di Storia Patria per le Province di Romagna* 45 (1995) 125–63.

Poletti, Vincenzo. "La Personalità di Pier Damiani." *Atti del Convegno di Studi nel IX Centenario della Morte*. Faenza, 1972, 115–33.

Polverari, Alberto. "Il problema della longevità di San Romualdo." *Fonte Avellana Nel suo Millenario. I. Le origini*. Fonte Avellana, 1981, 245–52.

Pomaro, G. "L'attività di Ambrogio Traversari in codici fiorentini." *Interpres* 2 (1979) 105–15.

Powell, John. *Spiritual Teaching of the Brief Rule of Saint Romuald*. Big Sur: New Camaldoli Publications and Tapes, 1993.

Proch, U. "Ambrogio Traversari e il decreto di unione di Firenze." *Ambrogio Traversari nel VI centenario della nascità*. Firenze, 1988, 147–63,

Prudenziano, Ariosto. *I Camaldoli di Nola*. Napoli: LER, 1993.

Quacquarelli, Antonio. "Sant'Albertino monaco di pace." *Sant'Albertino e il Suo Tempo (XIII Secolo)*. Fonte Avellana, 1994.

Quirini, Pietro. "An Unknown Letter of Pietro Quirini to Gasparo Contarini And Niccolo Tiepolo (April, 1512)." *The Catholic Reformation: Council, Churchmen, Controversies*. Ed. Minnich. Brookfield, Vt.: Variorum, 1993.

_____ e Giustiniani, Paolo. "Epistolicum Commercium." *Annales Camaldulenses* VI, App., col. 446–611.

_____. *Lettera al Papa; Libellus ad Leonem X [1513]*. Trans. Bianchini. Modena: Artioli, 1995.

_____. "Libellus ad Leonem X." *Annales Camaldulenses* VI, App., col. 612–719.

Radicchia, Gian Luca. *Il Sacro Eremo di Monte Corona; Capo dell'omonima Congregazione Camaldolese (1530–1861)*. Perugia: Edizioni Guerra, 1997.

Ragusi, Lucia. "Le origini di S. Maria degli Angeli attraverso i documenti più antichi." *Vita Monastica* 168–69 (1987) 30–44.

Rao, I. G. "Ambrogio Traversari al Concilio di Firenze." *Firenze e il Concilio del 1439*. A.c. P. Viti. Firenze, 1994, 577–97.

Razzi, Silvano. "Vita del reverendissimo Padre Don Ambrogio Generale Camaldolense." *Le Vite de' Santi e Beati Dell'Ordine di Camaldoli*. Fiorenza: Giunti, 1600.

_____. "Vita di Pietro Delfino Viniziano, Generale de Camaldoli Quadragesimo Quinto & ultimo de' perpetui." *Le Vite de' Santi e Beati dell' Ordine di Camaldoli*. Fiorenza: Giunti, 1600.

Redi, F., and others. "San Michele in Borgo (Pisa). Rapporto preliminare 1986." *Archeologia Medievale* 14 (1987) 339–69.

Resnick, Irven Michael. *Divine Power and Possibility in St. Peter Damian's "De Divina Omnipotentia."* New York: Brill, 1992.

Ricci, I. *L'Abbazia camaldolese e la cattedrale di Sansepolcro*. Sansepolcro, 1942.

_____, Pier Giorgio. "Ambrogio Traversari." *La Rinascità* II (1939) 578–612.

Righi, Vittore Ugo. *Biancospino in gennaio; vita del Beato Angelo da Gualdo Tadino, 1270–1324*. Milano: Ancora, 1968.

Robert, P. "Camaldules (Ordre Des)." *Dictionnaire de Spiritualité*, II, col. 50–60.

Rodolfo, Beato. "Constitutiones Camaldulensis a 1080 e 1085." *Annales Camaldulenses* III, App., col. 512–51.

_____. *Le Regole della vita eremitica*. Edizioni Camaldoli, n.d.

Roggi, Clemente. "Il B. Pietro Dagnino." *Camaldoli* 30 (1952) 91–96.

_____. "Vita e costumanze dei Romualdini del Pereo, di Fonte Avellana e di Camaldoli." *Benedictina* 4 (1950) 69–86.

Roselli, Piero e Micali, Osanna Fantozzi. *Le Soppressioni dei conventi a Firenze*. Firenze: LEF, 1980.

Rossi, Giustino e Spinelli, Giovanni. *Alle Origini di Vallombrosa; Giovanni Gualberto nella Società dell'XI Secolo*. Milano: Jaca, 1984.

Rudolph, B. *The Constitutions of Bl. Rudolph*. Big Sur, unpub., n.d.

Russell, Kenneth C. "Peter Damian's *Liber Gomorrhianus*: The Text vs. The Scholarly Tradition." *American Benedictine Review* 49 (1998) 299–315.

_____. "Peter Damian's Whip." *American Benedictine Review* 41 (1990) 20–35.

Ryan, J. Joseph. *Saint Peter Damian and His Canonical Sources: a Preliminary Study in the Antecedents of the Gregorian Reform.* Toronto: PIMS, 1956.

Salari, Paola Mercurelli. "Iconografia e econologia di S. Albertino da Montone." *Sant'Albertino e il Suo Tempo (XIII Secolo).* Fonte Avellana, 1994, 417–40.

Samaritani, Antonio. "Contributi di Pomposa alla storia del sec. XI." *Analecta Pomposiana* I (1965) 37–72.

Sancassani, G. "Badia della Vangadizza negli statuti veronesi del secolo XIII." *Atti e Memorie del Sodalizio Vangadiciense* II. Badia Polesine, 1982, 443–51.

Sansterre, J. M. "Le monastère des Saints-Boniface-et-Alexis sur l'Aventin et L'expansion du christianisme dans le cadre de la 'Renovatio Imperii Romanorum' d'Otton III. Une revision." *Revue Bénédictine* 100 (1990) 493–506.

_____. "Otton III et les saints ascètes de son temps." *Rivista di Storia della Chiesa in Italia* 43 (1989) 377–412.

_____. "Recherches sur les ermites du Mont-Cassin et l'érémitisme dans l'hagiographie cassinienne." *Hagiographica* 2 (1995) 57–92.

Santagostino Barbone, A. "Il Giudizio universale del b. Angelico nel monasterio Camaldolese di S. Maria degli Angeli." *Memorie Domenicane* 20 (1989) 255–78.

Savelli, Divo. *Il Convento di S. Maria Degli Angeli a Firenze.* Firenze: Tornatre, 1983.

_____. *La Rotonda del Brunelleschi; Storia e Documenti.* Firenze: Esuvia, 1992.

Savioli, Antonio. "Itinerari iconografici per San Pier Damiani." *San Pier Damiano Nel IX Centenario Della Morte (1072–1972).* Cesena: Centro Studi e Ricerche, 1972: I (271–75), II (307–18); 1973: III (179–92); 1978: IV (123–36).

Saward, John. "Joy, Mirth, and Folly in the Hermits of the Eleventh Century." *Perfect Fools: Folly for Christ's Sake in Catholic and Orthodox Spirituality.* New York: Oxford, 1980, 48–57.

Schmidtmann, Christian. "Romuald von Camaldoli. Modell einer eremitischen Existenz im 10/11." *Studia Monastica* 39 (1997) 329–38.

Schnitzer, Joseph. *Peter Delfin, General Des Camaldulenserordens (1444–1525).* München: Ernst Reinhardt, 1926.

Sebastianelli, Sandro. "La confisca napoleonica dei beni camaldolesi." *Lo Stato Della Chiesa in Epoca Napoleonica.* Fonte Avellana, 1995, 451–60.

_____. "Monsignor Albertino Bellenghi scienzato camaldolese." *Il Lavoro nella Storia della Civiltà Occidentale* I. Fonte Avellana, 1993, 237–52.

Semoli, Paola. *Codici miniati camaldolesi nella Biblioteca Comunale 'Rilliana' di Poppi e nella Biblioteca della Città di Arezzo.* Poppi, 1986.

Senyk, Sophia. *A History of the Church in Ukraine* I. Roma: Pontificio Istituto Orientale, 1993.

_____. "San Bruno di Querfurt e le sue missioni." *Vita Monastica* 152 (1983) 73–83.

Seven Hermits of St. Romuald. "The Camaldolese Come To America." *American Benedictine Review* XII-1 (1961) 40–54.

Sheils, W., ed. *Monks, Hermits and the Ascetic Tradition.* London: Blackwell, 1985.

Simi Varanelli, E. "Spiritualità ed arte di Fonte Avellana." *Le Abbazie delle Marche, Storia e Arte (Italia Benedettina 12).* Cesena: CSBI, 1992, 397–410.

Siren, O. *Don Lorenzo Monaco*. Strasbourg, 1905.

Smits Van Waesberghe, J. "Guido of Arezzo and Musical Improvisation." *Musica Disciplina* 5 (1951) 55–63.

_____. "The Musical Notation of Guido of Arezzo." *Musica Disciplina* 5 (1951) 15–53.

_____. *De Musico-Paedagogico et Theoretico Guidone Aretino: eiusque vita et moribus.* Florence: Olschki, 1953.

Società Torricelliana di Scienze e Lettere. *S. Pier Damiani: Atti del Convegno di Studi nel IX Centenario della Morte.* Faenza: Lega, 1972.

Somigli, Costanzo. "Le lettere di Ambrogio Traversari a Mariotto Allegri (1423–1439)." *Vita Monastica* 168–69 (1987) 154–236.

_____. "L'opuscolo 'Forma perfectionis eremitarum' di Girolamo da Praga." *Camaldoli* 8 (1954) 26–31.

_____. *Un amico dei Greci: Ambrogio Traversari.* Camaldoli: Edizioni Camaldoli, 1964.

Somigli, Costanzo e Bargellini, Tommaso. *Ambrogio Traversari, Monaco Camaldolese: la Figura e la Dottrina Monastica.* Camaldoli: Edizioni Camaldoli, 1986.

Soranzo, Giovanni. "Pietro Dolfin, Generale Dei Camaldolesi e il suo Epistolario." *Rivista di Storia della Chiesa in Italia* XIII-1 (1959) 1–31; XIII-2 (1959) 157–95.

Sottili, Agostino. "Ambrogio Traversari, Francesco Pizolpasso, Giovanni Aurispa: Traduzioni e letture." *Romanische Forschengen* 78 (1966) 42–63.

_____. "Autografi e traduzioni di Ambrogio Traversari." *Rinascimento*, Seconda Serie, V (1965) 3–15.

_____. "Il Laerzio Latino e Altri Autografi di Ambrogio Traversari." *Vestigia; Studi in onore di G. Billanovich.* Roma: Edizioni di Storia e Letteratura, 1984, 699–745.

Spagnesi, Enrico. "Fonte Avellana nella storiografia Camaldolese (secoli XVI–XVIII)." *Fonte Avellana nel suo Millenario. 1. Le Origini.* Fonte Avellana, 1981, 27–62.

Spinelli, Giovanni e Rossi, Giustino. *Alle Origini di Vallombrosa; Giovanni Gualberto nella Società dell'XI Secolo.* Milano: Jaca, 1984.

Stinger, Charles. "Ambrogio Traversari and the 'Tempio degli Scolari' at S. Maria de Angeli in Florence." *Essays Presented to Myron P. Gilmore.* Firenze: La Nuova Italia, 1978, 271–86.

_____. *Humanism and the Church Fathers: Ambrogio Traversari (1386–1439) and Christian Antiquity in the Italian Renaissance.* Albany: SUNY, 1977.

Stocco, G. and Guerra, M. *L'Abbazia della Vangadizza: i suoi potenti protettori, i suoi Implacabili avversari.* Badia Polesine, 1981.

Sweringen, Randy. *The Camaldolese Benedictine Threefold Good: Seeds of Growth for The Christian People.* Thesis. Berkeley: GTU, 1999.

Sydow, Jürgen. "Problemi della missione Camaldolese in Oriente." *Vita Monastica* 73 (1963) 51–59.

Tabacco, Giovanni. "La data di fondazione Camaldoli." *Vita Monastica* 71 (1962) 147–53.

_____. "*Privilegium Amoris*: Aspetti della Spiritualità Romualdina." *Il Saggiatore* IV (1954) 1–20.

_____. "Romualdo di Ravenna e gli inizi dell'eremitismo camaldolese." *L'Eremitismo in Occidente Nei Secoli XI e XII.* Milano: SEVEP, 1965, 73–121.

_____. *Spiritualità e cultura nel Medioevo; Dodici percorsi nei territori del potere e della fede.* Napoli: Liguori, 1993.

_____. *La Vita di San Bononio di Rotberto Monaco e l'Abate Guido Grandi (1671–1742).* Torino: Università di Torino, 1954.

_____ e Cannata, Pietro. "Romualdo." *Bibliotheca Sanctorum* XI. Roma: Città Nuova, 1968, col. 365–84.

Tamburini, Vittorio. "Prefazione" all'*Hodoeporicon* di Ambrogio Traversari. Firenze: Le Monnier, 1985, 1–20.

Tassi, Ildefonso. *Ludovico Barbo (1381–1443).* Roma: Edizioni di Storia e Letteratura, 1952.

Tierney, Brian. *The Crisis of Church and State 1050–1300 (with selected documents).* Englewood Cliffs, N.J.: Prentice-Hall, 1964.

Tocci, Luigi M. *Eremi e Cenobi del Catria.* Pesaro: Cassa Di Risparmio, 1972.

Tolra, H. *Saint Pierre Orseolo, Doge de Venise . . . Sa Vie et Son Temps (928–987).* Paris: Thorin et Fils, 1897.

Torresin, Pierluigi. *Ed è Subito Sera; Esperienze di vita camaldolese.* Cittadella (Pd): Bertoncello, 1981.

Tosatto, Clemente. *Eremo di Monte Rua; Richiami di storia e di spirito.* Padova: Edigam, 1980.

Tramontin, Silvio. "Un programma di riforma della Chiesa per il Concilio Lateranense V: il *Libellus ad Leonem X* dei Veneziani Paolo Giustiniani e Pietro Quirini." *Venezia e I Concili.* Venezia: Quaderni del Laurentianum, 1962, 67–95.

Traversari, Ambrogio. *Hodoeporicon.* Firenze: Le Monnier, 1985.

_____. "Hodoeporicon." *Ambrogio Traversari e I suoi tempi.* A.c. Dini-Traversari. Firenze, 1912.

Traversarius, Ambrosius. *Ambrosii Traversarii Generalis Camaldulensium . . . latinae epistolae.* 2v. Ed. Mehus. Bologna, 1968.

Turner, D. H. "A Twelfth-Century Psalter from Camaldoli." *Revue Bénédictine* 72 (1962) 109–30.

Urbanelli, Callisto. "Gli eremiti camaldolesi di Monte Corona e le origini dei Cappuccini." *Aspetti e Problemi del monachesimo nelle Marche.* Fabriano: Montisfani, 1982, 257–94.

Vagaggini, Cipriano. "Liturgia e questione monastica." *Vita Monastica* 55 (1958) 165–73.

_____ (Cyprian). *Theological Dimensions of the Liturgy: a General Treatise on the Theology of the Liturgy.* 4e. Trans. Doyle. Collegeville: The Liturgical Press, 1976.

Valentini, Ubaldo. "La figura di S. Albertino attraverso i racconti agiografici." *Sant'Albertino e il Suo Tempo (XIII Secolo).* Fonte Avellana, 1994, 217–36.

Vandenbrouke, François. *La Morale Monastique du XI au XVI Siècle.* Louvain: Editions Nauwelaerts, 1966, 33–43.

Van Engen, John. "The 'Crisis of Cenobitism' Reconsidered: Benedictine Monasticism in the Years 1050–1150." *Speculum* 61 (1986) 269–304.

Vasari, Giorgio. *Lives of the Most Eminent Painters Sculptors and Architects*. Vols. 2, 3. London: Philip Lee Warner, 1912.

_____. *Le vite de' più eccelenti pitori scultori e architettori*, v. 2, 3. Milano: Edizioni Per Il Club del Libro, 1962, 1963.

Vedovato, Giuseppe. *Camaldoli e la sua Congregazione dalle Origini al 1184; Storia e Documentazione* (Italia Benedettina XIII). Cesena: Centro Storico Benedettino Italiano, 1994.

_____. "Camaldoli nell'età comunale (1088–1250)." *Il monachesimo italiano nell'età comunale (Italia Benedettina 16)*. Cesena: CSBI, 1998, 529–62.

_____. "L'inizio della presenza camaldolese nel Veneto (1186–1250)." *Il monachesimo nel Veneto medioevale (Italia Benedettina 17)*. Cesena: CSBI, 1998, 85-120.

Vespasiano da Bisticci. "Commentario della vita del B. Ambrogio Traversari." *Leggende di Alcuni Santi e Beati Venerati in S. Maria Degli Angeli di Firenze* I. Bologna, 1864.

Vigilucci, Lino. *Camaldoli: Itinerario di Storia e di Spiritualità*. Camaldoli: Edizioni Camaldoli, 1988.

_____. *Camaldoli: Journey into its History and Spirituality*. Trans. Belisle. Big Sur: Source Books/Hermitage Books, 1995.

Virgili, E. "L'inventario dell'Abbazia di San Zeno di Pisa (1386)." *Bollettino storico pisano* 54 (1985) 117–29.

Visentin, Aldo. *Paolo Giustiniani Eremita*. Padova: Edizioni dell'Eremo, 1987.

Vita Monastica. Trimestrale di spiritualità—liturgia—ecumenismo. Camaldoli: Edizioni Camaldoli, 1952– .

_____. XLI, 168–69. *Ambrogio Traversari Camaldolese: nel VI Centenario dalla Nascità 1386–1986*. Camaldoli: Edizioni Camaldoli, 1986.

Viti, P. "Ambrogio Traversari al Concilio di Ferrara." *Ferrara e il concilio, 1438–1439*. A.c. P. Castelli. Ferrara, 1992, 95–119.

Voigt, *Brun von Querfurt, Mönch, Eremit, Erzbishof der Heiden und Märtyrer*. Stuttgart, 1907.

Wenskus, R. *Studien zur historisch-politischen Gedankenqelt Brunos von Querfurt*. Münster–Köln, 1956.

Whitney, J. P. "Peter Damiani and Humbert." *The Cambridge Historical Journal* I (1925) 225–48.

Wilson, N. G. *From Byzantium to Italy: Greek Studies in the Italian Renaissance*. Baltimore: Johns Hopkins University Press, 1992.

Wiseman, Nicholas, Card. *Recollections of the Last Four Popes and of Rome in Their Times*. New York: Joseph Wagner, 1858.

Wong, Joseph. "Identità camaldolese e formazione." *Camaldoli Ieri e Oggi: L'identità camaldolese nel nuovo millennio*. A.c. Emanuele Bargellini. Camaldoli: Edizioni Camaldoli, 2000, 29–54.

Zaccaria, R. "Dolfin, Pietro." *Dizionario biografico degli Italiani* XL. Roma, 1991, 565–71.

Zanetti, G. *I Camaldolesi in Sardegna*. Cagliari, 1974.

_____. "La vicaria o priorato camaldolese di S. Nicola di Trulla in Sardegna." *Bollettino storico pisano* 43 (1974) 57–93.

Zaninotto, Gino. *Un Contestatore ortodosso . . .* Roma, 1972.

Zattin, G. *Il Monastero di S. Maria delle Carceri.* Padova, 1973.

Zavaglio, Angelo. *Il Card. Placido Zurla.* Crema: Buona Stampa, 1935.

Zeri, Federico. "Investigations into the Early Period of Lorenzo Monaco." *The Burlington Magazine* CVI (1964) 554–58; CVII (1965) 3–11.

Ziegelbaur, Magnoaldo. *Centifolium Camaldulense, sive notitia Scriptorum Camaldulensium.* Venetiis: Albrizzi, 1750.

Zurla, Placido, Card. *Il Mappamondo di Fra Mauro Camaldolese.* Venetiis, 1806.

Contributors

Fr. **Alessandro Barban** is the Camaldolese prior of the Italian Hermitage of Fonte Avellana. In addition to teaching theology, he has published *La Fede Pregata* and numerous articles, and has edited R. Kearney and G. Lafont's *Il Desiderio e Dio*. Alessandro is a gifted teacher and lecturer in systematic theology.

Fr. **Emanuele Bargellini**, monk of Camaldoli, Italy, has been Prior General of the Camaldolese Benedictine Congregation since 1987. He is a liturgist and part-time professor. In addition to many articles on liturgical and monastic spirituality, Emanuele has also recently published *Camaldoli ieri e oggi; l'identità camaldolese nel nuovo millennio*.

Fr. **Bruno Barnhart**, former prior of New Camaldoli Hermitage, Big Sur, California, is the author of *The Good Wine: Reading John from the Center* and *Second Simplicity: The Inner Shape of Christianity*. As well as teaching and lecturing, Bruno is presently working on a collection of Bede Griffiths' writings and an ongoing project concerning the rebirth of the Christian sapiential tradition.

Fr. **Peter-Damian Belisle**, monk of New Camaldoli Hermitage, is the author of *Into the Heart of God* and *The Wheel of Becoming* (both under the name Augustin Belisle) and numerous articles. He also translated from the Italian, Lino Vigilucci's *Camaldoli: a Journey into its History and Spirituality*. Peter-Damian is an artist and poet, as well as teacher and translator.

Fr. **Cyprian Consiglio**, monk of New Camaldoli Hermitage, is the postulant director and liturgy director at Big Sur. A gifted musician and vocalist, Cyprian has published a number of musical compact discs (under both the names Daniel and Cyprian), including his recent CD, *In the Heart of the Desert*.

Sr. **Donald Corcoran** is the Camaldolese prioress of Transfiguration Monastery in Windsor, New York. She has taught spirituality for many years and is a well-known retreat director. Her present interest is the comparison between Benedictine monasticism and Confucianism. Besides many articles, Donald has published *Spiritual Sisters: A Benedictine and a Buddhist Nun in Dialogue*.

Dr. **Michael Downey** is professor of systematic theology and spirituality at St. John's Seminary, Camarillo, California. He is a noted author whose works include:

Trappist, Understanding Christian Spirituality, The New Dictionary of Christian Spirituality (editor), *Hope Begins Where Hope Begins,* and *Altogether Gift: A Trinitarian Spirituality.*

Fr. **Michael Fish,** a former Redemptorist from South Africa, is a Camaldolese monk of New Camaldoli Hermitage where he serves as oblate director/chaplain and assistant guestmaster. Michael is a dynamic speaker and noted retreat director.

Fr. **Robert Hale,** monk of New Camaldoli Hermitage, now resident at Incarnation Monastery, is a professor at the Graduate Theological Union in Berkeley. He has published *Love on the Mountain: The Chronicle Journal of a Camaldolese Monk, Christ and the Universe,* and *Canterbury and Rome: Sister Churches,* in addition to numerous articles. Robert is a former prior of New Camaldoli Hermitage.

Br. **Bede Healey,** monk of New Camaldoli Hermitage, is the novice master at Big Sur. Formerly a staff psychologist at the Menninger Clinic where he was director of the psychiatry and religion program, Bede now gives retreats and workshops in addition to his formation work. He has published various articles and book chapters on psychological themes.

Fr. **Thomas Matus,** American monk of Camaldoli, Italy, is an accomplished musician and linguist, in addition to his teaching and writing. As well as many articles and other books in Italian, Thomas has published *The Mystery of Romuald and the Five Brothers, Nazarena: An American Anchoress, Yoga and the Jesus Prayer Tradition,* and with Steindl-Rast and Capra, *Belonging to the Universe.*

Ms. **Jeffry Spencer,** widow and mother of three grown children, is a Camaldolese Benedictine oblate. She held many positions during her long teaching career and is presently professor emerita at California State University, Bakersfield. In addition to numerous reviews and essays, Jeffry has published *Heroic Nature: Ideal Landscape in English Poetry from Marvell to Thomson.*

Fr. **Joseph Wong,** a Chinese Camaldolese monk from Hong Kong, is the junior master at New Camaldoli Hermitage and the director of the Camaldolese Institute for East-West Dialogue. He has published *Logos-Symbol in the Christology of Karl Rahner,* as well as many articles. Joseph has taught systematic theology in Rome and periodically teaches at the Seminary of Shanghai, China.

Index